ONE FINE STOOGE

ONE FINE STOOGE

LARRY FINE'S FRIZZY LIFE IN PICTURES

An Authorized Biography

Steve Cox and Jim Terry

CUMBERLAND HOUSE
NASHVILLE, TENNESSEE

ONE FINE STOOGE
PUBLISHED BY CUMBERLAND HOUSE PUBLISHING
431 Harding Industrial Drive
Nashville, TN 37211

Cover design: Gore Studio, Inc.
Book design: Mary Sanford

Library of Congress Cataloging-in-Publication Data
Cox, Stephen, 1966–
  One fine Stooge : Larry Fine's frizzy life in pictures : an authorized biography / Steve Cox and Jim Terry.
      p. cm.
  Includes index.
  ISBN-13: 978-1-58182-363-9 (hardcover : alk. paper)
  ISBN-10: 1-58182-363-0 (hardcover : alk. paper)
  1. Fine, Larry. 2. Motion picture actors and actresses—United States—Biography. 3. Three Stooges (Comedy team) I. Terry, Jim, 1923– II. Title.
  PN2287.F47C69 2006
  791.4302'8092—dc22

                                                        2005038041

Printed in the United States of America
1 2 3 4 5 6 7—12 11 10 09 08 07 06

For my brother Brian, who introduced me to the Three Stooges; for my Dad, who took me to meet them; and for my great friend Kevin Marhanka, who kept the fascination alive.

—Steve Cox

• • •

For my beautiful wife, Doris, who loves to laugh.

—Jim Terry

Contents

Larry Fine, pushing his book in a 1973 television commercial.

PREFACE

by Steve Cox

Hi, I'm Larry of the Three Stooges. I just wrote a book called A Stroke
of Luck. *It's all about my life with the Three Stooges. It also contains
over one hundred and twenty rare and collector item photos from all
of our movies, many with Curly and Shemp. Now here's how you can
get your book: Send seven dollars and ninety five cents to me, Larry,
Post Office Box 313, Hollywood, California, nine hundred and
twenty eight. Thank you.*

And so went the brief television commercial starring Larry Fine, broadcast to
limited markets in 1973, to advertise his published memoirs. Little did audiences know that Larry was basically forced to deliver the lines. No, he didn't
have a gun to his head, but he might as well have.

The single-camera commercial, shot outside on a clear California day, was
seen in several states and scattered cities, including his hometown of
Philadelphia. It was an uncreative, straightforward advertising plea. In a fair
closeup was Larry, now an old Stooge sitting in a wheelchair, delivering the
dialogue as clearly as he could articulate. He read from a cue card, and his
speech was somewhat thick but discernable; he sat without much movement,
squarely, having donned his best brightly colored shirt. His signature frizzy
hair had been scrunched up for the camera—probably the only time he tousled the graying strands as a partially paralyzed resident of the Motion Picture
Country Home in Woodland Hills, California. For the most part, he now kept
his hair trimmed short, but for this commercial spot he let it grow in order
to tease it up so he'd be recognized as Larry, the Stooge, for what would be
the last time.

What audiences were witnessing in this commercial was Larry, the Stooge
in the middle, known for taking all of the bops and bruises dished out for
decades on film, now in his seventies; he had suffered a major stroke, but
amazingly came to terms with his ambulatory condition and attempted to
give it a positive spin and refer to it as his "stroke of luck." Most people die

from strokes, Larry told friends at the retirement home, so he considered himself a survivor—and now an author. You see, Larry's pride was torn. He was delighted by the fact that he was the first of the famed comedy team the Three Stooges to publish his memoirs; he one-upped his longtime partner, Moe Howard, with this dubious little hardback book, *Stroke of Luck,* a nostalgic look at his life of Stooging that even featured a foreword by longtime director and producer Jules White. And despite the fact that White's heading was misspelled "Forward," the producer/director's one-page contribution of insights into the world of comedy was about the only professional element found between the covers. The book's first photograph was indicative of what was to come—a peculiar full-page closeup of Larry wincing, in what can only be described as resembling the pain from constipation. So few good choices were made in the development of this publication.

Many fans had asked Larry to pen his memoirs, and he hoped this would satisfy them as well as generate income. As far back as 1971 he was planning a book; he flirted with the title *What You Always Wanted to Know About a*

Surrounded in *Back to the Woods* (1937).

Stooge, But Were Afraid to Ask! but decided against it. The reason for a memoir, he expressed in his typed eight-page outline, "is the same reason the midget gave when he said he married the fat lady in the circus: My friends put me up to it!" He wished to answer all of the questions, from kids of all ages, contained in the massive amounts of fan mail he was now receiving in his retirement.

The book, sadly, was a disaster, and Larry knew it. He was helpless at this point, and for reasons unknown to most around him—even his longtime partner and friend, Moe—the frizzy-haired Stooge was forced to hawk the book and could do nothing to prevent its release. Larry really was truly a "victim of circumstance."

Although Moe Howard congratulated his disabled partner on the book, he was quietly disgusted by the publication, and for good reason—it was riddled with errors, rushed into publication with little to no care for detail, and cheapened their lifetime careers in show business, he felt. Maybe Moe's feelings were laced with a little jealousy—who knows? Moe had been taking his own notes, putting memories down on scraps and notepads, and assembling photographs for his own autobiography (tentatively titled *I Stooged to Conquer*) through the 1960s. His intention, as he warned Larry for years, was to leave his memoirs to his kids as a gift, even a source of income for their future. (His hardback pictorial, *Moe Howard & The Three Stooges* was eventually completed by his daughter, Joan Howard Maurer, and published posthumously in 1977—a hugely successful book which went back to press literally dozens of times over the next couple of decades.)

Sure, Moe Howard had a copy of Larry's book. He read it. He probably wanted to vomit. Privately, Moe thought Larry's book was a pernicious publication, backhanding it, never offering a positive word about its content. He didn't dare help Larry publicize the book because he simply wished it to crawl away lame and die a natural death as most books in the publishing business do.

The photographer catches Larry in an unusually cross moment during production of *Have Rocket, Will Travel.*

When *Stroke of Luck* was published in 1973 by Siena Publishing Company of Hollywood and the first copies rolled off the presses, Larry was devastated. There was absolutely no sentimental value attached to this abomination, and he felt utterly used in the endeavor. His family was equally unhappy and bewildered by the outcome. Moe Howard was ready to pull someone's hair out.

The name of Larry's collaborator, James Carone, was surprisingly emblazoned on the cover as the author, and the copyright was secured in Carone's name instead of Larry's. Inside it explains the book is written by Carone, "as told by Larry Fine." The book contained so many senseless typographical errors, run-on sentences, and misuses of punctuation, it was an embarrassment. Many of the photographs were mislabeled, films and actors were misidentified, and stories in general were jumbled into a hardback mess. The cover, colorful enough, was painted by a talented young artist from Los Angeles whom Carone had commissioned. The vibrant cover depicts Moe, Larry, and Curly as jack-in-the-boxes; Moe is brutally sporting a baseball bat and Curly is sprouting devil horns with a splatter of pie dripping from his head. The back of the dust jacket featured a huge portrait of a smiling, wavy-haired James Carone. What happened to Larry Fine?

Larry disliked it, but he was forced into promoting the product. And yet, starving fans loved it because it was ultimately the only thing out there . . . and it came from a Stooge.

The book sold mildly, by mail order only, and Larry received no monetary advance and no profits following publication. Although most of the photo-

Stroke of Luck, Larry's ill-fated hardback book published in 1973.

graphs that producer Jules White contributed to the book were returned, many of Larry's personal photos—as well as any earned royalties from even modest sales of the publication—were hidden and eventually stolen by Carone. Larry eventually discovered that in reality, Carone had commissioned a book binder and was distributing the book himself, as his own publisher, rather than working with an established publishing company with legitimate, effective distribution. Confronted by the wheelchair-bound invalid several times, an indignant Carone threatened to break Larry's legs if he interfered with the book's sales or potential progress. This violence was no Stooges stunt. Larry was quietly scared and angry and desperately wanted to drag Carone into court to put an end the entire deal, but he had no financial means. The book mirrored every Stooges comedy Larry ever made—he was, yet again, caught in the middle . . . a victim of circumstance.

When Michael Mikicel, a fan visiting from Canada, probed the book battle with Larry in a taped interview in 1974, a more courageous and fed-up Stooge this time spoke openly about the ordeal: "[Carone] threatened to sue me if I write another book. He vanished. My daughter said, 'I hope he comes out of the woodwork, we'll sue him.' Sure, he stole my book. I don't know how many it sold, he never gave me an accounting. Never got any money from it at all. I want to nail him. He would sign my name on checks that came in for individual orders on books."

Very few people knew it, but Larry was planning another book and had already begun the process.

It is this book, *One Fine Stooge.*

Larry Fine's original *Stroke of Luck* is a rare find today, a gem fetching upwards of $400 in good condition on eBay or in rare bookstores—certainly not due to its literary superiority, but because of its genuine scarcity. Thirty years later it remains one of the most detestable of all products bearing a picture of Moe, Larry, and Curly. At the same time, the book also boasts a reputation as one of the most sought-after and pricey of all Stooges memorabilia. A copy actually autographed by Larry himself? You might as well be prepared to cough up half a grand or more. Funny, but that fact alone might have irked Moe the most.

• • •

In this book lies a thirty-year hidden history. I may be the only Three Stooges fan to research and nail down the sad facts surrounding *Stroke of Luck* and its conception. In the late 1970s, my fascination for the lives and career of the Three Stooges was burning inside me. Not so weird, I thought. Most kids my age loved the Three Stooges. It never occurred to me that they were considered lowbrow, and the "violence" was just not a factor. I held them up as true classics, a comedy trio to be respected and researched.

In fact, I distinctly recall where I was when I heard that Moe Howard had died—I was just a goofy kid of nine who played with friends in the neighborhood and went to school. I'm not that different from many fans my age in that I experienced the Three Stooges in reverse of their actual career: some of my earliest television memories were of watching their 1960s color cartoons. During the grade-school years, I watched the vintage Three Stooges shorts after school, and nothing—and I mean nothing, not even my accordion lessons—kept me from watching them on television with my brother. I was at a friend's house about to choose a flavor and enjoy a homemade crushed-ice snowcone on a sweltering summer day. My friend's mom delivered the news, in passing, that she'd heard on the radio a report that Moe of the Three Stooges had died, and I remember the feeling that accompanied that grape snowcone. From the dead, it seemed, Moe delivered a one-two blow to my own stomach and then, after I thought about it a little, it hit me even harder as I realized I was too late to ever meet him or Larry, who I found out had recently died as well. Up to that point, it hadn't occurred to me that these goofs flickering in front of my eyes in black and white were still alive . . . and now, in one poof, they were sadly gone. The whole fantasy of meeting the Stooges seemed to be created and crushed in the time it took to consume one snowcone.

The fascination set in quickly. I really wanted to know who these guys were. Did Moe wear a wig? What happened to Curly? What was up with Joe

One Fine Stogie Larry quietly enjoys his cigar on the set of *Phony Express* (1943).

Besser?! Outside of a few books published in the 1970s with a single chapter devoted to the Stooges, there was virtually nothing extensive available to devour. When Moe Howard's book was published in 1977, I couldn't ride my bike fast enough to the library to sign that baby out. And renew it, and renew it again until I just had to buy my own and begged my parents for some cash. The cost of that: one painted garage door.

After poring through Moe's photos and reading about the lives of the Stooges, I remember consciously forming an entirely different perspective, more of a realistic attitude regarding my favorite comedy team. They ceased being cartoon characters, and that was a jolting realization for me. It was about that time that I discovered the joy—and power—of the written word, and I guess that might have been the spark of my career as a journalist. I began corresponding with those who knew the Stooges or worked with them,

Larry Fine's brother, Morris "Moe" Feinberg, was a positive force for keeping the Stooges' torch lit with his national fan club in the 1970s and '80s.

and in years to come, my fascination would eventually lead me to writing and actually meeting two of them: Joe Besser (who came from St. Louis, I was impressed to discover), and the last Stooge, Curly-Joe DeRita. It was also about that time that I discovered the wonders of long-distance telephone calls, and the sizeable fallout at the end of each month when the bill arrived.

To the hunt! Those years were bliss for me as the Stooges became a great hobby and researching them was half, well, maybe *most,* of the adventure. My dad and I took an adventurous father-and-son vacation together and flew to Los Angeles, where I was fortunate to arrange a meeting with Curly's second wife, Elaine, and I also became acquainted with Shemp's widow, Babe, a remarkably wise lady. I interviewed the surviving Stooges, as well as many of their relatives and, of course, those talented individuals who worked alongside the Stooges, some of whom took those punishing pies like troupers—great spirits like Emil Sitka. I was in awe of Jules White, Edward Bernds, Elwood Ullman, all of whom made up the backbone of the Stooges comedies and, better for me, all of whom were patient with this young giggly and awkward kid who possessed an over-active curiosity.

In 1980, I was in eighth grade, and lots of great opportunities started opening up, including the chance to assist a fellow named Moe Feinberg, who was Larry Fine's brother—not to be confused with the Stooge with the bangs himself, Moe Howard. He lived in Philadelphia and was a huge proponent of

The Stooges scrap over a "Scrappy" doll, a cute merchandising item based on an early Columbia Pictures animated film character.

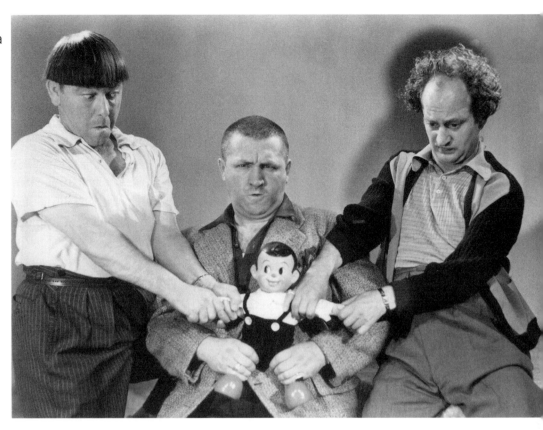

The Stooges are dwarfed by famous boxing champ Primo Carnera.

keeping the legend of the Stooges alive. Our joint mission was to reorganize and relaunch the original Three Stooges Fan Club, which had fallen, briefly, into limbo. My parents encouraged my hobby and so did my teachers, believe it or not, because they helped me rent some of the Stooges shorts from the local library and run the 16mm prints for our class—but that didn't go without assignment: one oral report, given in front of the class, all about meeting the Stooges.

Moe Feinberg dubbed me his "teen vice president," and I was proud to be working with the brother of a Stooge. To listen to Moe Feinberg on the telephone was like listening to Larry himself—their voices matched that closely. Moe taught me some Yiddish: he said I possessed "chutzpah" which, he explained, meant great enthusiasm or drive. Together, albeit mostly by long distance and through the mail, Moe and I assembled stories, recruited new members, and got the Stooges fan club newsletters up and running. Moe and I received written contributions and blessings from surviving Stooges Joe Besser and Joe DeRita, as well as many other descendants of the Stooges.

It wasn't long before I realized the name James Carone was a bad word within the Fine family, and with Moe Howard's kin as well. (Surviving Stooges Besser and DeRita were indifferent about the whole thing, although they'd felt bad for Larry when the book was published.) That lasting bitterness piqued my curiosity. Regardless of the acrid feelings Carone's name stirred, I thought I would try to track down James Carone, the man who collaborated with Larry on *Stroke of Luck,* because I was determined, at the very least, to secure a copy of the rare book for myself. And I wanted to ask him about the experience of working with Larry at the Motion Picture Country Home. It wasn't too difficult, and after some searching I found Carone living alone in the Pittsburgh area. Shortly thereafter he moved into a retirement home in Hawthorne, California (where he died in the early 1980s). We struck up a correspondence and talked on the phone many times.

Moe Feinberg warned me, like a wise old grandfather, to beware of Carone, but those signals only served to electrify the situation and incite my curiosity. I really wanted to get Carone's side of it all, quiz him about Larry's final years, and primarily find out if any copies of the rare book had survived.

Carone proved to be a big talker, and I suspect he enjoyed the attention from a young kid inquiring about his work. After a few conversations and some correspondence, I was able to ask him about working with Larry on *Stroke of Luck.* It might have been more of an interrogation—at that age, my level of tact wasn't that of a seasoned journalist or gentleman. My youth and inexperience afforded me latitude because people knew my intentions were good and my heart was in it. Deep down, I really wanted to contribute something worthy and notable to the history of the Three Stooges. And I was hungry to know more about the team in general.

Carone explained it all to me: "I never wanted to get involved with the book in the first place. It was my wife's plan and she was friends with Larry, so I was doing it as a favor to her and him. Larry wasn't very grateful. I admit I really didn't know what I was doing with that book because I wasn't a fan of the Three Stooges at all. I thought I could do Larry a favor and put this book out, but it fell apart. The manuscript I'd written was supposed to go to a copy editor before it was published, but instead the thing went directly to press. And then the publishing company burnt down and there was no money to be made."

Carone agreed that Larry's participation in the whole endeavor was hardly comprehensive. While convalescing and gaining strength and spirit, Larry was simply inspired to put together a book for fans, hundreds and hundreds of them, who were writing him and quizzing him about his career. He was drowning in correspondence, but attempted to answer it all, which was actually great therapy. He felt the book would solve his problem.

While at the Country Home, Larry met and befriended a female volunteer there named Helen Carone, who convinced him to work and collaborate with her husband, James Carone, on an autobiography. It seemed perfect. Helen brought her husband out to the home to meet with Larry and talk over what the book might entail and discuss how Larry envisioned it. Carone, who grew up in Pittsburgh, seemed to hit it off with the Stooge, and the men appeared to have a lot in common. Larry signed a deal with Carone and, hurriedly, the two began to prepare the text for publishing. Carone visited with Larry intermittently over a period of a couple of months and interviewed him, taking notes, gathering photographs, and assembling the book. It's a mystery, however, why the book was published absolutely void of any proofreading. Larry was not savvy about the world of publishing at all . . . what did he know? He was a Stooge all of his life. He made movies.

"Larry bugged me about royalties, but there weren't any," Carone told me. "I'd say there probably wasn't more than five thousand books printed, which really isn't that great a number."

Because I knew for a fact how scarce the book was, that was about the only statement I fully believed. I acted as though I bought into it all of Carone's ramblings, but as I learned, he wasn't altogether truthful in his explanations. The book must've done at least fairly well, because it sold well enough to warrant a third printing in 1976, the year after Larry's death. What happened, I wondered, to *those* profits? The publishing company was actually Carone's company, but he referred to it as someone else's establishment.

Vernon Dent as Emperor
Octopus Grabus in
Matri-Phony (1942).

He dismissed the thought of any profits and stressed that any money made on the books was negligible at best. He eventually sold all of Larry's precious photographs, so there was proof of some latent profits.

During my phone conversations with Carone, I realized the man was a blowhard, and that I couldn't take his explanations for fact, so I read between the lines. It was an exercise in psychology, really. He claimed to be a close friend of Frank Sinatra and fed me a tale about how he was busy flying in Sinatra's private jet, taking around a television pilot (titled *No, No, Daddy!*) at the time, in talks with NBC, all this hot air. Carone, then in his late seventies I think, was kind enough to me, but he much preferred talking about his ailments, some sports, money, and such things. I remember him explaining to me that a thousand dollars was called a "K." Like "5K" means five thousand. He was a talker. Funny how you remember minute details like that.

And I soon realized that Larry Fine was not his favorite topic, unless it meant money. Carone fancied himself as an accomplished writer and even a singer; however, his only other book was actually self-published, that same year as *Stroke of Luck.* It was an instructional book on methods of singing, titled *Master Vocal Study* (published by Siena Publishing, Carone's own company). Carone, according to his own biography in the book, was a professional singer, proficient in the opera style, and the former director of an opera company.

The whole thing seemed laughable. How this conniving Caruso got caught up with the Three Stooges is as convoluted as any flimsy Stooges storyline.

And as for books . . . yes, I was excited to find out a few unopened boxes of books survived in a basement at his sister's home near Pittsburgh and I was welcome to purchase them. He told me when those were gone, that's all there were to be had, so I needed to jump. There were about 150 copies, and I took the idea of acquiring these to Moe Feinberg, who, needless to say, was hot to get his hands on some of his brother's long-lost, pristine *Stroke of Luck* books, too. I borrowed $750 from my parents and Moe and I secretly pooled our equal funds, knowing that if we marketed the books together within the fan club, we'd make our money back. It was Stooge subterfuge.

Terrified at the thought of losing his cash to Carone, Moe Feinberg agreed, but stipulated that he remain a silent partner throughout the entire deal. He demanded this, and I was happy to oblige because I wanted things to go just as smoothly. If Carone discovered that one of Larry Fine's family members was involved, he might have nixed it altogether. There was that much bad blood.

It wasn't long until the deal was made, the money was covertly secured and exchanged, and the books arrived safely. Moe Feinberg's name was protected, although it became clear later on that we were in cahoots when we jointly offered the copies to Stooges Club members at thirty dollars a copy. At that point, Feinberg did not care. He'd gotten his books. We sold out almost immediately, earning just about twenty dollars'

Larry admired this special double-exposure portrait. It could be found framed in his homes and later in his room at the Motion Picture Country Home.

profit on each book, which we divided equally. We thought we did pretty well and everyone was happy. I remember Moe Feinberg took his profits and purchased a little room air conditioner for his home office so he could finally toil over the Club's Journals in some comfort during the hot summers. I kept visualizing this little old balding man in a sweater, plunking away at his sturdy manual typewriter, cutting and pasting type, and sweating as he slaved to get the Three Stooges Club Journals to his neighborhood printer and ultimately in the hands of the fans. Moe's heart was really into those homemade fan club newsletters—typos, mismatched print, and all.

When Moe Feinberg died in 1986, a Philadelphia relation, Gary Lassin, took over the chores and steadily built the not-for-profit organization into a healthy fan club which still serves an impressive worldwide membership today.

• • •

That's not the end of the story.

Let me explain: the little-known background regarding *Stroke of Luck* is intertwined with the long lost "blueprints," you might say, for this book. It

Left, Larry takes in some sun at the Country Home in 1974. *Below right,* Larry told a reporter: "I call it 'a stroke of luck.' I was lucky because I'm alive. I've heard that nine out of ten stroke victims die from it." *Below left,* Fans drop in on Larry and pose for a snapshot with their idol.

took thirty years for these paths to cross, but it finally it occurred, and thanks to a man named Jim Terry, who preserved Larry's materials, this book is a reality.

One Fine Stooge is probably more in tune with what Larry Fine actually desired in a memoir. Jim and I hope so, anyway. The title, perfectly appropriate, was Larry's own invention and the epithet he actually preferred for his memoirs. The photographs and ephemera featured within, for the most part, were culled directly from Larry's personal collection, saved by the Stooge himself, carefully tucked away for publication one day. When Larry finally realized it was best to wash his hands completely of *Stroke of Luck* in 1974, he began a new book, with new elements, different stories, a different collaborator, and a fresh approach. You see, though *Stroke of Luck* left a sour taste in Larry's mouth, his appetite for publishing was unsatisfied. He expressed to friends that he wished to write a *new* book, something different, with more of his own ideas and personal photographs, and certainly with accuracy. This is where Jim Terry and Larry Fine's paths crossed.

Terry, then in his early fifties, was a Los Angeles businessman, entrepreneur, and former television producer. Terry co-wrote *The Busby Berkeley Book* in 1973 and while publicizing it, he met one of Larry Fine's friends, Gwen Seager Tayler, a former Busby Berkeley dancer. Of course Larry had known "Buzz," the famous stage and film choreographer, having worked with him at MGM with the Stooges and Ted Healy. (In fact, Buzz was the godfather of Ted Healy's only son.) Larry looked at the lavish hardback book Terry had assembled about Busby Berkeley's films and wanted a pictorial just like that about his own career and life.

Recalling the first time he met Larry, Terry says: "Gwen and I became friends, and she said she had this man named Larry Fine she'd like to introduce me to. I confessed that I was never a fan of the Three Stooges or their movies, but I'd love to meet him.

"I went out to the Motion Picture Home and he was the sweetest little guy. He was in a wheelchair. Larry loved the Busby Berkeley book and told me, 'Jim, I'll give you the memorabilia I have and I wish you'd do a book on me.' He told me how disappointed he was with the first book. I signed an agreement with him and his daughter, Phyllis, and I met with her and she gave me a box of materials. And that's how I got acquainted, and I took a friend of mine, writer Norman Stanley, and we began recording interviews. I'd have lunch with him there and we'd stroll the Motion Picture Home. There were a lot of old-timers out there, well known actors. I remember Mary Astor was there. She had her own private apartment."

Terry also recalled Larry's great concerns about another book. "Frankly, he was so unhappy with the man who did the first book, *Stroke of Luck,* I cannot tell you. And also, something you should know . . . he was not happy with his partners, the other Stooges. He had some hard, unhappy, very ill feelings towards them, maybe about business. I felt sorry for him because he was just almost bitter about his two partners."

It wasn't long after that Larry suffered additional strokes and could no longer continue working on the book. Larry Fine died in January 1975. "I went to his funeral at Forest Lawn in Glendale, up in the hills," says Terry, "and the other two Stooges were there I remember. Larry was laid out in the casket, he looked fine, and it was a very nice service as I recall."

Terry and writer Norman Stanley attempted to launch Larry's story, but no publishers were interested and the two men all but abandoned the project in frustration. The rare materials, clippings, photos, and memorabilia sat in storage, hidden away in a cardboard box, for almost thirty years until Terry recently decided to finally dust it all off and do something creative with it.

By pure happenstance—you might even call it a stroke of luck—I was introduced to Jim Terry in 2002 by a mutual friend in Los Angeles, and the possibility of a collaboration instantly intrigued me. I think of it as a gift from Larry.

Now living on the West Coast, my life had taken different roads and I thought the Stooges were a past passion for me. But as a writer (and an unabashed fan of the Stooges no matter what), I found it hard to resist. I've been a freelance writer since I graduated college in 1988, and I assisted several other writers with their books about the Three Stooges. So this would not be my first book, but it would take me back to my first love—the Three Stooges. Moreover, the rare, unpublished photographs in Larry's collection jumped out at me. These amazing images were like eye candy, and I knew these elements alone would make a fascinating pictorial. Larry's story needed to be told.

Jim and I have carefully compiled Larry's personal mementos, meshed them with his personal remembrances, and this is the result. Yes, this is a book about Larry Fine, but also about his partners in comedy. You can't take Larry out the Stooges and you certainly could not take the Stooges out of Larry. They were one. They were essential to one another.

Much like Cole Porter, who commonly recalled stages of his life by what songs he was writing at the time, an examination of Larry's life is reflected and often marked or gauged by what he was doing with the Stooges at that time. In fact, when one fan asked Larry what he thought about when he watched the Stooges shorts, he said "Sometimes I'm thinking about what was happening in my life at the time, you know, marriage and kids. A lot of actors who have been in films for a long time do that." Anyone who exported as much celluloid over decades, such as Larry and his partners did, can attest.

Most people know him just as "Larry," the charming, disarming, and amusingly odd member of the high priests of low comedy, the Three Stooges. He was the Stooge caught in the middle, between the slaps and movie mayhem that have transcended decades and curiously survived. Behind that mask, you'll discover there was a life full of wonder, fame, and sometimes soured luck and tragedy. And while *Stroke of Luck* almost exclusively explored his working career as an actor (virtually no mention was made of his children and very little about his home life), Jim and I have expanded the scope of this book to provide a more detailed perspective on Larry's life; we've augmented his personal notes with reminiscences and additional photography contributed by some of Larry's friends who trekked out to the Motion Picture Country Home and conducted taped interviews with him in the early 1970s. We are grateful to the members of Larry's family and close friends who have also shared their candid and loving memories of the late comedian. It's a fascinating, unparalleled journey.

Mabel and Larry celebrate Larry's fiftieth birthday at Ciro's in Hollywood with friends Dr. Eddie Goursin and wife (October 5, 1952).

If you think about it, no one can be so grand as to postulate that Larry Fine dedicated his life to comedy . . . it just happened that way. His mug, like that of his partners Moe and Curly, became a well-ingrained part of American pop culture. He personified the word *stooge,* and along the way he evolved into a comedy legend—this little man with the electrocuted locks.

ACKNOWLEDGMENTS

"For duty and humanity!"

Foremost, hats off to Larry, the lovable Stooge in the middle. Here's how! (We *know* how!) Without Larry, naturally this book would not have been possible, the Three Stooges might not have become comedy icons, and the landscape of American comedy would have been oddly lacking.

The authors wish to offer gracious and heartfelt gratitude to all of the following individuals and organizations for their collective assistance over the years. Whether they were a friend of Larry's, a fervent Stooges fan, or maybe not a connoisseur of slapstick at all—these folks generously helped to create this unique memoir celebrating the world of entertainer Larry Fine and his lifelong partners in comedy. The authors also want to extend thanks to members of the Fine/Feinberg families—from both coasts—for their encouragement and support. We sincerely hope this book will be a keepsake for Larry's grandchildren, great-grandchildren, and descendants for generations to come.

Academy of Motion Picture Arts & Sciences; Frankie Avalon; Nick Barker; Buddy Barnett; Milton Berle; Busby Berkeley; Tom Bertino; Edward Bernds; Ernie and Joe Besser; Carol Brady; Nate and Lyla Budnick; Kevin Burns; Mickey Carroll; Brian Chanes; Richard Cohen; Ned Comstock; Connie Cezon; Columbia Pictures Industries; Blanche and Jerry Cox; Brian Cox; Eddie Crispell; Aaron Cushman; Bernadette and Dave Dalton; Megan Dalton; Eunice Dent; Jean and Joe DeRita; Moe and Elaine Howard Diamond; Ralph Dimsal; Rick Eberenz; Moe Feinberg; Harry Fender; Michael Fleming; John Flinn (at Columbia Pictures); Bob Frischmann; Paul Gierucki; Mark Gilman Jr.; Phyllis and Don Goldbloom; Jane Howard Hanky; Darrell Herbst; Geri Howard; Jill Howard; Gertrude "Babe" Howard; Helen and Moe Howard; Paul Howard; Sandie Howard; Donald Jacka; Alex Jackson; Laurie Jacobson; Carol Heiss Jenkins; Ted Knapp; Christy Kraus; Lew Kraus; Robert Kurson; Phyllis Fine Lamond; Susie and Don Lamond; Tiny Landers; Robin and Gary Lassin; Laughsmith Entertainment; Greg

Lenburg; Jeff Lenburg; Vicki Trickett Lindblad; Kevin Marhanka; Norman and Joan Howard Maurer; Ed McCollough; Marlin McKeever; Scott Michaels; Helen Molenaar (at Columbia Pictures); Jim Neibaur; Julie O'Neil; Lee Orgel; Jim Pauley; Dean Rasmussen; Joel Rasmussen; T. Todd Reboul; Tommy Richards; Kirk Robbin; Jim Romanowski; Ambrose Rose; Gino Salomone; Ray Savage; Ralph Schiller; James Scott; Marilyn Howard Server; Burt Shaw; Emil Sitka; Saxon Sitka; Carol Christensen Sneed; John Solomon; Tim Stocoak; Edson Stroll; Gwen Seager Tayler; The Three Stooges Fan Club, Inc.; Doris Terry; Turner Classic Movies; Twentieth Century Fox Productions; Elwood Ullman; USC Cinema-Television Library; Joe Wallison; Chandler Warren; and Jules White.

Special thanks go to: Bob Saget, Jim Malinda, Walter Mitchell, Michael Mikicel, and Scott Reboul, all of whom generously shared their unique personal experiences and Fine interviews from the Motion Picture Country Home; also to research consultants Trent Reeve and Brent Seguine for allowing us to pester them with questions. For further information about The Three Stooges Fan Club, Inc., inquire at: P.O. Box 747, Gwynedd Valley, PA, 19437.

A warm thank you to Tod Johnson and Norman Stanley for all of their efforts.

And finally, great thanks go to our courageous publisher, Ron Pitkin, our talented editor/designer Mary Sanford, and all of the supportive folks at Cumberland House Publishing.

ONE FINE STOOGE

Following their split with Ted Healy, the team of Howard, Fine & Howard (Shemp, Larry, and Moe) appeared in the stage show *Masquerade* in 1931. The show was a Publix Theaters production staged by Carlton Winkler, who later worked for Florenz Ziegfeld as a technical director on Broadway.

ALONG CAME LARRY

The single most important factor that sets the Three Stooges apart from any other movie comedy team is their unequaled longevity. It's debatable, but you can't deny them their advantage: a stretch in the spotlight that burned their image into the American popular culture, possibly forever. It was accomplished flicker by flicker, drip by drip, administered in a healthy dose in theaters, then in live performances, then on television and back to the big screen. This unique Stooge equation, in which the team paralleled and then transcended the movie medium—they entered with the talkies, and forty years later they vanished with the advent of home video—puts them in a mighty position. They've become mythical figures that the ages now respect—an earned dimension to their legacy.

Larry Fine was the stooge "in the middle," some say. He may have been a Stooge, but he was no dummy. Larry, the performer, knew his position and his character and how it fit into this troika. He almost never wandered. The Three Stooges was an all-encompassing, embracing, even defining, part of the life of Larry Fine; so it's impossible to detach Larry from the Stooges . . . or filter out the Stooges from Larry.

Larry Fine's life, as that of his partners, truly was a span on earth spent in motion pictures. You might even say that his life really began when he started making movies. He liked how his name was centered, aside from the rest of the cast, in his big-screen movie debut, *Soup to Nuts,* in 1930. Everything about the movies was young, and Larry's life would fly alongside the medium in its greatest era, touching down often until his death in 1975.

Larry has always been in good company. As long as there has been the art of comedy on film, there have been kooks and flakes like Larry and the Three Stooges. The world of television is also loaded with flakes like Larry. Harpo Marx was a flake. Lucy—a flake. *Seinfeld*'s Kramer was a lovable flake. Ed Norton and Ralph Kramden were the best of flakes.

Director Edward Bernds, who guided the Three Stooges on film at Columbia Pictures for many years, happily explained that moniker pinned on Larry with a wink: "Larry was called the third Stooge, or the Stooge in the middle, and lot of the time he was a little flaky and a lot of his ideas were so off the wall that we couldn't use them. But it just wouldn't have been the same without him. Although he didn't do as much as the other two, he had to be there. . . . Even in story conferences when I would call the boys in, I'd call them because I'd get ideas, I'd get material and Larry always came up with the strange ideas and once in a while would come in with something good that would possibly trigger some ideas. Moe would call him stupid or say to him, 'Keep your mind on what you're doing. . . . You're not listening!' Larry would just hang his head. Moe was just the same offscreen as he was on—the boss, the tough boss."

Larry believed that he collaborated with the others at work just fine. He didn't have to act, as he really wasn't a thespian in the sense that he attempted to dig deep or enrich the characters he played. He was an entertainer. Actor . . . well, yes, he *acted*. But his talents weren't of the depth you'd recognize within a trained actor, nothing in the sense that he could have mastered the nuances for dramatic performances. Probably not. It's doubtful Larry devoted much time or effort to bettering his skills as an actor, although he certainly needed offer no apologies for his work. (Except to Moe, when he was off watching the ball game instead of rehearsing.) Larry was a self-assured actor and comedian, dripping with confidence in his pratfalls. He didn't have to dig deep for his laughs, the talent was of natural stock. Comedy was his forte, an effortless attribute for the most part. Isn't that an indication of natural talent? He never appeared to act. His character on screen—basically the same lovable patsy in most any adventure starring the Three Stooges—really wasn't that much of a stretch from his own personality. No matter what was happening at home in his personal life—and there was tragedy—it never came across in his performances, and in the end, that's all that mattered.

The man with the frizzy hair connected with audiences simply because he was the "everyman" of the group, the simple one just trying to get along and get by in life with little turmoil. Larry was the glue between the boss and the comic. Everyone can associate with the guy in the middle at one time or another, victim of circumstance or not. His unpretentious charm made him approachable, even lovable, quirky, and bizarre at times. There was the hair, the rubbery face, the pointed nose that attracted abuse, and that smooth, sloping, perfectly rounded pate, which seemed to just beg for a smack. And of course, there was his voice: that pleasant, unusual nasal tone (with an occasional gasping snort); he created a Stooge that was inimitable, different from the other two, and ultimately a mainstay. While Moe was gravelly and Curly's voice had that high-pitched, melodious tone, their voices boisterous and usually cut hard, Larry's voice was a richer, warmer product of the pipes than his partners. From their first film on, they harmonized beautifully. Kids especially took to Larry's kindly nasal tone later in his life; that quality permeated every song and narrated children's record album they made in the 1960s. Backed by an orchestra, Larry's charming solo version of "Mairzy Doats" on the children's album *The Three Stooges Nonsense Songbook* is as mellifluous as it gets.

There's an art to appreciating the comedy of the Three Stooges. True, it's a "guy thing"; the Stooges are an acquired taste and simple polls show that their comedy is favored more by males. In sheer volume, the Three Stooges took low comedy to new heights, contributing unbounded celluloid to American film comedy for repeated generations to pore over. The extensive library has meant a feast for lovers of slapstick. Anyone who has watched a Stooges short subject film and laughed at the vintage buffoonery can attest: for the most part, there lies a tendency to follow one particular Stooge throughout the story, keenly watching his reactions. Maybe Curly was your favorite, and you unconsciously kept an eye on him. Then, as you gradually watch the films repeatedly, like an old *Gilligan's Island* rerun, you peripherally notice the other citizens. Then you switch Stooges.

When you follow Larry as the central Stooge, it's easy to appreciate his reactions and his well-chosen movements, wasting little in his performance. "Larry had more talent in his hands, with expressiveness, than Moe did with his face," said actor Jim Malinda, who was close friends with Larry in the comedian's final years.

Larry used his talents well and chose his actions wisely and that discriminating nature is the hallmark of a seasoned performer. Although he almost never discussed his craft in these terms, he implemented the talents he honed in front of live audiences. His lengthy film career was an education on the acute awareness of his own face and body on camera, to know what intimate and genuine movements drew laughs on film; on stage he knew how to yank a yuk from a large audience with overblown, over-the-top horseplay. And he knew how simple to keep it. All of the Stooges did. They performed comedy

Mural, Mural on the Wall Adorning a building that marks the birthplace of Larry Fine in Philadelphia is a massive twenty-foot high mural of the city's native son, created by artist David McShane. The building, located at Third and South Streets in Philadelphia is now the home to a popular bar and grill.

that required no thinking because there was simply no time for anything else. They subscribed to the old Mack Sennett theory of fast-paced silent comedy: if you're spending time thinking, you're not laughing.

Penn Jillette (the taller, vocal half of the comedy/magic duo Penn and Teller) agrees that for a while he leaned toward Curly as his favorite Stooge, "like everyone else," he told writer Paul Fericano. "But then a friend of mine who really has done a lot of work looking into what Larry's done, helped me understand how Larry is possibly the most skilled and most eccentric of the Stooges. He constantly has something going on that's interesting and pretty wild in every scene. . . . He's a very odd actor; he keeps going with what you think would be distracting and upstaging stuff, but it all fits into the texture of the Stooges. I mean, the Stooges have this really thick, messy texture. The Marx Brothers have focus every second. It's like the Three Stooges are the Rolling Stones to the Marx Brothers' Beatles."

Later, in his retirement, fans loved Larry for something more tangible: his accessibility and candor. In an interview with one fan, he tried to describe Moe, Curly, and Shemp's true personalities. Larry cracked, "Well, their mother and father were cousins. You know what *that* means, don't you?" Although he'd suffered a stroke, the line was delivered with precision and timing. It got a laugh, and it was fact. The matriarch and patriarch of Stoogedom, Moe, Shemp, and Curly's father and mother, Solomon and Jennie Horwitz, a loving Jewish couple who hailed from Russia, were cousins who married and made a family—a family of famous comedians, it turned out.

● ● ●

He was born Louis Feinberg in South Philadelphia. Inside the very two-story brick row house in which young Louis Feinberg was born is now Jon's Bar and Grill. The local landmark, located at 606 South Third Street, now features a huge wall-size mural of Louis Feinberg, known to all of us as Larry Fine, just in case a visitor to the establishment is not aware of the hallowed ground on which they stand—or stagger.

Louis—sometimes called "Louie" by his family and "Whitey" because of his very blond hair when he was young—was born October 5, 1902. Larry was the oldest of four children born to Joseph and Fannie (née Lieberman) Feinberg. Joseph Feinberg was a jeweler and watchmaker and ran a store on the first floor of their building, while the family lived above in an apartment on the second floor.

Larry's younger brother Morris "Moe" Feinberg arrived on September 5, 1904. The Feinberg's third son, Philip, born December 21, 1906, died when he was just thirteen, a victim of the 1919 Spanish Flu epidemic. Young Philip died on the very day he was to be bar mitzvahed. Fourteen years after Philip was born, Fannie became pregnant quite unexpectedly and on November 24, 1920, gave birth to a daughter, Lyla.

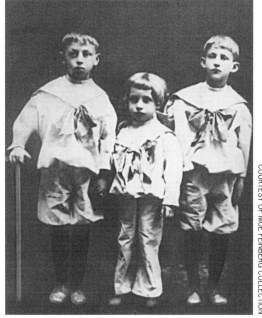

The Feinberg boys: Morris (age 7), Phillip (age 5), and Larry (age 9) in 1909. Sister Lyla arrived years later in 1920.

Oddly, from his birth until he was in his thirties, Larry and the family celebrated his birthday on September 4, 1902. No one knows how or why his birth date became switched, but clearly something happened. For years tradition dictated that Larry and his younger brother, Moe, born in September two years later, celebrated their birthdays together around the same time, on the 4th or the 5th. It was when he searched for his birth records years later, in 1939, that Larry discovered a monumental discrepancy in birthdates. In preparation for the Stooges' overseas tour, Larry had to send for his birth records to apply for a U.S. passport. He was perplexed when he found out that his actual birth date was October 5, 1902. Despite knowing the actual date, Larry continued to celebrate in September with his brother, nicknamed Moe, for many years to come.

One childhood moment in particular, one serendipitous event in Larry's youth, pointed the way for a career in the entertainment business. When he was just a tot of four years old, Larry nearly lost his left arm to an accident that occurred while he was in the back of his father's jeweler's shop. He recalled:

When I was a child, my father was a jeweler and was using oxalic acid to test gold. That acid is the only thing that won't turn gold green. I grabbed the bottle and spilled it on my left arm. All of my family is left-handed except me. Because of this accident, I had to develop my right hand and arm. The accident burned my whole arm and all the muscles in the left arm. They had to do a skin graft on it. A Doctor Segal in Philadelphia performed the skin graft operation. That doctor later suggested to my mother I take up boxing to develop my left hand. So, in a local gym, I made friends with a man named Phil Glassman, and I fought under the name of "Kid Roth" so my parents wouldn't know. When I had my first professional fight, my father attended. I won the fight, but lost to my father. He dragged me right out of the ring. It was my last fight.

Lefty Larry became right-handed, but the ability he carried naturally in his left hand and arm only made him extremely ambidextrous. He could write, if necessary, with both hands, although he developed his right hand to such an extent that he mastered a beautifully symmetrical, slightly slanting penmanship that he preferred to his final day.

Fannie Feinberg and her boys, Philip, Louis, and Morris, circa 1913. Young Philip died of influenza at age thirteen.

Larry's parents thought violin lessons might effectively strengthen his left arm without getting his pointy beak broken in the process. Music therapy worked wonders for Larry, who took to the fiddle like a Stooge to a disaster. They became inseparable. Over time, Larry became a gifted musician, with a knack for reading music as well as playing perfectly by ear.

"One of my earliest memories is of a scrawny, blond kid sitting in bed, slowly sawing away on a quarter-size violin, only eight inches long," wrote Morris "Moe" Feinberg in his 1984 book, *Larry, the Stooge in the Middle.* "Larry's first real performance was as a violinist at a children's concert with the Philadelphia Orchestra. Larry was nine years old. And he did the solo on 'Humoresque,' a Late Romantic piece by the Czechoslovakian composer Anton Dvorak. Mother and Dad were ecstatic."

Up to the age of nine or ten, Larry and his younger brother Moe were about the same height. "I'd had an operation on my adenoids and tonsils and somehow or other, that gave me a little spring," recalled Moe Feinberg when he was eighty. "Larry used to get a kick out of introducing me as his 'little' brother, but I was a head taller than him. We had a strong facial resemblance. My hairline was the same with the high forehead. My younger sister looks more like Larry than I do. We sound exactly alike. I've been mistaken for Larry on the phone more than once.

"Larry actually started show business from about age nine or ten. He was a ham from day one and he always wanted to be in show business. He actu-

ONE FINE STOOGE

ally really started when he was about seventeen; he got into an act, a school act. It was on the premise of the old minstrel show. This act had desks on either side of the stage and the kids were sitting there. The school teacher was like the interlocutor and then there was a comedian on one end and another comedian on the other end. Larry was the sissy kid. Then there was a Jewish kid on another end, that was Jules Black. That's where he learned some training and timing."

Larry attended Philadelphia's South Walk Grammar School and later Central High School, but he did not graduate. By his own admission, he was too distracted by music, sports, women, and other interests, to concentrate on his education, a reality he later said he regretted. During the pre-Depression years, it was sometimes more important to carve out a career and earn money than it was to pursue a proper education. Larry's parents were not poor, but the family lived by modest means.

• • •

In the middle and late 1920s, radio was the mass medium taking off in America, bringing the nation closer together while producing a brand new spectrum of entertainment stars. It was a medium Ted Healy and the Three Stooges allowed to let pass them by, mainly because their humor was more visual than verbal. The Stooges didn't have an aversion to appearing on radio—they appeared on local radio shows while touring the country and

Larry (far right) with the group he joined shortly after he left the School Act.

LARRY ON LARRY

The following biographical sketch is a narrative that came directly from Larry Fine, in his own words. In it, he condenses his early years and hits some highlights based on his own memory and what he felt was important or interesting. This oral narrative is from 1960 and it should be noted that while Larry retained a fairly good memory of events from his past, his recollections were not infallible. For Larry, it seems, life began with high school, when he decided to drop out to pursue a career as a musician.

I started as a musician, always played the violin in school bands. I also conducted the orchestra. My violin teacher was the father of the actor who played in *The Moon Is Blue*. He had great hopes for me to become a concert violist. However, my tastes ran to jazz and I would sneak off from school and go to the music publishers and get professional copies. I was about thirteen years old and about 4 feet 2, and I taught some of the boys in the school (grammar school) band to play jazz, much to the discomfort of my teachers and, of course, my music teacher.

Then I met Gus Edwards, in a music publishing firm. I was thirteen. One of the reasons I gave up serious violin was an idea that my teacher wanted me to go to Europe to study. This was during the World War years, 1917, and my mother didn't want me to go.

Gus Edwards was replacing his original School Act and besides playing violin I could dance and do Jewish dialects. Then I eventually joined The Newsboy Sextet, which he put out under the supervision of his brother, Ben. Before that I used to appear in the movies with the slides and sing—that was my first professional job, when I was about fifteen. It was 1921. I appeared at the Keystone, Alhambra, Broadway, Nixon's Grant, Allegheny, and other theaters in Philadelphia. I used to get paid about two dollars a performance. That was audience participation.

I also plugged songs in five and dime stores; in 1921 I was with the Gus Edwards Newsboy Sextet for one year. In those days, you played twelve weeks in Philadelphia, twenty weeks in New York, and about ten in Boston. That was as far as I got with that act.

In 1922, my father decided I should join his jewelry business. I lasted three months. The boss came to me one day and gave me two weeks notice and salary and an extra bonus of $100 to go on the stage, because I kept everyone laughing in the place and they were getting no work done.

Then I went around to the theatrical agencies to try to get a job. I met this man, Jules Black, and his partner, Jolly Joyce, now a famous theatrical agent. They were organizing a School Act and they knew I'd been with the Gus Edwards kid act, and he asked me to join his act, which consisted of him as the comedian. I was the sissy in Lord Fauntleroy clothes, and he had a sister team called the Haney Sisters and Marty Bohn, who became a successful café operator in Wildwood, New Jersey. This is where I met my wife, Mabel Haney.

In 1922, when I joined the School Act, I fell in love with my wife, but we were way too young; we both had to get permits from the Board of Education to work, and then four years later we were married. We got married much later because we were both very young and there was a difference in our religion. We finally got married on June 22, 1926, in Philadelphia. My wife, who was Irish Catholic, turned Jewish, and we were married by a Rabbi Krause.

When we got married, we left the School Act and formed a trio, the Haney Sisters and Fine. We did an act called "At the Crossroads." It was an act consisting of the two sisters as traffic cops on the road to music land. My wife directed traffic toward the jazz section, and her sister Loretta toward the classical. I came in the middle of the road and they each tried to convince me which road to take, so my wife did a jazz dance, which I played for her. Then my sister-in-law, a beautiful dancer, did a classical dance while I played on the violin for her. I wrote this act myself, including the music.

One of Larry's earliest portraits, and a photograph inscribed to him by his dear Mabel, a young and beautiful flapper in the roaring twenties.

Then we joined and did a combination on jazz and classical, singing and dancing. We introduced the Charleston in vaudeville in Charleston, South Carolina. That was quite a coincidence and we got a lot of write-ups on it. We introduced it in vaudeville. It started in the Broadway show *Good News*. Then we went together as a trio until 1928, all over the country, the RKO circuit, the Orpheum, and the Keith-Orpheum.

One of my greatest disappointments was in 1927 when I was signed to emcee in Detroit, Michigan. I called my father to tell him the good news and he asked me how long the contract was for, and I said one year. He said to me, "I guess that means I'll never see you again." I told him, "Don't be silly. A year isn't so long. He told me, "Maybe I'll come out to see you." And the next day, he died. He never saw me do comedy. I was working with the girls. He only saw me play violin and sing. My mother saw me do comedy years later, and working in pictures, too.

We got a booking from the Paramount Theatre in

Larry actually mastered the difficult Russian Cossack dance—even with a fiddle—in his early days of performing.

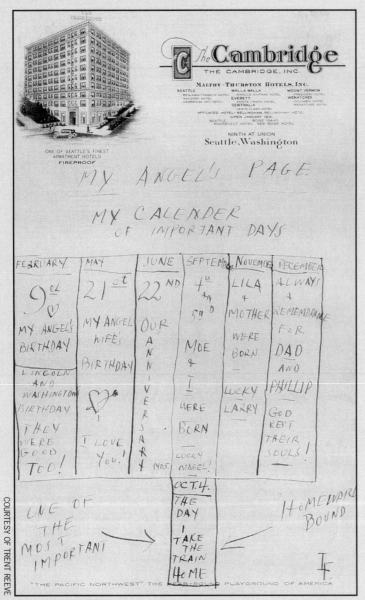

While in Seattle, Larry drew this calendar and sent it to his young daughter, Phyllis, who constantly asked when he'd be returning home from touring. Note that Larry still mistakenly assumed his birthday was September 4 and his brother Moe's was the 5th. It wasn't until 1939 that Larry discovered his actual birthdate (October 5, 1902). Larry commonly initialed notes and artwork with his trademark integrated initials *LF*, shown at the bottom right.

Toronto, Canada, where a friend of ours, Eddie Laughton, was an emcee. He was a very popular one in those days, and while we were appearing there Sol Berns, who was out booking the circuit, caught our act and offered us fifteen weeks on the Canadian Circuit from Toronto through to Vancouver. However, my sister-in-law Loretta refused to do it because she was engaged to a boy in Philadelphia and she promptly went right back to Philadelphia, breaking up the trio. My wife and I stayed on in Toronto with our friends the Laughtons, and he was running an amateur contest that night. I wanted to see a movie. So I went to another theater before the show went on. During the performance in the movie house, they flashed on the screen: "Larry Fine wanted at the box office." I got panicky and ran out and asked "What's the matter?" the man said, "Eddie Laughton just called and wants you back at his theater immediately." I ran back during the terrible snowstorm, and I got there in his theater, the Paramount. I asked him "What the matter?" and he told me that because of the storm in the outlying districts where most of the amateurs were coming from, some of them couldn't get in, so he wanted me to go on as an amateur. Well, I was embarrassed; I had just played the theater, and I said "They'll recognize me as a professional." Well, Eddie knew me well, and he knew that during our act, the Haney Sisters and Fine, we worked in a unit with a blackface comedian called Mel Klee, who worked along with us for almost a year. So he said, "Put the black on and go out there. Do Klee's routine!" and he introduced me as Joe Roberts.

Well, my wife was sitting with Eddie Laughton's wife in the box, and when she saw me come out, she ran down the aisle. She didn't want to watch, but she never got out of the theater because I started to get laughs right away and she came back, and naturally, doing this professional's act, I was a riot. Then, Eddie put me on the spot because when it came time to win

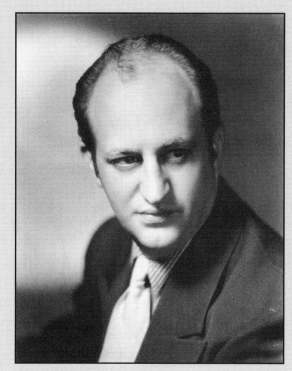

Although Shemp, Moe, and Larry were "Three Lost Souls" for a time, they did have a straight-man, Jack Walsh, to help point them in some direction in the early 1930s. *Right,* Larry Fine in a rare formal portrait circa 1935.

Larry in his late teens, trying to look older and make a name for himself in vaudeville. "When I first got into show business, I met a girl named Wynona Fine. No relation, but the same name. We didn't want to use Fine & Fine, because in those days, people saw a girl in the act, if they thought she was married they'd lose interest. So we called our act Fine & Dandy, but people kept calling me Mr. Dandy."

the prize, he didn't want me to win because he couldn't bring me back. So he held the card over my head for the applause, and as it started he would switch the card to the girl next to me and had her win the prize.

Later, that evening, we had a party at Eddie's home and Sol Berns had been in the audience and he was questioning Eddie about how he could get in touch with the blackface comedian. He said to me, "If I didn't know you were part of the Haney act, I'd swear it was you." Never having done blackface before, I left a little of the black in my ears and he finally noticed it and knew it was me who had done the act. He said to me, "I'll give the fifteen weeks I was going to give the trio and for the same money, just work as a single."

So I talked it over with my wife and she called Philadelphia to tell her parents that she would go on with me, just travel with me as a single. Well, I played about two weeks when my wife got a call from her sister, who said she'd had an argument with her boyfriend and would like to go back on the road. Well, I was all set as a single now and my wife's other older sister, Rose, who was also a performer, was married to Harry Romm, a theatrical agent. He suggested that he could book the two sisters without me for the same money we were making as a trio. My wife and her sister, Loretta. We finally agreed that I would finish out the fif-teen weeks as a single and my wife would go and do a sister act with Loretta. So she went back and I contin-ued on.

By this time it is two weeks before Christmas and they are working for Mike Fritzel, who owned the Chez Paris in Chicago. My wife called me in Canada and said to me, "This is going to be our first Christmas that we'll be apart." So she said, "Why don't you quit and come to Chicago?" I'm sure they can get you lots of work around here. So I got in touch with Sol Berns—luckily he was a friend, and he let me out of my single book-ing and I went to Chicago to join my wife.

In Chicago, I belonged to a club called the Comedy Club. And I was playing cards with Fred Mann, who owned the Rainbo Gardens, an exotic night spot (a combination café and jai-alai games); LeRoy Prinze, the producer; and Mort Hyman, the publicist. I was playing cards with the three of them and the new revue at Mann's Rainbo Gardens was opening that night. They were relaxing with the card game in the afternoon, when they got a phone call that Ray Evans, the comedy star and emcee of the show, refused to go on during rehearsal because Ruth Etting, who then was becoming a great attraction, was billed as the star of the show. Ray quit because he wanted top billing. Mr. Mann said, "Let me talk to him." and the stage manager told him

This is Chicago's Rainbo Gardens, where Larry became a Stooge, as it looked in March 2002. The building was demolished in November 2003 despite efforts to pre-serve it as a city landmark.

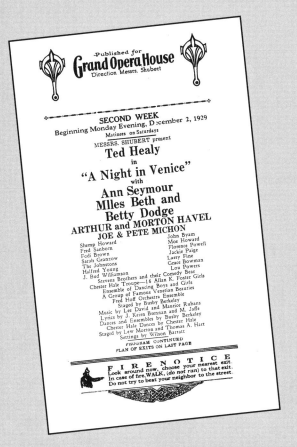

that he'd already left. So now they were stuck and they had to go back to the café. I said to LeRoy Prinze: "Hey, how about giving me the job?" He said, "My God, there are six numbers to learn." I told him, "I can do it, and I can play violin and dance."

Fortunately, LeRoy had the script with him since he was the producer of the show and we went to a music publisher's and I got a copy of the songs and sang them for him. They knew me there and knew I could play the violin. I got the job. I went on that night and was quite a hit. Mr. Mann signed me to a three-year contract.

He kept the original Rainbo Gardens in Havana, Cuba, where jai-alai (pronounced hi-li) games come from, and I was to play between the two Rainbo Gardens, in Chicago and Cuba, for the next three years. I stayed there quite a while, and Ted Healy appeared in Chicago at the Cohens Theater with a show called "A Night in Spain," with Shemp Howard, Moe Howard's older brother, as the show's main foil. However, Shemp had received an offer from another agent to do a dou-

ble act, at a much bigger salary, so he gave Healy his two weeks notice and coincidentally, that night, they threw a party at the Gardens for the cast of "A Night in Spain," the old chicken a la king; and Ted Healy and Shemp attended. Al Jolson was with the show and he came too. Healy and Shemp took one look at me and Shemp, who was about to leave, suggested to Healy that he could use me and called me to their table and offered me the show. However, when I mentioned it to Mr. Mann, he refused to let me out of my contract.

On the next Wednesday matinee, Healy invited me over, and when I saw Shemp and the show, I went backstage and told Healy I didn't think I could do it. Shemp was so great. I explained to him I couldn't get out of my contract anyhow. However, I had dinner with them, and Healy was very nice and then took a cab to my café. When I got there, it was closed tight and there were signs posted all over by the Internal Revenue office, that they had closed them on account of they sold liquor. This was during Prohibition. It really was the manager and the waiters who were in on it. Mr. Mann knew nothing about it.

I immediately called LeRoy Prinze and asked him how I stood with this contract. The place was closed, so was I still on salary or not? He told me very sadly that Mr. Mann committed suicide from the shame. I immediately took another cab back to the theater to tell Mr. Healy the situation. He let me stand in the wings again and watch the show and then hired me. I stood in the wings and behind me was Al Jolson, who was the star appearing there. I stood in the wings so Healy could see me. I wanted to tell him I'd take the job. He saw me out of the corner of his eye and he gave Jolson the signal to push me out there onstage. I was dressed for winter, overcoat and hat. He was a great ad libber. He pushed me right into the scene. The audience knew I didn't belong.

I watched the show the next evening. During intermission, he called me into the dressing room with Shemp and we talked over the other bits Shemp had to do in the show. Healy said I was going on. Now! I got very upset, but I went on and finished the show. The next evening I did the show and Friday night I did the whole show and then Shemp left. I walked right into the show and stayed with "A Night in Spain" thirty-five weeks and then was in "A Night in Venice," on Broadway, and it ran from 1929 into 1930 and we toured with that show.

Shemp had been doing the act with Healy's brother-in-law, Sam, and a dancer named Paul Louise. When we came out here to Hollywood as a trio, we worked in "A Night in Spain" at the Biltmore Theatre in Los Angeles. On the way back, Shemp had broken up with his partner and was waiting so he could join our show again. It was then Shemp, myself, and Paul Louise until we began "A Night in Venice" in 1931. Moe then joined us in New York for that and it became Shemp, Moe, and me.

Shemp and Moe came back to Healy and we formed a trio, so it was called Ted Healy and his Stooges. We also called it Ted

The BIGGEST LAUGH IN NEW YORK
•
A NIGHT IN VENICE
•
Now at the SHUBERT THEATRE
Matinees Wed. and Sat.

TED HEALY *and his three Southern Gentlemen*

A promotional postcard for their stage show, "A Night in Venice," circa 1929.

Healy and His Three Southern Gentlemen. During that period we were signed by the old Fox company to do our first motion picture, called *Soup to Nuts,* written by Rube Goldberg, the famous cartoonist. That was in 1930. We came out to Los Angeles and did the picture partly at the old Western Avenue studio and partly at what is now the main studio, but then was called "the ranch." The Cafe de Paris, the studio commissary, was just opened, and while there we met some wonderful people who were getting started just as we were, like Raoul Walsh, Al Green, Leo McCarey, Sidney Lanfield, John Wayne (who was then in the prop department, just out of college), and Winfield Sheehan, then the head of Fox. Mr. Sheehan saw the picture and decided he wanted us and not Healy, which aggravated Mr. Healy no end. So Healy left for New York that same day, but

before he did, he went in to see Mr. Sheehan and told him he thought it wasn't all right to take his boys away from his act, so Mr. Sheehan cancelled our contract. Meantime, Healy went to New York, so we were left out here.

However the William Morris office booked us into the Paramount Theatre, locally, for two weeks. And incidentally, Fox was very nice. They gave us all fare for us and for our wives to go back to New York and about $300 apiece for expense money. We did that act for about six weeks, and from Paramount we worked in theaters in San Francisco and Seattle. Mr. Healy got an injunction against us claiming we were using his material. We had to go back to New York for an arbitration case, which we won. Then Shemp, Moe and I continued as a trio, calling ourselves The Three Stooges. We worked quite a lot, but Healy kept hounding the theaters, threatening lawsuits and injunctions against them. It didn't make it easy for us.

In fact, I think that period was the greatest struggle in my career, when Healy was making all the trouble for us and we couldn't get work for a while because he was suing and threatening to sue. I had my wife and child to take care of and was too proud to ask my folks for help, and we missed a lot of meals. A man can stand that for himself, but not for his wife and children.

In 1933, Mr. J. J. Shubert offered us a show called "The Passing Show" in conjunction with Healy, to star Healy and us. We then went back with Healy and during rehearsals, the other star—I can't remember the name of the other star, a woman—got sick and Mr. Shubert asked us to postpone the show. While waiting, Mr. Healy booked some theaters in Chicago with Balaban and Katz.

He was paid $6300 net for the four of us. He had signed a contract with Shubert for $3,000 for the four of us. When he realized how much more money he could get out of the show, he then found a loophole in his Shubert contract and he broke it. Shubert was mad and sued. During the litigation, Mr. Shubert saw that he couldn't win the case. So he offered Shemp the starring part in the show at quite a lot of money. Shemp promptly gave Healy his notice and that's when Jerry, known as "Curly," Moe's younger brother, replaced Shemp.

We came out to Hollywood to work in the Club New Yorker, and during that period, Bryan Foy had a picture called *Tomorrow's Children* and he was throwing a big party at the Rancho for all his producer friends. He had produced the picture independently and was trying to sell it to a major studio. Mr. Foy had gone to school with Ted Healy, so he asked him to do him a favor and entertain that night and put on a show, which we all did. At the end of the act, when we were swamped by Jack Warner, Louis B. Mayer from MGM, Harry Cohn of Columbia, all the majors were offering us jobs and contracts.

We went home and talked it over and decided on MGM. They signed us to a contract. The first picture we made, it was so bad, I think they burned it without ever releasing it. It was so terrible. They fired the director and us but Healy offered Louis B. Mayer to make another picture for free to prove that we were funny and we came up with the idea for *Nertsery Rhymes,* in color. Then, incidentally, we made a picture with Walter Lang at MGM; it was called *Meet the Baron,* it was Jack Pearl's first starring role, with Edna Mae Oliver.

Ted Healy, Bonnie Bonnell, and the Stooges, circa 1933.

We made a series of pictures at MGM: *Turn Back the Clock, Hollywood Party.* Then we went into a picture which was advertised as the first million-dollar musical ever made, with Joan Crawford, called *Dancing Lady,* co-starring Clark Gable, Fred Astaire, Franchot Tone, Nelson Eddy and many others.

I played the piano in the picture *Dancing Lady.* Harry Rosenthal was the name of the piano player I replaced in the picture. He was signed for the picture and he was given a leave of absence from the show "The Moon Is Blue" for the picture. During the start of the picture, Clark Gable had appendicitis and was operated on. *Dancing Lady* was postponed eleven weeks,

Larry Dearest Larry takes his scenes with Joan Crawford quite seriously in MGM's *Dancing Lady.*

so Mr. Rosenthal couldn't continue in the picture and I played his part. I coaxed and begged Joan Crawford and Robert Z. Leonard, the director, to let me do the part. The part was a piano player and a Jewish comedian, who during the whole picture was working on a crossword puzzle. The puzzle turned out to be Adolph Hitler. I didn't work with Moe and Curly in that picture, I worked alone in that without them.

We got caught in an exchange deal between Columbia and MGM. Columbia had a pictured called *Transcontinental Bus* and MGM had a picture called *It Happened One Night* so they exchanged pictures and MGM also gave Columbia Clark Gable as the star for *It Happened One Night*. We made the picture *Transcontinental Bus* [renamed *Fugitive Lovers,* 1934] with Robert Montgomery. The bus never got anywhere. Actually, it never started. The picture went nowhere and *It Happened One Night* won Academy Awards all over the place.

About this time, Healy found out that MGM was going to release Jimmy Durante and he figured that they must have some stories lying around for Durante, so that he would have a better chance without us and we parted company with him. We signed with Harry Cohn at Columbia in March of 1934 and stayed at Columbia until January 1958, without a break. I think it's the longest studio contract ever held by a team, or any actor.

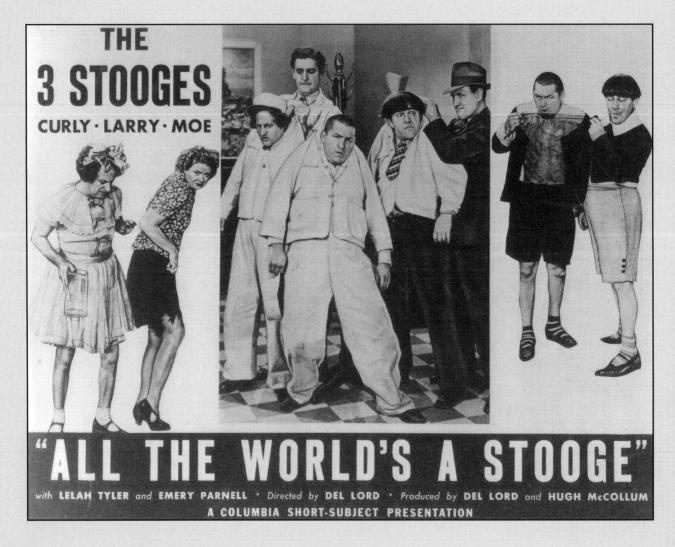

plugging their performances in each city—they just never completely adapted their routines for microphone banter alone.

With Healy, the Stooges performed onstage and molded the characters and appearances that we now know. Moe adopted his sugar bowl haircut and Shemp just let his long greasy locks fly where they may. Larry recalled how the frizzy hair became his trademark: "When I was in 'A Night in Spain' with Ted Healy, I was washing my hair in the dressing room and then it was drying while we were talking. It stood up in curls. Mr. Shubert saw it and said, 'What are you doing?' and I said, 'I just washed my hair and it's drying. I'll comb it down.' He said, 'No, no, leave it that way!' And ever since I've had to wet my hair and let it dry naturally during every performance so it would curl and stand up." Eventually, Larry got to the point where he could simply tease it up with a comb quickly, if needed, but for the full effect in films, he wet it down and let the natural perm do its wild thing. When he wasn't working, Larry combed his hair straight back with no part, much like Moe Howard did when not in character.

Moe, in a radio show interview years later, remembered how another Stooge trademark came to be: "The poking in the eye was discovered in a card game. Playing contract bridge. Larry claimed he had four honors when he only had three. Shemp proved to him that he had and Larry still insisted that he had four. So Shemp threw his fingers at him and poked him in the eyes. Shemp went deep right into Larry's eyeballs. Larry had tears coming from his eyes for a week. It struck me so funny I leaned backward in a chair and went right through a glass door."

● ● ●

The close of the twenties marked not only the approach of a new decade, but the invention of sound motion pictures; it also proved to be a great turning point in Larry and Mabel's life together. Mabel Fine gave birth to their first child, a daughter they named Phyllis, in the Atlantic City Hospital on February 9, 1929. Telegrams poured in from Larry's friends and relatives and the new parents couldn't have been happier. Larry was absolutely taken with his little blonde-haired "angel baby," as he called her. He was forever "Daddy" to her, and the two shared a special bond that endured.

WSB Presents These Stars

Shemp, Moe, and Larry were headlining vaudeville theatres in the early 1930s as "Three Lost Souls" or "Howard, Fine & Howard." While appearing at the Paramount Theater in Atlanta, Georgia, in June 1932, the trio broadcast their antics on the WSB radio program *Paramount's Radio Party.*

Larry was invited to join the cast of "A Night in Venice," a J. J. Shubert Broadway revue starring Ted Healy. He was reluctant to leave his wife and the new baby daughter, but Mabel convinced him to take the job because there were plenty of relatives around to help her with the baby. Their Broadway revue opened in May 1929 and later toured until just after the Wall Street crash in late October of the same year. They continued to perform onstage at the Palace with Healy as his "Three Racketeers" or "Three Southern Gentlemen," and these performances led to an offer to appear in their first motion picture, *Soup to Nuts,* made in 1930. Mabel and the baby joined Larry in his trip across country to Hollywood. The Stooges were breaking into the movies and the excitement among Healy and all three of the Stooges and their wives was palpable.

Soup to Nuts, written by cartoonist Rube Goldberg and directed by Benjamin Stoloff, had a flimsy story at best, involving the Stooges as firemen. Released in September 1930 to smaller areas and a wider release on October 29, the film was, for the most part, lambasted by critics. *Variety* at the time called it "an abortive comedy . . . a two reel Keystone of the silent days padded into over six reels with dialogue."

Moe, Larry, and Shemp appeared onstage at Seattle's RKO Orpheum Theatre during the premiere weeks of the film *Lost Squadron* in 1932.

The film was mostly forgotten over the years, by audiences and by the Stooges, obviously shelved by the studio—but not destroyed, thankfully. The Stooges themselves never saw it again. Moe speculated the studio "made guitar picks out of it." Film historian Richard Finegan described *Soup to Nuts* in 1991 when the film finally resurfaced after decades: "The plot of *Soup to Nuts* can be summarized easily: Proud old shopkeeper Charles Winninger refused to work under a young creditor who has

ONE FINE STOOGE

come to take over the shop. But, fortunately, the Stooges have enough time to do their stuff between plot developments. They play firemen and waste no time in the very first scene of the movie, delivering routines and gags. . . . The highlight of the movie is the Stooges' appearance at the Fireman's Ball. Ted Healy sings a song, then motions for his three stooges to come on the stage with him and they go into many familiar but funny routines, made all the more memorable as they are appearing for the first time on film."

Finegan further pointed out that the routines performed by Healy and the Stooges in *Soup to Nuts* are "valuable to Stooges fans and historians because just like the similar sequences in 1933's *Plane Nuts*, they provide a record of the Stooges' vaudeville act with Ted Healy."

Writer/inventor/artist Rube Goldberg, known for his elaborately designed kinetic motion gadgetry (think of the children's board game Mousetrap or Vincent Price's elaborate machinations in the film *Edward Scissorhands*), wrote *Soup to Nuts* with Ted Healy in mind as its star, as evidenced in the script's twenty-two-page first draft treatment dated May 1930. (Goldberg appears in the film in a brief cameo in the restaurant, reading his mail.) There were no "stooges" in the first script; however, additional firemen did have lines and action. In a later draft, dated June 6, 1930, only Shemp had lines; the additional dialogue for Moe and Larry came shortly thereafter. The seventy-minute film was shot in just a matter of weeks at the old Fox lot in Culver City, with street scenes filmed in a downtown Los Angeles area known as "Little Tokyo"—doubling as Brooklyn, New York, where the story is set.

Larry recalled little of the film's production in his later years; however, he did remember the opening preview in San Diego, mainly because it involved the loss of cash—and eventually, a sabotaged opportunity to sign a contract with Fox studios. The studio had chartered a Santa Fe Railroad car to transport the cast, an orchestra, young girls, and plenty of champagne for a two-hour party excursion to San Diego. Larry recalled:

> The cast was taken down on a special train. Having never been in San Diego before, we didn't know Caliente in Mexico was so close. We crossed the border over to Caliente with only about $50 between the

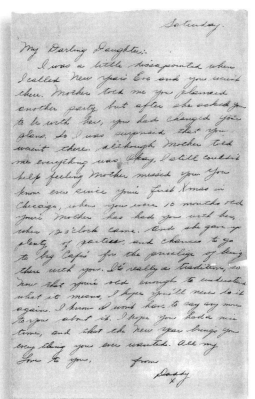

This letter from Larry gently admonishing his young daughter, Phyllis, illustrates the affection he showed his children.

three of us. After a visit to the races, we were broke, because Lenny Sachs, Jack Dempsey's manager, had told us not to bet until he gave us the information on who to bet on. Of course, you guessed it, we lost. There was a private club room where big shots could go, but we weren't permitted in. Moe threw my straw hat over the fence and I went over to get it and ran right into the room where Sheehan [Winfield Sheehan, Fox's head of production], our writer Rube Goldberg, and Al Rocket [associate producer] were. I told Rocket I wanted to borrow $300 and he gave it to us. I told him we would pay him Monday. Of course, we lost the $300. When we got back to Hollywood, we went to pay Rocket back his money. Mr. Rocket wasn't in but had left an envelope for us with $500 in it. He felt bad about our losing our money. We were stunned, but we actually came out with a profit.

The Stooges couldn't believe their ears when they received word that Sheehan had decided to sign them to a contract with Fox, but not Healy. The contract would be a handsome seven-year deal with an escalating salary and options. Infuriated and jealous that the studio would "break up the act," Healy threatened to sue the studio, and consequently the Stooges' offer was withdrawn. This was not just a mere shot of seltzer in their faces, it was a powerful triple slap.

Healy suddenly headed back to New York, leaving his boys in the messy legal aftermath. Since some documents had been signed and the Stooges left hanging, the studio apologized and issued first-class fares for the trio and their wives plus handsome compensation for the trouble. The studio also arranged for them to appear at the Paramount Theatre before heading back to the East Coast, and Moe, Larry, and Shemp felt better about how things

Larry, Shemp, and Moe make it to the silver screen in *Soup to Nuts* (1930). Larry's first words on film: "Me too."

ONE FINE STOOGE

Not seen since 1930, *Soup to Nuts* was buried deep in the vaults of 20th Century Fox Film Corporation in the form of a single, dangerously unstable nitrate negative. Not until the 1990s did Fox, in conjunction with UCLA's Film and Television Archive, restore and preserve the motion picture. The film was screened for a live audience for the first time in sixty years at a Three Stooges convention; eventually it was given a television broadcast debut on American Movie Classics cable network.

ALONG CAME LARRY

worked out with the studio—but not about Healy. They were angry and fed up with him. The Stooges' wives pleaded with their husbands to break the ties completely.

"Healy put an injunction against us for using 'his' material," recalled Larry. "So we went into the musicians' pit and worked different material and worked six weeks before we had to go back to New York for the Board of Arbitration. We were vindicated and they told us we would have the right to work alone. That was a huge relief for us because Healy couldn't touch us now."

Shemp was actually afraid of Ted Healy, who was known to be a great drinker in his day. Healy was loud, volatile, and obnoxious, and he loved to play tricks on his "boys." He had a penchant for lighting small fires in hotel rooms as a gag; he laughed hysterically as he jettisoned heavy wetted-down telephone directories from hotel room windows targeting unsuspecting passersby five stories below. There was definitely a malevolent streak in Healy; he could be humorous, but also quite menacing. For example, in December 1935, Healy spent a good portion of his Christmas holiday in a Los Angeles jail, arrested for arson. According to the *Los Angeles Times,* a drunken Healy busted into the home of his girlfriend, Marion "Bonnie" Bonnell, through a glass front door and set fire to a pile of her clothing and other paraphernalia on the kitchen stove.

Director Ben Stoloff poses with the Stooges' wives on the firehouse set of the team's first film, *Soup to Nuts.* Left to right: "Babe" Howard (Shemp's wife), Stoloff, Helen Howard (Moe's wife), and Mabel Fine (Larry's wife).

The Stooges stayed far away from Healy for a stretch and retooled their act; they knocked out audiences with a hilarious new stage act where they portrayed musicians in the pit. A riot would break out and mayhem took over as they broke instruments over their heads and a fight erupted among them. The hysterical act took off, and the theater management booked them into venues up the West Coast from San Francisco to Seattle. From there, they headed back to the East Coast. When they were working at the Capitol Theatre in New York, a crazed Healy threatened the Capitol's manager that he'd throw a bomb in the theatre if the Stooges appeared.

The boys received an offer to play some dates in Detroit, and as Larry described, "We were only happy to get out of New York." Years later, Larry remembered the sleeping arrangements quite clearly on this trip heading to Michigan. "They only had one upper berth and one lower berth," he described in his book, *Stroke of Luck.* "So Shemp and I took the lower berth, and Moe took the upper berth. I woke up the next morning around 9 a.m.

ONE FINE STOOGE

Shemp had been up for some time, and I noticed the bed was soaked and I was wet halfway up my back.

"Shemp, who was still nervous and frightened from our previous day's experience, had wee-weed all over me during the night. Shemp had already cleaned up so I got up also and cleaned up."

But here's the kicker: To cover his embarrassment and explain the soiled bedding, Shemp told the porter that Larry was sick all night and put the blame on him.

A Fine Romance Larry and Mabel couldn't get enough of the warm weather.

Healy felt betrayed, jealous, and angry that the Stooges—the act he created—would go out on their own. And succeed to boot. The Stooges felt vindicated all the way around. They figured if things had been the other way around, if the studio had signed Healy without them, he would have readily accepted and they would have had no choice but to go out on their own anyway. But it didn't work out that way. Following the Detroit dates, the Stooges were gaining popularity on their own and headed back East, where they appeared in an act called Howard, Fine & Howard, as well as "Three Lost Souls" with straight-man Jack Walsh for a time. Healy, at the same time, began breaking in new "stooges" in his own act for a Broadway revue at the Imperial Theater.

In 1932, Healy apologized sheepishly and asked Moe, Larry, and Shemp to rejoin him for a new production called "The Passing Show of 1932." A truce was called. The Stooges were skeptical, but forgiving. While in rehearsals for the new production, Healy received a more handsome offer to go on the road with the Balaban and Katz theatre chain and his manager, Paul Dempsey, ferreted out a loophole in the Shubert contract so he could exit "The Passing Show." A few weeks into the show's Detroit previews, Healy left and urged the Stooges to hit the road with him. But Shemp's patience was nearing an end; he'd had enough of Healy's threats and pranks. Shemp's wife, Babe, who was always protective of her husband no matter how quirky he could be, urged her husband to contemplate a break with Healy.

When an offer came from the West Coast for Healy and the Stooges to play at the Club New Yorker in Hollywood (a basement club in the Christie Hotel), Shemp refused to go. It was a great loss to the team, and maybe even more so to Healy. Shemp had been his original Stooge, and Healy felt abandoned and lost without his main boy to bat around. A tempting offer came Shemp's way in 1933, to appear in some talking short-subject comedies for Vitaphone Studios in Brooklyn, and this became his ticket out. (Shemp began carving out a nice career of his own at Vitaphone and went on to appear in short-subject comedies alongside Roscoe "Fatty" Arbuckle, Jack Haley, Ben Blue, Bert Lahr, and even Dizzy and Daffy Dean.)

Enter Moe and Shemp's youngest brother, Jerome . . . a.k.a. "Curly."

• • •

Moe Howard brought in his younger brother, Jerome—sometimes called Jerry—who shaved his own head without any wheedling. It was a fashion of his own invention and it led to his nickname, "Curly." Jerry had been a comedy orchestra leader appearing with the Orville Knapp Band and had developed a comic timing all his own. He stood about the same height as the other guys and was a heavy guy, but he wasn't obese. Curly carried his extra pounds with a tight gut and moved gracefully with his extra weight; he had a full head of dark brown hair and sported a nicely groomed and waxed handlebar mustache. On paper, he didn't exactly scream "Stooge." But despite Healy's initial reluctance, Moe urged him to take a look at Curly and once Healy got a dose of his younger brother's abilities, he agreed to have him join as the new third Stooge.

There was one performance, one monumental moment in time, when the three Howard brothers—Moe, Shemp, and Curly—appeared onstage together as a team of three stooges. No one recalls exactly what they called themselves or where it took place, although Larry's notations indicate it probably occurred just before Shemp left for New York. They just didn't click, and of course this worked in Larry's favor. Larry recalled years later: "They did have an act, they did a trio. It lasted one show and the manager threw them out. There was a riot in the dressing room. I wasn't there, but Healy told me. I said,

The Stooges, Ted Healy, and Jimmy Durante *Meet the Baron* (Jack Pearl) in MGM's 1933 feature film. *Bottom:* Also from *Meet the Baron,* Ted Healy and the Stooges tackle some plumbing issues in the girl's dormitory.

ONE FINE STOOGE

'Where are the boys?' and he told me, 'They're out doing a trio. . . . I guarantee they'll be back in an hour.' Sure enough, that same night, he said 'They're available.' They just couldn't get along. It happens to a lot of brothers. I'm surprised the Marx Brothers got along.

"I think Shemp and Moe got along because I saw to that," Larry explained. "I was the peacemaker. I'd break the tie sometimes, you know what I mean? They'd accept my word. In the early days Moe was an awful coward and so was Shemp. If theater managers wanted to fight, they'd throw me at them and I'd fight with the managers. Moe would say, 'Larry, go ahead!' I didn't take no shit from anybody."

A genial type, Curly submitted to his new name, his new look, and his new job. His appearance was just as goofy as the other guys, but it took some time to adjust. Larry further observed, "At first, Curly was very sensitive and embarrassed about his crew cut hair. For months he would never take his cap off; however, as soon as he got popular in the movies, he was proud of his appearance and wouldn't keep his cap on so everyone would immediately recognize him."

Healy and the Stooges rehearsed with Curly and opened at the Club New Yorker on March 2, 1933, to an enthusiastic audience full of Hollywood stars and studio executives. Also featured in the musical show was Bonnie Bonnell, Betty Grable, Glen Dale, Doris Roche, Velma Wayne, and the Jed Warner Orchestra. Healy and the boys were later invited to play a benefit performance at a party where they were once again a smash hit.

Attending the party were some of Tinseltown's most powerful men: studio moguls such as Jack Warner, Harry Cohn, Louis B. Mayer, and Carl Laemmle. The audience roared with laughter and immediately the studio execs came knocking; by the next day, Healy and the Stooges had become part of Metro-Goldwyn-Mayer's stable of stars. MGM was the biggest, most majestic studio of them all, shepherded by the great Louis B. Mayer, and the Stooges had an inkling their stardom was twinkling as Tinseltown finally embraced their knockabout comedy style.

While Larry resided in hotels in Los Angeles, Mabel stayed at the Haverford Apartments in Atlantic City and later relocated to the posh President

This rare page from the original treatment for the MGM comedy short titled *Beer Garden* (dated April 1933, written by Robert Hopkins), shows the first time Moe, Larry, and Curly were officially labeled "The Three Stooges" in type. This film, renamed *Beer and Pretzels*, is considered by many to be the best of the Ted Healy/Stooges shorts.

Above left, Ted, Bonnie, and the Stooges perform portions of their live stage act in the MGM short *Plane Nuts* (1933). *Above right,* Shot in a new two-strip Technicolor process, the Stooges with Healy and Bonnell star in the short-subject *Nertsery Rhymes* in 1933 at MGM.

Hotel. They maintained their apartment at the President, and eventually Larry sent for Mabel and young Phyllis to join him in Southern California. Little Phyllis took to life in California quickly and loved having Moe's daughter Joan as a playmate because she was close in age.

From 1933 to 1934, the Stooges, along with Ted Healy and his girlfriend, Bonnie Bonnell, made five short films at MGM, including: *Nertsery Rhymes, Beer and Pretzels, Hello Pop!, Plane Nuts,* and *The Big Idea.* Two of them, *Nertsery Rhymes* and *Hello Pop!* were shot in experimental two-strip Technicolor. With Healy, the Stooges also appeared in six feature films during this year: *Turn Back the Clock* (solo), *Meet the Baron, Dancing Lady, Fugitive Lovers, Hollywood Party,* and *Myrt and Marge.*

Beer and Pretzels, their second MGM short, was written in April 1933 and released in August of that year. Originally titled *Beer Garden,* it was written for Healy and the Stooges by veteran MGM gag man Robert "Hoppy" Hopkins, who became the first to officially call the troupe by their rightful title, "The Three Stooges," in print, or at least in a script. In MGM's vault is the original seven-page treatment, dated April 15, 1933, in which they are referenced by that new title for the first time. Granted, the name is there mainly for camera position, but still, it is the first script in which that title is used. Later scripts, such as the April 26, 1934, continuity script for *The Big Idea,* follow suit and refer to them as "Three Stooges" ("Three Stooges raise their hats" . . . "in walk the Three Stooges playing trumpets").

The original May 10, 1933, treatment/script for *Nertsery Rhymes* was written by Ted Healy, Marty Brooks, and Moe Howard. Later, a more polished July 13, 1933, script became *Nertsery Rhymes* and it included the "Little Fly Upon the Wall" poem, delivered by Moe. (Later, Curly recited the ditty with more attitude and humor in the Columbia short *All the World's a Stooge*.) Larry retorts with his own version: "Little fly upon the track—the train came along and broke his back." *Hello Pop!,* the final musical short the Stooges made with Healy at MGM, has yet to be discovered: no prints are known to exist in studio vaults or private collections.

Concurrently, the Stooges were appearing in several MGM films, their first being *Turn Back the Clock* with Lee Tracy and Mae Clarke. In *Meet the Baron* (original title, *Oh What a Liar*) a film designed for Jack Pearl and Jimmy Durante, the Stooges and Healy met and worked for producer David O. Selznick, who later made the classic *Gone with the Wind*.

In *Dancing Lady,* Larry's favorite of the early MGM work, he acts separately from his partners. The script describes the role as: "Harry, the Jewish piano player at rehearsal who's also working on a puzzle." One scene called for Larry to play opposite Joan Crawford, and much more dialogue was filmed than ended up in the finished product—a great disappointment to Larry. Since this was a box office smash for MGM, starring Clark Gable and

Puzzling Larry's role as "a Jewish piano player" was cut short in *Dancing Lady* with Joan Crawford and Clark Gable. *Above*, A scene from *Dancing Lady* with Crawford, Ted Healy, and the Stooges.

Joan Crawford (also produced by Selznick), the few scenes in which the Stooges did appear provided massive exposure for the team.

It is a little-known fact that prolific humorist, writer, actor, and critic Robert Benchley, a member of the famous New York Algonquin Roundtable, wrote dialogue in August 1933 for Healy and the Stooges in *Dancing Lady*. MGM's vault copies of the scripts for *Dancing Lady* illustrate such dialogue contributions made by the respected writer. Benchley was brought in to rewrite and add to existing Healy/Stooges material in the early scenes where Healy enters. Unfortunately, much of Benchley's contributions were cut, and he did not receive screen credit in the final film. (Benchley, who won an Academy Award in 1936 for his short film *How to Sleep*, died in 1945.)

A rare candid photograph of the Stooges with cinematographer Allen Siegler, Ted Healy, and producer David O. Selznick, on the MGM lot during production of *Meet the Baron* in 1933.

In *Hollywood Party* (originally titled *Hollywood Revue of 1933*), Ted Healy joined five other writers developing comedy bits for the movie, even suggesting a bit from "A Night in Spain," although it had almost nothing for the Stooges to do. Eventually, Healy and Moe Howard collaborated on a treatment of old stage bits and routines and handed this in to MGM on April 19, 1933, but none

This interesting character study in Stooge, captured in 1934 by famous MGM photographer Clarence Sinclair Bull, was one of Larry's preferred portraits.

ONE FINE STOOGE

of it made it into the film. The final cut, starring Jimmy Durante and Jack Pearl among others, includes the Stooges in a brief cameo, as well as Laurel and Hardy, Joe E. Brown, Robert Young, and Arthur Treacher. Per early treatments and story sessions, *Hollywood Party* was supposed to feature a host of cameos from Gary Cooper, John Barrymore, Cary Grant, Marie Dressler, Clark Gable, and even Mae West that, alas, ultimately never materialized.

MGM's publicity for *Hollywood Party* described it as a multi-star extravaganza and even a "novelty." It was hyped as "the largest all-comedian cast ever assembled . . . a spectacular musical with an army of ravishing sun-kissed beauties." The studio's press releases even mention the appearance of Mickey Mouse in a musical number called "Hot Chocolate Soldiers," with songs from Richard Rodgers and Lorenz Hart and more. The Stooges and Healy are last on the studio's list of potential press-attractive names.

Ted, Bonnie Bonnell, and the boys work together for the last time in the Universal feature film, *Myrt and Marge* (1934).

Healy and the Stooges ended their association with the Universal Studios film *Myrt and Marge*, released in December 1934. "Ted Healy found out that MGM was going to release Jimmy Durante," Larry explained, "and he figured that they must have some stories lying around for Durante and that he would have a better chance without us." Healy and the Stooges parted company and it wasn't very long before Moe, Larry, and Curly signed with Columbia Pictures to star in two-reelers—on their own at last. Healy went on to appear in twenty-five more films, including *Bombshell* with Jean Harlow, but the cantankerous comedian never roped the success he had hoped for, the success he achieved with his Stooges.

If the Stooges thought perhaps they hadn't heard the last of Ted Healy—they were right.

MOE ON THE HOWARD BROTHERS

*In 1973, Moe Howard discussed his brothers and the art of comedy in an
interview with longtime Stooges fan Mike Mikicel.*

Curly was my younger brother and Shemp was my older brother. They were two different types of individuals. Shemp was more the deadpan, expressive type. Curly, half the time, we never knew what he was going to do. He was what we call "a hard study," which meant he didn't absorb the lines so quickly and solidly.

Curly would adlib, but not in words. If he felt that he had to speak—his line was due and he couldn't think of it—he'd go into anything. He'd fall on the floor and spin around like a top, or he'd go into the back-kicking business, fall on his back and roll all over the place. It was everything we could do to contain ourselves when he'd go into this. I knew why he was doing this. He was trying to catch up on the dialogue. Curly was very inventive, as far as expressions, actions with his hands. Barking. Wave in front of you. He could have fractured my skull in two if he wanted to, considering his size, but the extent of his reactions was sounds and motions.

There's quite a difference between *comedian* and *comic*. A lot of people don't realize that. A comedian has to have jokes written for him. If you look at Bob Hope, Johnny Carson, any of those standup comedians, at the end where the credits are given, you'll see that each one of them has about nine writers. But what you can't take away from them is the fact they're selling their personality more than anything else. So they depend on the humor that's written for them. But they have a sensational delivery of that humor. Those are comedians.

A comic, for instance . . . Curly is a comic. We are too, for that matter, because we can take a situation and make it funny. You don't have to have words, to speak funny words, to make things funny. Even to the point where many times, if we did something and then the thing wouldn't get a laugh, we found a way of either to hit Curly in the stomach and have a barrel noise, or grab him by the nose. It was always action going on. The tempo. That was the difference between us and Laurel and Hardy. Laurel and Hardy did great things. They could look at each other for the count of three and built up to a terrific laugh. But if we had to count thirty before we got a laugh, we'd faint. *Bang! Bang!* Laughs come more often. When you have fifteen minutes of film, you then have time to create a comedy situation that deals laughs along the way. There's a lot of psychology in the work we do. I mean, it doesn't just happen.

Larry snapped this extraordinary picture of the three Howard brothers—Moe, Shemp, and Curly—on the set of the short subject *Pardon My Scotch* in April 1935.

32

2

ON THEIR OWN

Without hesitation, Larry always said his favorite Stooge to act with was Curly. This was not a verbal slap in the face to Moe, with whom he'd worked a lot longer. Moe understood. He even agreed: his favorite was Curly as well. The funniest one was the last to enter.

This statement of preference also carried with it no disrespect toward the other "fill ins," you might say, for Curly Howard. Shemp Howard, Joe Besser, and Joe DeRita—all of whom eventually replaced Curly and completed the team for a spell—were certainly talented in their own way. Curly was simply their favorite, and the chemistry they had with Curly was perfection, at times, for all three. Moe couldn't have done enough to help his younger brother Curly, and Larry loved him like a brother, too, unabashedly admiring the rotund Stooge for his talent for uproarious ad-libbing when the cameras rolled or the curtain parted. Offstage, Curly was quiet, insecure, and reserved, cutting up much less than his partners.

Without question, Curly was a comedy genius on film, having created an original—truly unparalleled—face of comedy, unique as Charlie Chaplin and crazy as Robin Williams. Inasmuch as Larry and Moe recognized that the most popular Stooge, hands down, was Curly, they also realized that each of them had something to contribute to the trio to make it harmonize.

Moe, Larry, and Curly were the most popular mutation of the trio. With those three, everything clicked. Popularity—and paychecks—proved it. The Three Stooges just knew they were onto something when they hit their stride making shorts at Columbia and touring the country throughout the later '30s and '40s—they worked as a well-oiled locomotive in high gear. And the time went fast.

Debarking the California Limited, the Stooges return home to Hollywood from a sixteen-week personal appearance tour through the East and Midwest (September 28, 1935).

They weren't sure where they were heading with their comedy, or how they would evolve. Destiny controlled that and history wrote it down. In their best days, at the pinnacle of their work, their sharpest of timing, they took the journey and ran the distance. You can literally witness the team, like a moving timeline, gain and then lose their steam as they progressed in age—some parts requiring replacing, of course—and with a final burst and a second wind, they slowed to an end, and poof! Forty-plus years of filmmaking and an era ended when both Moe and Larry, the mainstays throughout, brothers in spirit and spit, died just months apart in 1975.

• • •

In 1960, the Three Stooges released an official biography to the press, a document that had been prepared under the guidance of Moe and Larry. In it, the story of their start with Columbia Pictures is told:

It was in 1934 that Ted Healy made his first film without the Three Stooges and decided to go it alone. The Three Stooges were promptly and simultaneously signed by Columbia and Universal International. Moe Howard signed the deal for them at Columbia, while Larry, unaware of this, signed for them at Universal. There was a big dispute between the two studios, settled only when it was discovered that Moe Howard had signed the deal for the trio three hours before Larry had signed the Universal deal. Columbia got them, and show-wise folks say Abbott and Costello would never have won their breaks if Larry's contract had prevailed. Abbott and Costello hit the big-time. The Three Stooges hit the far end of double feature bills with 200 two-reelers they made during 24 years with Columbia until the recent re-release of their shorts to TV—which brought them a new and fervid generation of fans throughout the world. The Three Stooges are just as popular on European TV since their two-reelers are so predominantly visual that Europeans who don't understand English can still understand and howl at the Stooges' physical shenanigans.

Moe and Larry always slightly exaggerated the number of two-reelers they made at Columbia. In all, 190 Three Stooges shorts were produced between

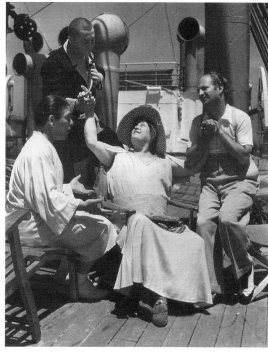

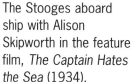

The Stooges aboard ship with Alison Skipworth in the feature film, *The Captain Hates the Sea* (1934).

"To the Hunt!" A rare behind-the-scenes snapshot of the Stooges getting crazy for the camera just outside the soundstage on the Columbia lot.

1934 until 1958, when their unprecedented contract was summarily terminated upon the death of studio head Harry Cohn.

Cohn was the president of Columbia Pictures, and Jack Cohn, his brother, was at one time the studio's vice president. Harry gained a reputation in Hollywood as that of a monster—intimidating, tyrannical, most always unsavory, and coarse. According to Larry, Cohn would routinely summon the Stooges to his office, where he sat at a desk on a raised platform. Their deal and continuous renewals always consisted of, on the surface at least, a simple

Here are some rare images of the Stooges performing with their stage straight man, Eddie Laughton, who also appeared with them in several shorts.

handshake all around. In reality, of course, contracts were drawn and signed by the Stooges: The team was to be paid on a fifty-two-week basis, and when the team wasn't in production on the short subjects (two-reelers), they were allowed to make personal appearances. All salaries derived from those appearances was their own. During the weeks they made personal appearances, the studio paid them half salary. That same contract included a clause that Moe later called "very mean," whereby the studio owned, as he said, "perpetual rights to your likenesses, your voices, in mediums now known or to be invented."

"How do you like that?" Moe said rhetorically to a reporter in 1970. "And of course, it could have been corrected [by] our charming governor, Ronald Reagan, when he was president of the Screen Actors Guild and a producer at the same time—which was a conflict of interest when he was producing pictures for General Electric—[but] he fixed it so nobody could get residuals, only in pictures made after 1960. Charming fellow." Larry remembered:

Harry Cohn signed us up at Columbia. He was the big boss then. Very eccentric. He thought we brought him luck. He was a god at the studio. If he didn't like you, you couldn't even get *in* the studio, let alone work for him. He was pretty hard-headed. And he missed a few opportunities because he was stubborn: We had Lucille Ball in a picture; we thought she was great. He didn't think much of her. He let her go. He let Marilyn Monroe go. I thought she was great. He had Sinatra, who won an Academy Award. He never bothered to sign him up.

He wanted to keep us exclusively making shorts. We wanted to do features, but he didn't want that. Even in pictures like *Start Cheering*, he had all of the good scenes taken out. He didn't want us to be too funny in features because other studios would pick us up.

He told us, "You boys will be here as long as I'm alive." And we were, because the minute he died, out we went. They didn't even wait until he was buried.

God help the guy that Harry Cohn caught lagging back on the job. He had a filthy mouth of the worst kind. Nobody seemed to like him, but we got along wonderful with him. You know, the funny thing about it, as mean a bastard as he was, he liked us. He used to like to have me come in his room, he had my favorite chair, which was wired, and I knew it all the time, but like a big kid, he'd get a kick out of seeing me sit down and *aaaahhhhh!* I knew what was happening. He'd say, 'Larry has been here twenty years and the dope falls for it every time.' One day, I came in and he said to me, "Don't take that chair. Put Moe in it. Sit over there." And I saw the wires on that one. He's giving the signal to everybody: watch Larry, he's gonna fall for it. I knew it. When I sat down, I jumped eight feet and he died laughing. That was his pet gag—fooling me. I let him think he was doing it, too. He was a big kid, you know.

If Cohn was the big kid on the block, then Ted Healy was the bully around the corner. Once the Three Stooges began production of shorts—starting with *Woman Haters,* released in May 1934—word made it to Healy that his boys were signed with Columbia and calling themselves "stooges." In June 1934, Ted Healy filed a lawsuit in Los Angeles seeking an injunction against Moe, Larry, and Curly and Columbia Pictures. Healy objected to their use of the name "Stooge," as well as any use of his name in association with theirs; Healy sought an accounting of their earnings to date as of February 1934. Cohn, always protective of his Stooges, instructed his legal team to shut down the suit immediately. Healy never collected a dime.

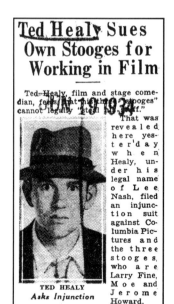

Ted Healy Sues Own Stooges for Working in Film

Ted Healy, film and stage comedian, feels that his Three Stooges" cannot legally "step out."

That was revealed here yesterday when Healy, under his legal name of Lee Nash, filed an injunction suit against Columbia Pictures and the three stooges, who are Larry Fine, Moe and Jerome Howard.

TED HEALY
Asks Injunction

In a complaint filed in Superior Court late yesterday Healy asked for an injunction to stop Columbia Pictures advertising the three comedians as "Ted Healy's Three Stooges," and he seeks an accounting for their earnings and judgment thereof since February 16.

The boys' break from Ted Healy was hardly a smooth one.

One Fine Day Larry reluctantly meets the family of the bride (Majorie White) in the musical rhyming short *Woman Haters* (1934).

Moe Howard, who had evolved into the team's spokesman, spent a lot of time clarifying the definition of the title "stooge" in the press during the next few years. Just in case.

"Everybody in the world has a stooge," Moe told *Detroit News* reporter George Stark in 1936 when the team appeared at the city's famed Fox Theater. "You take a president of a bank, for instance. Well, all the vice presidents of the bank are stooges for the president, and if it wasn't for the vice presidents, where would the presidents be? The president of the United States has a lot of stooges, too. They're in the Cabinet and in Congress. They have to play kind of dumb while the boss cracks wise. That was true of Mr. Hoover as well as Mr. Roosevelt, so there's nothing political about these reflections.

"Stooge," explained Moe quite seriously in further definition, "dates back to Shakespeare's day, when there were three classes of actors. There were the principals, the supers, and the students. The principals, of course were the boys who walked out on the stage and made important speeches. The supers were the boys who just walked on and waved banners and held spears. Sometimes they had a line or two to speak like 'Hail to the king!' Or 'Here comes the emperor!' But the students, they didn't do anything but be students. They just hung around and studied how to be supers. The word student eventually was contracted to stooge, and there you are. And so today we have in the theater, stooges—or guys who just hang around the stage and say

The Stooges stop what they're doing to pose for a picture backstage at St. Louis's Missouri Theatre. Moe's daughter, Joan, recalled the Stooges' functional stage wardrobe: "Their costumes were incredible . . . dirty old frock coats with shirts that were never white, always sweaty and yellowed, and around the necks they wore ugly black plastic ties."

Clockwise from top left, Larry smiles for MGM photographer Clarence Sinclair Bull in this 1934 portrait. Bud Jamison administers initiation rites for membership into the Woman Haters club in the Stooges' first Columbia short subject, a musical comedy, in 1934. It's three against one in this snapshot taken in Cleveland, Ohio, in January 1938.

nothing. Just act dumb. And if you think that's an easy thing to do in the theater, you try it some matinee."

Today, of course, the word "stooge" almost always signifies one of three things: Moe, Larry, or Curly. Verify it in an encyclopedia, Google it, wherever you look, it won't vary. The Three Stooges adopted the term as their own, using it as their umbrella almost exclusively from the time they were let loose on the Columbia Pictures lot in 1934.

In his 1978 book *The Great Movie Comedians,* Leonard Maltin noted: "Clearly the Stooges were hampered in developing a comic style of their own as long as they had to play off Healy and allow him to remain top banana. When they finally split the Stooges' individual personalities came into sharper focus and gave them a much stronger impact."

The Stooges take time from filming *Pop Goes the Easel* (1935) to step outside of the soundstage and pose with a painting created by a visiting fan, Joe Coscio.

Trading Spaces, Stooge Style Moe and Larry proceed to wreck the home of newlyweds Elaine and Curly Howard in 1937.

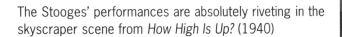

The Stooges' performances are absolutely riveting in the skyscraper scene from *How High Is Up?* (1940)

Moe quickly took over the Ted Healy role, the boss of the group. Curly became the favorite, an endearingly clever comic who formed a style all his own. Maltin furthered: "Larry is the least distinct character of the trio, but he adds a pleasing touch by siding with either Moe or Curly, depending on the situation, thereby enabling him to show moments of lucidity as well as lunacy."

At one time, Larry considered the team's first Columbia short, a musical novelty called *Woman Haters*, his favorite, but not just because he was featured a little bit more than Moe and Larry. "I liked *Woman Haters* the best for the simple reason that being our first one, it was more difficult," he told Mike Mikicel nearly forty years after he made the film. "And I think we did a helluva job. It had music and it was really a showcase for us. We only signed a contract for one short. If they didn't like it, we were through. Instead we stayed there twenty-four years."

Larry usually laughed when he spoke about the sets used in the Stooges shorts. "The stories of our shorts involved the sets that they had on hand at the time," he explained. "Our first picture, *Woman Haters*, was made on account of a picture called *Twentieth Century* with John Barrymore and Carol Lombard, which took place on a train. So we made a train picture. From then on, any time they had a big picture, we knew what we were going to have to do . . . all through our career. We never had any original sets. When they had built sets for *Pal Joey*, with Frank Sinatra, we made apartment pictures.

"We made eight pictures a year and it took us five days to make a picture, that's forty days a year," he added. "After the first or second year, they didn't let us lay around. They gave us permission to go out on a personal appearance tour. They saved money and we made money, because they gave us half salary while we were gone. It was a good deal for them and a great deal for us. That was one of the sweetest deals in Hollywood."

Moe often cited *Punch Drunks* as one of his favorites. "We wrote that one, almost completely, script and all," he told Mike Mikicel in an August 1973 interview at his home. "Although basically, we wrote about ninety percent of the films we did on what they call a treatment basis. Our scripts were usually twenty-nine pages and we always wrote a nine-page treatment embodying what the background would be and different pieces of business, and that kind of stuff. And then we'd turn it over to a screenplay writer who would put it in shooting script form. Then of course, we'd take the first draft of that and we'd take it back and put the speeches where they belong, because you couldn't have Larry using any tough language to me because that's not the way we'd operate, you see? We'd change the dialogue and put the words where they belong and to whom they belong and then they'd take it back for a second and final draft, shooting script. But we always sat in with the great writers, Felix Adler, Del Lord, Charley Chase. A couple of them were writers for Harold Lloyd."

All three Stooges were exceptionally proud of the Hitler/Nazi spoofs in two shorts, *You Nazty Spy!* (1940) and its follow-up, *I'll Never Heil Again* (1941). It was their unique and blatant contribution to the World War II propaganda effort. They were the first to mock the fascists, Hitler, and the Third Reich on film. Captured in black and white, just like the newsreels of the actual dictator, Moe's performances poking fun at the Fuhrer opened up a whole new performance realm for the Stooges and for American filmmaking as well. Up until that point, such parodies were verboten. Even today, it's almost creepy to watch Moe apply the little dark mustache, comb his hair to one side, and take on that Hitleresque scowl—barking out double-talk German in a beautifully accurate parody.

Jules White, the man who started the studio's short-subjects department, gladly produced both of the Nazi parodies. He directed many of the comedies with Curly, and dabbled with the later 1950s Shemp Howard and Joe Besser Stooge comedies; White's comedies were among the team's most violent. Jules was known to be a director who demonstrated exactly what he wanted and how it was to

Midget "Little Billy" (real name Billy Rhodes) is the bite-size bellboy in *You Nazty Spy!* (1940). Rhodes was a well-known actor in the 1930s and '40s who starred in the low-budget western *The Terror of Tiny Town* and later became a Munchkin in *The Wizard of Oz.*

"Hail! Hail! Hailstone!" The Stooges were the first to courageously satirize Hitler on film in *You Nazty Spy!* released in January 1940, nine months before Charlie Chaplin's *The Great Dictator* hit theaters. (Note: In this rare outtake or wardrobe/makeup test photo, Moe and Larry are wearing mustaches. However, in the actual dictator of Moronica scenes, they are not. Obviously, the mustaches were ix-nayed. It's too bad, because Moe, with the little black mustache and his hair partially combed back, bore an eerie resemblance to Hitler.

THE MYSTERIOUS DEATH OF TED HEALY

Larry, Moe and Curly were on the road, specifically at a train station in New York, when they received the news that their former stage and film partner, Ted Healy, had died following a beating at a Los Angeles nightspot. The Stooges were stunned. The news was especially painful to Moe, because he and Ted (real name: Charles Ernest Nash) had been friends since childhood in New York. Larry said he was ambivalent; the years of slaps to the face—both physically and mentally—had numbed much of the admiration that he had once had for the man.

The entertainment world mourned this popular, rising star. Healy had made his name in vaudeville and was now establishing a decent motion picture career for himself. It was a tragic end to the comedian's life; it was news that hit hard in newspapers and radio news programs around the country. Sadly, Healy was only forty-one and his only child, a son named John Jacob, had been born just days before.

Curly Howard, speaking from New York, was quoted in a news wire story the next day: "His death can't be on the level. He was all right, that guy, and I never heard of him being seriously sick or having anything the matter with him that would cause him to go so quickly."

Although the beating Healy received was ultimately ruled out as a cause of his death, a small mystery began to take shape, one that has yet to be unraveled, even today. It's easy to see that the events surrounding Healy's death were probably not fully explored and investigated by authorities. The situation is likely never to be fully and accurately documented.

Larry had this candid photo of Ted Healy tucked away in his scrapbook. The picture showed Healy at age forty-one, not long before his mysterious death.

The late Milton Berle, who revered and even emulated Healy, was convinced there was mob involvement in the death of his comedy idol. Comedy writer turned television star Morey Amsterdam claimed his friend Healy died at the hands of the late Hollywood agent who had known ties to the mob, Pasquale "Pat" DiCicco. (This was the same Pat DiCicco who later married Gloria Vanderbilt, but the marriage ended in divorce the year she inherited four million dollars.) Others have speculated that MGM star Wallace Beery had a hand in the fighting during Healy's final night out, and that the studio paid to hush the situation to preserve the polish on their silver screen star.

The day after his death, the *Los Angeles Times* reported, "Circumstances leading to the sudden death of Ted Healy, famous stage and screen comedian, continue to puzzle police this morning. . . . A bizarre chain of circumstances, marked by a stormy tour of Hollywood night clubs, was being checked by police."

Healy had been out drinking heavily Sunday evening, December 19, 1937, most likely celebrating the birth of his son. His wife, Betty Hickman Healy, was still in University Hospital in Culver City when she was informed of his death. According to friends, Betty was eager to return home to Ted and spend the Christmas holidays introducing the new baby to family members. Instead, she found herself a widow and new mother, burying her famous husband on Christmas Eve.

According to eyewitnesses, Healy was hitting the nightspots—the Seven Seas, the Brown Derby, Clara Bow's It Café, and the Trocadero among them. No official reports surfaced of Healy fighting before he arrived at the Trocadero, located on Sunset Boulevard. It was after midnight, inside the Trocadero bar, where Healy started a fistfight with Albert Broccoli, a twenty-nine-year-old "scion of a wealthy Long Island family," reported the *Los Angeles Herald-Examiner*. Broccoli, nicknamed "Cubby," was the cousin of Pat DiCicco, who was reportedly also at the scene. And yes, this Albert Broccoli is the same "Cubby" Broccoli who would later became a highly successful film producer and lord of the 007 James Bond motion picture franchise.

Broccoli, at the time, publicly denied causing a laceration above Healy's left eye, noting that he and the comedian had fought but also made up inside the bar. He noticed no injuries on Healy following the incident. Broccoli told the press his account:

> I was standing at the bar in the Troc late Sunday night when Healy entered. I knew he had become a father only two days before, so I said to him in friendly fashion, "Have a drink, Ted." He seemed quite unsteady. He turned to an attendant and said, "Who is this fellow?" I laughed that off and offered my congratulations about the baby.
>
> Healy staggered toward me and punched me on the nose. My nose began to bleed. The next thing I knew, he had hit me in the mouth. And he followed that up with a stiff punch to the chin, which nearly knocked me out. I shoved him away from me, because I didn't want to hurt him and the attendants led him to an ante-room. Pretty soon, they came back and said Ted wanted to see me. I walked in and shook hands. Then Ted went out and got in a taxicab and that's the last I saw of him. As I recall, he wasn't marked up when I last saw him.

Newspapers quoted another eyewitness inside the Trocadero, who saw a drunken Healy start trouble with another table of patrons, two men with their dates, before being led out of the establishment by attendants. The two men followed the comedian outside and

After Ted and his Stooges disbanded, Healy wasted no time going forward with his own fairly successful career on stage, in radio, and in a dozen or so feature films. In *Bombshell*, Healy costarred with Jean Harlow and Frank Morgan (1933).

took turns delivering punches to Healy's head and stomach. A cab was called for Healy and he left, bleeding and dazed.

Several hours later, friends found Healy staggering in front of the Hollywood Plaza Hotel. A friend of his, vaudevillian Joe Frisco, helped take Healy to the home of Dr. Sydney L. Weinberg, who closed the cut over his eye with stitches and tape. (One report said he just clamped the wound closed and bandaged it.) The doctor told the press that Healy indeed had been drinking and mentioned the fight, "but was unable to say who his opponent was."

The doctor did not feel it was necessary to hospitalize Healy and the comedian returned to his home at 10749 Weyburn Avenue in Westwood bruised and bandaged. Throughout Monday December 20, Healy's condition steadily worsened and he went into convulsions and delirium. The family physician, Dr. Wyant Lamont, who had delivered Healy's son just days before, was called to the comedian's bedside in the evening. Ted's sister Marcia, who was caring for him, felt helpless with her brother. Lamont arrived at Healy's home and immediately phoned another doctor, a heart specialist named Dr. John Ruddock, to rush over. At 3 o'clock early Tuesday morning, December 21, while still in bed at his home, Healy suffered an attack and lapsed into a coma, never regaining consciousness. Why he wasn't rushed to a local hospital during this period is not known. With two physicians attending, it seems only logical that an ambulance should have been summoned.

Healy's body was first brought to a mortuary in Culver City, where it was embalmed. Then, the order for an autopsy arrived and the body was moved to the Los Angeles County Morgue. The postmortem examination concluded that Healy died of acute toxic nephritis, caused by acute and chronic alcoholism, which weakened his heart, kidneys, and liver. The coroner, Dr. A. F. Wagner, a surgeon who performed the autopsy in the presence of two Los Angeles police detectives, declared that no injury to the skull or brain had caused the comedian's death and signed the death certificate. Despite the fact that the body had been embalmed prior to the autopsy, Wagner ruled out any blood clots or cerebral hemorrhages that would have contributed to his death. It's unclear whether the embalming process posed any problems in terms of producing an accurate autopsy. The body was returned to the Noice, Smith and Salisbury mortuary and funeral services were planned.

On December 23, the 10:00 a.m. services, held at St. Augustine's Church in Culver City, were led by Father John O'Donnell. Pallbearers included MGM executives Eddie Mannix and Billy Grady and actors Dick Powell, Frank Fay, and Bryan Foy. Newspapers reported that about three hundred were in attendance, including Healy's close friends actress Patsy Kelly, film and stage choreographer Busby Berkeley, Ted's sister Marcia Healy, his first wife Betty Braun Healy, and of course his widow Betty Hickman Healy, who held their newborn son, John, tightly during the Catholic ceremony. Many cast members of his final film, *Hollywood Hotel,* attended the mass, as well as Healy's newest set of film "stooges" with whom he was currently working (Dick Hakins, Sam Wolfe, and Paul Garner); his new boys all sat in a pew together and shook their heads,

all three bewildered by the death of their boss. The real Three Stooges—Moe Howard, Larry Fine, and Curly Howard—continued on their tour through parts of the East Coast while their wives attended the funeral ceremony on their behalf.

Immediately following the services, Healy's first wife, Betty Braun Healy, angrily challenged the coroner's conclusion in a series of newspaper interviews. She demanded a grand jury investigation and charged that the beating must have been more extensive than the coroner revealed. "I'm convinced there was foul play in connection with Ted's death," she told the *Los Angeles Herald-Examiner.* "I hesitate to accept the autopsy verdict. I saw Ted last Saturday night and he never looked better. He told me he never felt better in his life. He declared he had been taking good care of himself and had not been drinking. . . . I'm convinced that the beating Ted got had a lot to do with his death. Who is being protected in the death of my ex-husband? I'm confident that someone is being protected."

Healy was looking forward to fatherhood and attempted to get his drinking under control. According to family members, including Healy's sister Marcia, the comedian had been on the wagon for more than six months leading up to the birth of his son. His drinking problem was no secret. "I'm satisfied with the police investigation," said the comedian's sister, Marcia. "If I thought he'd been murdered I would be the first to demand an investigation."

Healy's young widow, while still in shock, spoke out to newspaper reporters in a story that ran the day after Christmas. "I resent bitterly the attempts made by Ted's former wife to inject mystery into the case," said Betty Hickman Healy. "She has no right to do so.

"Ted had not been drinking for eight months until the baby was born. Then he took a few drinks to celebrate our happiness, which has ended in such appalling tragedy. But he must have been in bad shape physically for a long time without letting me know it."

• • •

In an editorial in the *Los Angeles Times* the day after he died, an unidentified writer described Healy as a per-

In the final scene from *Beer and Pretzels* (1933), Ted and the boys are thrown out into the alley after they are fired from their jobs as waiters in a night-club.

former who helped take care of his own: "Although Healy's salary was large, he chose his friends without regard to wealth or position. True to the tradition of vaudeville folk, he never forgot his pals. A considerable portion of his earnings went to help less fortunate troupers."

Unfortunately, when Ted Healy died, he died broke. The press eventually reported that at the time of his demise he was pulling in a salary of $1,750 a week, but despite that fact he left his widow penniless. He should have been a millionaire.

His business manager, Jack Marcus, confirmed to the press his client's salary, adding, "But somehow, he got rid of it. He supported ten or twelve families other than his own and only last week, for example, doled out $300 for people he never had heard of, who wrote him seeking Christmas aid. He never learned to save money. He always said: 'Next year we'll make a million and everybody will be happy.'"

Promptly, many of Healy's show business friends went into high gear to raise funds. Unsolicited contributions were coming in to his friend at MGM, casting director Billy Grady, who also set up a committee to solicit further funds from friends who knew and worked with Healy. Several of Healy's costars at MGM and Warner Brothers organized a testimonial benefit show that took place in mid-January at the Warner Brothers Hollywood Theater. Proceeds from the all-star benefit show went to Healy's widow and baby. The testimonial was a first class Tinseltown affair, which united Hollywood royalty in honor of their friend, a fallen comedian. Entertaining at the program were Jack Benny, James Cagney, Pat O'Brien, Dick Powell, Al Jolson, Burns and Allen, Fanny Brice, George Jessel, Rudy Vallee, Spencer Tracy, Clark Gable, Ray Bolger, Bert Lahr, the Ritz Brothers, Robert Taylor, Sophie Tucker, Olsen and Johnson, John Boles, Milton Berle, Bert Wheeler, and Bob Hope.

be done rather than relying on the actor's instincts or creativity within the scene. He would act it out for the actor, shoves, slaps, the whole shebang. White was detailed in his description as to how it should appear on film and how the tempo should proceed in a scene, where a hit should land and what reaction it should elicit from which Stooge. This lack of imagination never distressed Larry, who was content to take the fastidious direction.

However, "Moe and Jules didn't get along," Larry said. "Jules was jealous of Moe's money, maybe. I never had no qualms with him. I never argued with him. I don't think Moe ever argued with him, he just didn't like him, or just didn't think the same way Jules did."

Cheek to cheek with Ruth Skinner, Julie Duncan, and Julie Gibson in *Three Smart Saps* (1942).

Edward Bernds, who worked his way up from soundman on several Frank Capra films at Columbia to director in the shorts department, was usually at odds with his boss, Jules White. "Jules's stuff was very violent. That was just his way of doing it. His stuff was just violent. He used a lot of things I didn't like and never used: the finger in the nose. Ice tongs in the ears. I talked it over with Moe on the first one I directed and said, 'Anything kids are liable to imitate and injure one another, I don't want to do.' And he agreed with me. So in my pictures, they don't do so much of the eye poking. Once in a while, in a flurry, he'd forget and give it to Larry or Shemp. But Moe didn't want kids to get hurt."

Another difference Bernds recalled between his own style and that of White's was the scripting process. "I'd call them in for story conferences. Jules would not," he said. "He'd just give them a script and say, 'Here it is.' Even before we did a script, I would call them in and get their ideas. Maybe I'd not have even a basic idea. I'd ask, 'Think we can get away with another "scare"?' and that would get them started. Moe would have a terrific memory and he'd remember the scare routines, and which ones were done previously in what shorts, and how long ago. Or if it was a 'high and dizzy,' one where it dealt with somebody out on a ledge, I'd have conferences so that I'd have a pretty good idea of what we were gonna do with their approval, and then I'd either write it myself or give it to another writer like Elwood Ullman, a very competent writer."

Things were going beautifully for Larry and Mabel, who now resided pri-

The Knickerbocker in Hollywood was home to Larry and his family in the 1930s, '40s, and again in the '60s. The Fines enjoyed a large apartment in the building with full services and amenities.

marily in the Hollywood Knickerbocker Hotel located on North Ivar Avenue in the heart of Hollywood. With its massive crystal chandelier in the lobby, the Knickerbocker was first a luxury apartment building, a landmark in Tinseltown since Rudolph Valentino frequented its grand bar and tangoed in the ballroom in the 1920s. The history swirling about the (some claim haunted) eleven-story building is legendary: In 1926, magician Harry Houdini's widow held a séance on the roof in an attempt to contact her dead husband; Marilyn Monroe and Joe Dimaggio honeymooned at the Knickerbocker in January 1954; Elvis Presley stayed in suite #1016 in 1956 while shooting *Love Me Tender.* (In the mid-'60s, sadly, Larry's old friend and neighbor from the Knickerbocker, Bill Frawley, collapsed and died of a heart attack on the street just outside the apartment building. Frawley, most known to television audiences as the lovable Fred Mertz on *I Love Lucy,* went to ball games often with Larry and the two showbiz hams ate lunch together whenever they could inside the building's cafe. Frawley worked with Larry and the Stooges just once, on *The Ed Wynn Show* in 1950.) The Knickerbocker was the temporary home to many celebrities over the years—including Frank Sinatra, Mae West, Barbara Stanwyck, Lana Turner, and of course, Larry Fine and family—off and on, until the late 1960s. But for the Fines, it was more permanent than temporary.

On March 15, 1936, Mabel gave birth at the Wilshire Hospital to their second child, a son they named John Joseph Fine. From day one, they called him Johnny, named after the pianist Johnny Green, an Academy Award–winning composer and orchestra leader who was a dear friend to Larry and Mabel. Johnny was an incorrigible child, full of rambunctious energy, who sported a thick head of dark brown curly hair, which he got from his old man. With Phyllis, who was born in Atlantic City, and the new arrival of Johnny in Los Angeles, Larry often joked to friends, "I have one from each coast."

Moe was starting a family as well; he and his wife Helen had two children, a daughter, Joan, and a son, Paul. Curly was married four times, with none of the marriages lasting very long. Curly fathered two daughters: Marilyn (with his second wife, Elaine) and Janie (with his fourth wife, Valerie).

In the '30s, Moe and Larry were both doting dads, each with a little girl at home to spoil and parade around, and eventually a son for each. Moe's daughter, Joan, recalled that Moe showed his love by buying gifts and surprising his children with mild extravagances. Mabel and Larry were more on the

ONE FINE STOOGE

Naki, Saki, and Waki
The Stooges are actors mistaken for Japanese spies in the hilarious wartime short, *No Dough Boys* (1944).

affectionate side, tactile parents, generous with kisses and hugs for the kids. While the Stooges' spouses never appeared in any of their films, Moe's daughter, Joan, and Larry's daughter, Phyllis, can be spotted briefly outside on a sidewalk playing hopscotch in the 1935 short *Pop Goes the Easel.*

In the summer of 1939, the Stooges boarded the luxury liner the *Queen Mary* and sailed to Europe for some dates abroad: the team played the London Palladium (June 4–18), the Palace in Blackpool, England (June 19–25), the Theater Royal in Dublin, Ireland (June 26–July 2), and the Empire in Glasgow, Scotland (July 3–9). "We were offered many other dates," explained Moe, "but we had to come back East because we had signed a contract before we left to appear in *George White's Scandals of 1939,* which, incidentally, was the last George White *Scandals* that ever came to Broadway." Larry, however, cited in *Stroke of Luck* that the urgency for the Stooges to depart was due to political unrest at the time and that plans were in the mix for the Stooges to continue on to Paris for more appearances.

The 1939 edition of *George White's Scandals* opened Monday evening, August 28, 1939, at New York's Alvin Theatre with the Stooges headlining the Broadway production alongside Willie & Eugene Howard, Ben Blue, Ann Miller, and fourteen additional acts. The boys performed some tried-and-true material, such as "The Stand-In" sketch, the "Curb your Dog" bit, and in drag the guys harmonized in a hilarious number called "Three Smart Girls."

Waiter, There's a Stooge in My Soup! This Chicago eatery was never the same after the Stooges got through with it.

Dublin the Fun During their 1939 overseas tour, the boys ran amok in Clery's, one of the more fashionable old department stores in Dublin, Ireland.

During the war, the Stooges obliged every USO invitation they could squeeze into their schedule. They played benefits for the soldiers and frequented the Stage Door Canteens in both New York and Hollywood. During the final weekend of March 1944, the Stooges appeared in a star-studded two-nighter show at New York's Stage Door Canteen with Morey Amsterdam, Ginny Simms, Buddy Lester, and Dick Haymes. It didn't matter where they appeared, the men in the military jammed venues to see the Stooges perform live. Remember, the Stooges have always been a "guy thing," and although the team avoided "blue" material, their act got a little raunchier onstage than film audiences were used to.

The Stooges continued making shorts at Columbia, but secretly yearned to make feature films like Abbott and Costello and the Marx Brothers. When they did appear in features, the finished product rarely allowed the team to shine. The pieces of the puzzle never seemed to fit.

On December 22, 1944, the Stooges completed filming a low-budget Columbia feature, *Rockin' in the Rockies* for producer Colbert Clark. The mediocre comedy western, costarring Mary Beth Hughes, Jay Kirby, Gladys Blake, Tim Ryan, and Vernon Dent, was released almost a year later in November 1945, and it held little expectations from the studio as well as its stars. The feature was a departure from the Stooges' usual twenty-minute comedies, but their material was not. Ill-equipped in the comedy without their usual team of writers and directors from the shorts department, the Stooges couldn't muster much comedy from the script; the director, Vernon Keays, most likely had no concept of how to draw out the best slapstick from the team. Reviews were mixed: A critic for the *Hollywood Reporter* noted, "Moe, Jerry, and Larry have a razzle-dazzle field day. . . . Their termite routine is zestful and their contribution considerable, even if some of the gags are moth-eaten." *Variety* felt the Stooges merely confused audiences with their appearance and branded it a bomb: *"Rockin' in the Rockies* is a poor example of film entertainment. It is an attempt to dress up a tired western plot with several specialties and tunes. The results are dull and too long. At best, it's minor filler and a credit to no one."

The Stooges were getting tired, wondering themselves if they'd worn out the welcome mat. The treads in their material were worn thin. Curly, most noticeably of the three, was beginning to suffer physical difficulties and slowing down to a point where his performances were downright pathetic.

● ● ●

Joan Howard Maurer, Moe's only daughter, remembers addressing her Uncle Curly as "Uncle Babe." (He was the baby of the Howard brothers and the

This rare wardrobe and makeup test still of Curly Howard, taken February 2, 1934, proves he began work on the MGM film *Operator 13,* costarring Ted Healy. Reportedly, Curly was released from this film—or the scenes were cut—after the Stooges severed ties with Ted Healy.

family affectionately called him Babe.) As Stooges go, Curly was her preference as well.

"My dad was naturally my dad," she says, "but Curly was my favorite as far as the Stooges were concerned.

"As I used to look at Curly, he had this foot that was injured when he was a kid, and he had a limp, but the limp he sort of covered up and the limp became part of his gait that was just part of him. I never was aware that really he was limping. The expressions on his face were incredible.

"When my dad would give him a really hard whack, you'd see this little boy look come over his face, his mouth wide open," she says, vividly recalling the Stooges' stage act. "Rarely did he express anger, just annoyance. The sound of the slap would reverberate through the entire audience and everybody would crack up and be laughing. And as I stood there—I can remember standing between the wings and the curtain, that space where you can stand and watch what's going on from the side—and as I stood there I could see the saliva fly out of his mouth. The slap was quite a push on the face, even though I'm sure it didn't really hurt him."

Joan says she adored her Uncle Babe, and her father, Moe, had a special,

By the late 1930s, the Stooges began inspiring popular merchandise made in their likenesses, like these hand puppets from Ideal Doll Company.

almost paternal relationship with him. "I don't know what the average person thinks he was, but I'll tell you something, he was very much the same person in life as he was on screen—he was a big kid. Everyone will say that. Curly used to aggravate the life out of my father because he did all of these wild things. My father worried about him constantly, because Curly was like a child. My father was more of a father to him than a brother."

Moe assisted Curly in many

Hats Off to Larry A rare lavish musical number from the Monogram Pictures feature *Swing Parade of 1946. Below,* Blanche Stewart and Elvia Allman chase the boys in *Time Out for Rhythm* (1941).

Below left, Dorthy DeHaven flirts with Moe and Curly while Larry takes a smoke break in *Three Little Pirates* (1946). *Below right,* Fourteen-year-old child actress Edith Fellows, a Columbia contract player, joined the boys for a photo session to publicize their Pillsbury/Farina "Moving Picture Machine," a cardboard cut-out giveaway product.

53

facets of his life; he routinely prepared his kid brother's income taxes, for instance, and made the major decisions for him—all except when it came to the creativity on the set or in front of an audience. Curly held his own in that department and Moe let him fly, allowing even himself to marvel at Curly's inventiveness. It was something that Moe loved to witness, savor, and even participate in like a game. On the stage, his brother was his equal, but at home, he needed assistance in his personal life. While Curly wasn't considered an alcoholic, Moe was bothered by the amount of drinking and carousing Curly did.

"I don't think Curly was a very strong person," confesses his niece, Joan. "Because of Curly's mother taking over his life as a young fellow and really not letting him to do his own thing, he never got a chance to really grow up. And then when he finally separated from his mother at one point in his life, my dad took over. My father took over his life as manager because Curly really was inept in many areas of his life. He needed somebody to carry him along."

Curly also loved dogs—it was a passion—and he owned many in his lifetime. Eunice Dent, the widow of longtime Stooges costar Vernon Dent, recalls that trait in Curly very well: "Curly gave us a dog, a little schnauzer, which I loved very dearly. His name was Pigeon, a wonderful dog, and both Vernon and I were dog lovers too. As long as we knew Curly, he had dogs in his home and he doted on all of them."

On May 6, 1946, the final day of shooting the film *Half-Wits Holiday*, while sitting alone outside the soundstage in a folding studio chair waiting to be called for the next scene, Curly Howard quietly suffered a debilitating stroke. He was just forty-two.

"It was a very sad day," Moe later recounted. "We were just finishing up this picture, with one more scene for Curly to finish. And the assistant director called for Curly. He was sitting out in the sun, outside the stage. He didn't answer, so I went out to call him. I tapped him on the shoulder. His head was on his chest. He looked up, his face was all distorted. He'd had a stroke in the chair."

Larry admitted that he and Moe knew there was something wrong with Curly's health during that period. Curly had suffered minor strokes in the two years leading up to his major collapse, but he continued to work anyway. In 1945, when it became apparent that he couldn't fulfill certain out-of-town personal appearance dates in between their shooting schedule, Moe knew changes were in store and began grooming his brother Shemp for a return. Shemp rejoined Moe and Larry for some personal appearances, out of town mostly, filling in for Curly for some of the live shows only. Curly continued to work in the films with Moe and Larry until 1946, but his appearance and performance were noticeably sluggish.

"You see, when you've got two other guys, you can cover up a lot, which we did for Curly," Larry later said, reflecting in 1973. "But it still didn't work out. His actions and reactions were too slow. After about a year, he got sick. He had some smaller strokes. Like earthquakes, you have a big one then some small tremors afterwards."

JAN. 18, 1945
THE TIMES-PICAYUNE, T

ments

satires, and The Martingales, adagio specialists.

Moe and Shemp Howard and Larry Fine, who were the origi-

The Three Stooges

nals in The Three Stooges act, compose the trio to appear here. Curley Howard, who took Shemp's place after the act had been organized some years and whose appearance is familiar to movie audiences, is not on the current tour because of illness.

The new screen show today at the St. Charles is "Bowery Champs," with Leo Gorcey, Huntz Hall, Gabriel Dell and Bobby Jordan.

This revealing clipping from a New Orleans newspaper in January 1945 proves that Shemp replaced his ailing brother Curly—in personal appearances, anyway—more than a year prior to Curly suffering a massive stroke on the film set in 1946. Notice the odd publicity still used in the ad—Shemp's head was simply pasted over Curly's.

Not even two months after he suffered the major stroke, Curly's third wife, Marion, filed for divorce. According to a *Los Angeles Times* story dated June 20, 1946, Curly was too ill to take the witness chair during the divorce hearing in court; however, his wife was eager to testify and laid out a laundry list of reasons she wished their marriage to be dissolved. She accused Curly of: "1. Pushing, striking, and pinching her; 2. Throwing cigars in the kitchen sink; 3. Screaming at waiters in restaurants; and 4. Sheltering two vicious dogs in their home." Curly's physician, Dr. Marcus Crahan, arranged for the partially paralyzed actor to testify from his chair seated next to his attorney. When asked about financial matters, Curly replied, "Ask Moe, he handles the business." In just a few words, Curly defended himself, informing the judge that his wife was cold and indifferent and insulted him in public. Nonetheless, the divorce was granted.

Curly improved slightly after he fully retired and his health stabilized for a few years. He remarried and almost two years to the day following his stroke, Curly and his new wife were blessed with a little girl on May 7, 1948. They named her Jane, and she was a smiley little charmer who put spark in

Curly's fourth wife, Valerie, Curly, and their collie named "Lady" in 1948. In his retirement, Curly lost a considerable amount of extra weight and preferred to let his hair grow.

Curly does his best Carmen Miranda in the feature film *Time Out for Rhythm* (1941).

Rudy Vallee and Allen Jenkins join the Stooges in a scene from *Time Out for Rhythm*.

the life of her ailing father during his final years. He was only in his mid-forties, and the vibrant, spinning comedy genius from the big screen was reduced to a man who walked slowly with the aid of a cane. His voice, once a beautiful instrument, was now a rusty creak, barren of any humor.

"I remember going to see Uncle Babe after I was married," recalls Joan Howard Maurer. "It was kind of traumatic to me because there was this vital man that I saw backstage reacting all of these incredible ways on stage and then suddenly to see him in bed.

Actress Evelyn Young and the Stooges in *Boobs in Arms* (1940).

"He had such difficulty speaking and expressing himself. He lost weight, but looked good, slim," she remembers. "The hair had grown in. He was not a bad looking man. Every once in a while you'd see he had a very strange expression on his face. He could never quite smile the same after his strokes."

Moe was crushed by his baby brother's sad condition. "I later learned from Curly's wife's sister—Janie's aunt—about that period of time in his life and it's not as down as I thought it would be," Joan says. "I think finally when he married Valerie, it was one point in his life where he was his own man and found some form of peace in that."

In 1950, Curly was admitted to the Motion Picture Country Home and Hospital in Woodland Hills; he returned home but his condition grew worse in mid-1951. His wife, Valerie, could no longer provide the full nursing care he required, so Moe arranged for Curly to be admitted to a hospital/sanitarium. He moved from one institution to another in the San Fernando Valley, and then in early 1952 Curly was transferred to the Baldy View Sanitarium in San Gabriel, California, where he could receive further treatment and therapy. After just a week, Curly died there on January 18, 1952, of a heart attack at the age of forty-eight. (Many newspaper obituaries incorrectly listed Curly's age as forty-six, but in fact he was born on October 22, 1903, which made him forty-eight at the time of his death.)

Curly, Valerie, and their daughter Janie in 1948. Janie was Curly's second child.

3

IN AND OUT

In the mid-1940s, Larry and Mabel purchased a beautiful Mediterranean-style two-story white stucco home at 2555 Aberdeen Avenue in the Los Feliz area of Hollywood (actually Los Angeles). Purchased from actor Fred Stone, the house was near Griffith Park, the observatory, and a golf course. The street was a beautiful residential winder with the houses escalating up into the hills, all beautiful homes with well-manicured lawns. There was a garage in the back that was detached from the house with a rumpus room above the garage where Larry had his pool table. In the back yard was an in-ground pool, which the kids, and later the grandkids, utilized much more than Larry and Mabel. The living room was the main gathering spot in Fine Manor, and next to that the most used room was the dining room, where, on Sunday nights, Larry and Mabel hosted card games, penny-ante poker nights, and even bingo nights—it was Larry's job to roll the ball and always pull the numbers out of the cage and make the calls. Mabel's sisters and brothers-in-law were fixtures at the Fines' home.

Mabel's widowed sister, Marguerite, lived in the maid's room, off the kitchen area, for a period of years, which pleased both Mabel and Larry. Marguerite and Larry shared most of the cooking responsibilities in the house, so when Larry played out-of-town appearance dates on weekends and sometimes stretches of weeks on more extensive tours, he felt that Mabel would be in good company with her sister. Mabel also worried Larry greatly, as she began drinking heavily and often; he soon realized it was more than just social drinking. Mabel's addiction was getting out of control, but Larry just learned to placate her during and following every binge. He didn't know what else to do.

Moe Feinberg (in glasses) stops by to see his brother, Larry, and the Stooges backstage at a theatre in 1949.

In *Hold That Lion!* (1947), Curly Howard comes back for a brief appearance as a crazy snorer (like a "cocker spangel") on a passenger train. Curly summoned his strength for this momentous scene—a rare film appearance with all three Howard brothers.

ONE FINE STOOGE

Even though they were Jewish, the Fines celebrated the Christmas holidays as a joyous gift-giving event each year. The bigger the tree, the better. Larry loved to decorate it himself, meticulously hand-placing the shiny icicles on each branch until the tree shined like polished chrome.

When Larry and Mabel's son, Johnny, was a youngster, he preferred living in the house as opposed to the luxury apartment. The house had a yard and a place to play. In Johnny's preteen years he, like many boys, went through a pyromania stage and was lighting fires at the house. It's possible Johnny was seeking attention. Mabel found it increasingly difficult to handle Johnny, and Larry, ever the softie, found it hard to administer strict discipline to their boy as well. They decided to enter him in a military school for a few years, much to Johnny's chagrin.

Phyllis Fine was too busy discovering men and going out on dates to be bothered with her younger brother's situation. The two got along terrifically as siblings, according to members of the Fine family, but in the late 1940s Phyllis's interests were naturally leaning more toward clothes, dating, and being with her friends. In early 1947, she met Don Lamond, who lived not far from the Fines in the hills of Los Feliz. Phyllis was having difficulty starting her car and pulled over to the curb. Lamond offered to give her a ride to the gas station, and that's how they met. The two dated for a year and married in 1948.

"The first time I met Larry," recalls Don Lamond, "was about three days after I met Phyllis. I met him at their house. I picked her up to go to dinner and that was the first time I realized who he was." Lamond recalls taking to Larry instantly, but says he always remained guarded around Mabel. After the young couple married, they lived on Commonwealth Avenue, also in the Los Feliz area. Eventually, Don and Phyllis gave Larry and Mabel their first grandchildren, Eric and Kris.

"Larry was the epitome of the spoiling grandfather," says Lamond. "Especially at Christmas time. There were gifts for everyone. He loved being Santa Claus, loved to shop for everyone and he had more fun than anyone doing it."

Lamond was interested in the entertainment field and accompanied his father-in-law to the studio on occasion to watch the Stooges filming shorts and study the whole process of filmmaking. By this time, Moe and Larry had

Larry's son Johnny, attending a military school at the time, visited his pop on the set of *Rockin' in the Rockies* (1945).

Larry and Mabel pose for a photographer with their daughter, Phyllis.

welcomed Shemp Howard back into the act and the team made a seamless transition following Curly's illness and death a few years later. Shemp had as much energy, if not more, than Curly and there was no problem keeping up with Moe and Larry in the configuration.

"Shemp was a sweet man," recalls Lamond. "He marched to his own drummer. He was funny as hell and a lot of fun to be around. He had phobias. He was afraid of everything, and yet he wasn't afraid to get hurt or get slapped by Moe. He was more afraid of getting sick or being bitten by a bug.

"I remember they were doing a scene and it involved an elixir of youth in a drugstore," Lamond recalls, referring to the short *All Gummed Up.* "They kept looking for Shemp and he was over on the side playing the piano on the cash register, and he wouldn't quit until he finished the tune. They kept calling for him.

"There was a scene I'll always remember watching, with Emil Sitka as an old man. They were pouring all of this elixir to make him young, it was a whole bunch of shit into a funnel, down his throat. They said, 'Emil, you won't be able to see with the funnel in your mouth.' Emil said, 'It's okay, I'll hold my tongue against it.' They jammed all this shit in there and then hit him in the stomach and he gulped and swallowed some of that crap. Poor Emil. I'll always remember that scene and what a trouper he was."

Lamond enjoyed studying the dynamics of the team. "There was a lot of harshness, sometimes indiscretions before they started to work, but it all disappeared when they went to work," he says. "It mainly came from Moe; he was exacting. Their timing was impeccable because they'd done it for so long.

Actress Vivian Mason flirts with the boys during filming of *Shot in the Frontier* (1954).

ONE FINE STOOGE

They would discuss a scene briefly and then do it. Moe was very businesslike when discussing the scenes, very serious and to the point. There wasn't much bullshitting with him when they were at work."

Emil Sitka, the Stooges' longtime foil who, by the time all was said and done, worked with all four sets of Stooge configurations and nearly became one himself, entered the picture at the end of Curly's moment in the sun. Ironically, Curly's final film, *Half-Wits Holiday,* in 1946, was Sitka's first with the Stooges. "I met Curly, who was very subdued. He was quiet. He called me 'sir.' He saved all of his acting and comedy for the camera. Moe was always talking, but business. Very serious most of the time, whether it be about acting, his home, and he had a lot of business ventures outside of his movie career. But on a personal level, I liked Shemp best. Shemp was the kind of guy who would tell jokes a lot. His voice was funny. The way he delivered the jokes was funny.

"Although Moe became my closest friend of the Stooges—we had lots of contact together—I still enjoyed being around Shemp because he was so much fun to work with, he had a great sense of spontaneity that I admired very much. When the time came to act in front of the cameras, he turned on a lot of things that you didn't know would come. He was the funniest, to me, and I especially liked watching him act. He'd have the director laughing long after the scene was cut."

Sitka, who died in 1998, remembered Larry as a carefree guy who would have rather been at a ball game than at work. "Many times he'd be at the racetrack, a baseball park, looking for a party and talking about sports, boxing, and anything other than acting," he said. "We'd be there waiting and we'd have to look for him many times, and when we found him, they'd put him to work. Larry was the type that if he came in with an idea, Moe would veto him immediately. Moe would say, 'What the hell's the matter with you? Where did you get that from?' Larry would say, 'I thought it was a good idea.' And Moe would shut him up and say, 'Well keep it to yourself.'"

28 The Atlanta Journal FRIDAY, FEBRUARY 27, 1948

STOP THE PRESSES FOR A SCOOP—The Three Stooges, Larry (left), Moe and Skemp, get a story like crazy ready for The Atlanta Journal. Larry had the wrong number, Moe filed the story in the wastebasket which was typed by Skemp, who used an improvised touch system. You'll find the story they wrote on Page 41.—Journal Photo by Bill Wilson.

"Stop the presses" is right! Someone thought his name was *Skemp*!

Clockwise from top left: A dapper Larry in the mid-1940s. Director Edward Bernds presents the Stooges another Laurel Award for the leading two-reel comedies on the set of *Three Arabian Nuts.* Moe and Shemp are *Out West* in 1947. The Stooges are *Income Tax Sappy* in 1954.

Director Edward Bernds took an extreme liking to Shemp as well, describing him as "one of the nicest guys I ever encountered." Bernds directed many of the shorts with Shemp, and wrote scripts as well during that period. "When Shemp came in, I don't think he objected to all of the violence in the act. He was willing to do it and didn't have to be talked into it. It never occurred to me to ask him, but from the way he acted, he couldn't have had any reluctance, because from the beginning, he was so professional and so willing. He took it for granted. He took the slaps and the pokes.

"Shemp was always *on*," recalled Bernds. "For instance, I remember that old gag where the Stooges all run toward a door and the door closes just before they get there and the Stooges slam into it. Well, Moe and Larry knew how to protect themselves. They could make like they'd hit their head, but Shemp didn't have quite the knack. So he bumped his head, cut it, and blood was streaming down his forehead. He swipes the blood and says, 'Whaddaya know . . . catsup!' Even bleeding, he had to be funny."

The mid-1950s widened the scope of employment for the Stooges. Television was burgeoning, and the Stooges jumped right in. As early as 1948, they appeared with their old pal, Milton Berle, on the *Texaco Star Theater,* broadcast live on NBC. Other variety show appearances followed, *The Eddie Cantor Comedy Theater* and *The Ed Wynn Show* among them. The television spots were paying well, too. For one night's work on the

The trio plays the Palomar Theatre in San Diego, California, in 1947.

The boys celebrate a birthday with Chef Joseph Milani, a local Los Angeles television personality.

COURTESY OF TRENT REEVE

Larry is jealous: His son Johnny is now taller than he is.

The trio placed this half-page ad in show business trade papers in 1954 to thank those individuals for helping them earn yet another Laurel Award for leading two-reel comedies.

Cantor show, the team received $1,250 for the team to split; the work was minimal and they were getting more and more exposure.

In 1949, Moe, Larry, and Shemp took a turn at TV in their own production. Before a live audience, they made their own television pilot, titled *Jerks of All Trades,* at ABC in Hollywood. Produced by Phil Berle, brother of Milton Berle, the pilot costarred Emil Sitka and Symona Boniface, but despite having a strong supporting cast and some funny sketches, the pilot fell flat. Even though short subjects, as a theatre attraction, were on the decline, the Stooges remained comfortable at Columbia making a steady job of films and personal appearance gigs, with occasional television appearances thrown in for good measure. As it was, their material had been burning up over the years and scripts were now being rewritten and rehashed in the shorts department at Columbia. Their tried-and-true material was getting tried too many times and the Stooges needed to find ways to reinvent their live act on stage. While preparing to break in new material at Lake Tahoe's State Line Club in August 1953, Larry told columnist Howard McClay of the *L.A. Daily News* in 1953, "It's tough enough inventing and rewriting gags for two-reel jobs without trying to do the same thing for a full-length film. We can make six short features out of material needed for one long comedy. Look what happened to Harry Langdon and Buster Keaton when they tried to be funny for seven reels. We're satisfied to keep 'em short."

In 1953 the Stooges unleashed two amazing shorts produced in the newly introduced process of 3-D. *Spooks* and *Pardon My Backfire* were both directed by Jules White, who enjoyed the filmmaking gimmick and how it applied to the Stooges' comedies. The actual filming was customized to capture the three-dimensional effect, and the theater audience wore special glasses handed out before the film; the display of depth on the screen was truly a feast for the eyes as the experience became a craze that swept the nation for a spell in the 1950s.

Emil Sitka recalled the experimental film process: "I made one of them in 3-D," he said. "They used two cameras, or one camera with two lenses; two cameras, side by side, like two eyes for 3-D, and they would shoot them simultaneously. The effect they were proud of was the things going into the audience so people scream. They had to devise in the script several things to go deliberately right towards the camera. Like say, they'd throw a spear, and they'd have it on a wire, of course, and it would go right between the two cameras.

"People didn't like wearing those infernal little glasses," recalled Jules White in 1980. "That's why 3-D didn't take off. I thought the few we did were hilarious. We did one with a gorilla, about a mechanic's garage. We had a crazy scientist. That was a very good one. Never, of the hundreds of pictures I've made, did I hear such shrieks of laughter as at the Paramount Theater in Hollywood than with that picture."

Today, Leonard Maltin praises the Stooges' brief but successful diversion into the film-enhanced fad. The movie critic recently wrote: "*Spooks* contains one of the single greatest moments in 3-D history, when a mad scientist extends a hypodermic needle toward the camera and holds it there with a menacing grin. How, I wondered, could the makers of a cut-rate comedy short understand what big-time directors failed to get: It takes time for your eyes to focus in 3-D. By holding that needle in place, it enabled the audience to zero in on the three-dimensional object, coming to feel as if it was jutting out into the theater! Far too many feature filmmakers believed, incorrectly, that one could achieve the same effect by throwing things at the camera. (The Stooge comedies also grasped the idea of simple mechanical tricks, like making the hypodermic needle absurdly long, or building a headboard for Moe, Larry and Shemp's bed in forced perspective.)"

• • •

One chilly evening, Larry telephoned Shemp to verify some out-of-town performance dates and was given the shocking news. Shemp had just died of a sudden heart attack (according to his death certificate; his family maintains it was a cerebral hemorrhage) in the back of a car coming home from the fights with a friend. He was lighting a cigar and slumped over. It was that

Larry and Mabel's two-story house on Aberdeen Street in the Los Feliz area of Hollywood, near Griffith Park, as it appears today.

One of Shemp Howard's final portraits, taken in 1955.

quick. Larry reckoned that Shemp's death, on November 22, 1955, was a blessing the way it occurred. "He wouldn't have been able to stand being sick for a long time," Larry said. The loss was another crushing blow to Moe and Larry. Shemp, at the age of sixty, left behind his wife, Gertrude (sometimes called "Babe"), and a son, Mort. Larry recalled:

When Shemp died, I don't think we were working. We had finished a picture. A man called me from Dallas, Texas, and they had a big show there for eleven days, a big show every year. It was a lot of money. I said, "Well, I have to call Columbia to find out our schedule, if it will permit us to go away for that length of time." I told him I'd call him back tomorrow. I immediately got on the phone and called Shemp's house and his wife got on the phone and I said, "Let me talk to Shemp." And she says, "He just left for the fights." There was a championship fight that night. So I said to her, "Have him call me the minute he comes home, it's very important." It got to be about 11 o'clock and I knew he should be home, so I got on the phone, attempting to ball him out. Moe's wife got on the phone and I said, "What are you doing there?" She said, "I just came over. Shemp's dead." I was shocked. I asked, "What happened?" And she told me that Moe was at St. Joseph's hospital right now. When Shemp died in the back of a car, they drove him right over to the hospital.

• • •

With Phyllis married and Johnny away as well, Larry and Mabel suddenly found themselves alone in their home on Aberdeen, and the Stooges were once again without a third. Larry felt his career winding down and actually contemplated abandoning film work altogether. At one point, Moe and Larry considered just calling themselves the "Two Stooges," but were quickly resigned to the fact that they wouldn't get anywhere with the handicap. Audiences wouldn't have accepted the loss.

Johnny Fine had grown up to be a handsome young guy. At

eighteen he joined the Navy and served as a Corpsman for almost two years. He had met a lovely girl named Christy Ann Watson, who grew up in Redlands, California. They dated and in 1957 the two, both still in their early twenties, got married and started a family soon thereafter.

"Larry was just superb to me," says Christy Fine Kraus today. "Mabel, well, I rarely saw a kind person in Mabel. I came from an alcoholic family, too, but mine was not like that. She was more of a mean alcoholic and I'd never in my life come across that before. I didn't know how to react to it. I was told by Lyla, Larry's sister, that she hated me because I took her little boy away. It took a while for me to adjust and I wanted to please Mabel."

Simple things such as cursing shocked Christy at that age. "We weren't allowed to cuss when I was growing up, so when I heard Mabel cussing all the time and their daughter Phyllis—well, 'shit' was every other word to her—it was something to get used to. Larry didn't cuss that much, and never in front of the grandchildren. He tried to be careful about that."

Christy recalled one instance where Mabel's drinking led to violence. "There were times when Mabel just wasn't a nice lady," she said. "I'm sorry, but things tended to get out of hand and poor Larry never showed what he was feeling. He was so even keeled and kept it all to himself.

"I had heard that Larry was out working at an election board one night. In those days they used to have to count the ballots and everything. Larry volunteered to work on the election board. I guess he came in late and Mabel had been drinking. She thought he was out with a woman and she threw a mirror at him and hit him in the head. Larry was telling Johnny about how violent she got and Johnny just put up with it too. He loved his mother, I know he did, but I remember him telling me that she used to put a guilt trip on him, telling him that she almost died when she had him. That used to drive him crazy."

When Christy was pregnant they lived for a few months in Los Angeles while Johnny traveled back and forth from Camp Pendleton in San Diego. After she had her first child, Christy Lynn, the couple moved back to

Top, The boys disappear in a box with Sheri O'Neil in *Fiddlers Three* (1948). *Above,* Devouring the marshmallow gumbo cake with Christine McIntyre in *All Gummed Up* (1947).

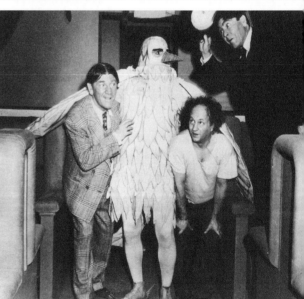

Clockwise from top left, Any self-respecting vaudevillian loved the opportunity to work in drag, and here are Larraine, Moella, and Shempetta in *Self-Made Maids* (1950). Evident on Shemp's lower left shin is a cyst that he had since his youth. Larry, Larry, Quite Contrary—the Stooges segue into their own brand of nursery rhymes in *Fiddlers Three* (1948). *Cuckoo on a Choo Choo* (1952) was one of Larry's favorites because he plays an unusually bitchy character in this bizarre short. Emil Sitka portrayed a scientist and Christine McIntyre was his daughter in *Fuelin' Around* (1949).

Claremont, about thirty miles outside of Los Angeles, and lived with Christy's mother. On weekends, Johnny and the family would drive into Los Angeles and stay with Larry and Mabel. Christy described Johnny as a good father and an earnest provider for the young couple. In August 1960, Christy gave birth to their second child, Phyllis Lorraine, and for a time, Mabel and Larry felt content with visitors to the house on Aberdeen, but they knew that they would be better off selling the house and moving back to the Knickerbocker, leasing another apartment. After fourteen years in the Aberdeen home, they sold it. The decision was not only a practical one, it was a financial one, as the house was getting too expensive to run with just Mabel and Larry residing there. Larry wasn't sure where his next paychecks were coming from, quite frankly. Christy said it was a sad time for Mabel and Larry, because they were forced to sell the house.

There is a misunderstanding, perpetuated by a few biographies of the team, that the Three Stooges signed with Columbia Pictures and never received a raise in the twenty-four years with the studio. Larry was even quoted saying offhandedly that there were never actual contracts, just handshake deals to renew with Harry Cohn each year. Neither was true. The Three Stooges *did* sign contracts and addendums to their agreements with Columbia, and they certainly received salary increases over the decades.

Shortly after making *Woman Haters* in 1934, Columbia picked up their option, and they were paid $1,000 per short for the team (split equally) ascending to $1,500 for the group by their seventh short. The next year, the group was paid in the form of a weekly salary totaling $20,000 per year for the group to produce eight shorts. Two decades later, each Stooge was taking home $20,000 a year. Their earnings from Columbia during that era, however, paled in comparison to what they brought in from personal appearance tours. But by the late 1950s, they were hardly making any live appearances anymore, so the Stooges—especially Larry—relied on their Columbia salaries to make ends meet.

On January 1, 1956, former vaudeville comic Joe Besser officially joined the group to fill in the gap for the next sixteen two-reelers. For a time, Larry could breathe a little easier since the

Fine Dining In *Horsing Around* (1957), the boys' little sister, Birdie, has been reincarnated as a horse.

Don't Ask, Don't Tell
Many fans didn't find Joe Besser's effeminate "sissy" style of stooging amusing. He was much funnier with Abbott and Costello, and he knew it.

next two years meant paychecks from Columbia, but the money was not what it used to be since they weren't touring.

Joe Besser, who hailed from St. Louis, had actually worked with Ted Healy and the Stooges on the same vaudeville bill eons before. He had subsequently carved out a successful unique style of comedy all of his own. He'd appeared with Milton Berle and Jack Benny on radio; Abbott and Costello had welcomed Besser many times to their radio and television programs. The rotund comic, who stood the same height as Moe and Larry, was making feature films and short subjects at Columbia when the opportunity to join Moe and Larry came around.

Besser's "sissy" style was much different from what Moe and Larry were accustomed to, and the newbie didn't want to suffer the slaps that his deceased predecessors did. Larry approached Joe and assured him that he would take most of Moe's abuse. The new team collaborated well, or at least with ease, and attempted to create a new relationship within the group, including a new look. In some of the shorts produced with Besser, both Moe and Larry combed their hair back for the first time on film. It was a look that didn't appeal to the regular customers. While Besser's comedy style could be funny at times, his brand wasn't what Moe and Larry preferred. He hit Moe in retaliation, screaming "Not so haaaaard!" or "Not so loooouuuuuuddd!" and swished around, jumping up and down like a little boy who couldn't wait to get to the bathroom to pee.

"Jules White and Harry Cohn asked me if I would do them a favor and jump in and work with Moe and Larry," Besser said in 1983. "Harry Cohn asked me if I would join them and carry out their last two years on their contract and I loved the boys so much. We used to have a lot of fun at the studio. They wanted me to go on the road and I couldn't leave my wife, who was sick at the time. I wouldn't leave her for anybody.

"During those two years, I loved every minute of it with them," Besser added. "They were the best. It wasn't difficult for me to join. I have my own way of working, which I've been the most copied comic in the world. I copy nobody. Nobody ever compared me with Shemp. To show you how wonderful they were, I never liked to be hit with anything and Larry used to say to me, 'Don't worry, Joe, I'll take it.' That's the kind of guy he was."

• • •

Above, Moe, Larry, and Joe are *Rusty Romeos* (1957). *Right*, The Stooges' longtime producer and director, Jules White, steps in front of the camera for a change in this rare candid photo on the set of *Fifi Blows Her Top* (1958).

Oil's Well That Ends Well with the boys in 1958. Joe Besser refused to suffer the standard smacks that were part of being a Stooge, so Larry absorbed much more of the abuse during that era. But every once in a while. . .

Buxom beauty queen Greta Thyssen, Miss Denmark of 1952, costars with Larry, Moe, and Joe in *Pies and Guys* (1958).

Larry once said he had the most fun making films, which usually involved costume changes, and not just the shorts in which the Stooges were in drag—although it was gleefully grotesque to see the Stooges in wigs, dresses, and heels with overdrawn lipstick. In one hilarious short, *All the World's a Stooge,* the boys dressed as little refugees to fool a potential adopting mother; Larry became little Mabel with a bow in his hair. (This was certainly a wink to his wife.)

The costumed shorts reflected the times, socially and historically. The Stooges took steps backward and forward in time, turning history on its ear and twisting it for good measure. For some reason they skipped Biblical times, but over the years they parodied the prehistoric age, prodded through the Pilgrim era, made merry in Olde England, and menaced the Old West. To watch the Stooges comedies released by Columbia (1934–1959) is to see a wildly warped reflection of American history, with stabs straight through the Depression, World War II, and into the be-boppin' '50s with nods to science-fiction, monsters, and outer space travel.

The boys are once again caught up in a maze of lunacy in *A Merry Mix-Up* (1957).

ONE FiNE STOOGE

Left, In possibly Joe Besser's funniest scene with the Stooges, he accidentally devours a Cuban cigar, turning ghostly white in *Quiz Whizz,* with costar Gene Roth (1958). *Below,* "I *knew* you were coming, so I baked a cake!" The Stooges compete for the affections of Connie Cezon in the 1957 short *Rusty Romeos.*

Strangely, Larry's choice of personal favorites could also be amongst the oddest—even worst—films the trio made. Usually confounding Moe in his selection, Larry really fell in love with a few of the trio's all-time stinkers, like the delusional *Cuckoo on a Choo Choo,* where Larry plays a T-shirted thug living on a stolen train car, showering himself with a bottle of beer and barking out orders. Supposedly this is Larry's nod to Marlon Brando in *A Streetcar Named Desire.* It's a Jules White acid trip and makes little sense throughout, but Larry loved it.

Another one of his picks was *Sweet and Hot,* the bizarre musical short made with Joe Besser near the end of their career as short subject stars. *Sweet and Hot* is one of the trio's most embarrassing films, but Larry preferred it because it spotlighted his musical talent with the violin in a finale he performed with Besser and portly costar Muriel Landers titled "The Heat

ABUSE ON THE LOOSE

It must be the most frequently asked question, the one posed to the Stooges time and again by interviewers and friends alike: Were you ever hurt while making the movies?

The Stooges were, not surprisingly, sick of the question. The mishaps that resulted from precarious pratfalls and punches were all hazards of their job. Nobody counted the broken bones, naturally. Larry didn't write down the date he got a tooth knocked out during a scene and simply swallowed it with a gulp to save the take. Moe didn't record which episode he dressed as a woman, bent his ankle, and ended up on crutches. It was all in a day's work as a Stooge.

Moe and Larry, without hesitation, blamed producer/director Jules White for much of the violence factor inherent in the earlier comedies, especially with Curly and Shemp. White was a film auteur with a penchant for violent comedy, and when he directed, almost no orifice was off limits, no gag was too gross. Of course there were limits. To hear White describe his years steering the Stooges, you'd think they didn't hurt a hair on their heads.

"The Stooges didn't get hurt very badly, thank God. Never," White insisted in 1980. "We inspected—both

In Dixie The Stooges are clever Union spies in *Uncivil Warriors* (1935).

the boys and I—any props that they were going to get hit with. You wouldn't want to throw boards of nails under your thoroughbred horse before it goes on the racetrack, so they were thoroughbred horses as far as we were concerned.

"They knew they were hitting each other, they weren't trying to knock each other out. Moe sometimes forgot himself and hit Larry pretty hard because as a rule, Larry was the recipient of the smacks. But Curly too, he got his share."

In interviews, strangely, both Moe and Larry would temper or tailor their answer to that eminent question, depending on who they were communicating with. For instance, if Larry was talking with a group of grade-school children, he would downplay the violence and sustained injuries and opt to reassure them that he didn't get hurt too badly because Moe was so precise with the punches and the pokes. It was true, Moe could glide his cupped hand across Larry's face to accomplish a slap on film when he wanted, but nine times out of ten, the whacks were real.

When Moe talked to a group of college students,

Larry lost more hair this way. . . .

he let the blood spill and revealed the gory details to the hungry adult audience. No doubt about it: Moe's hits could be caustic, and the props they bopped each other with weren't always so obtuse that they didn't cause injury. Larry's nose was broken once due to a pop from a hard rubber mallet with a wooden handle. There were so many instances that Larry said he lost track, and over the years the stitches, the arm slings, and the bruises all ran together in some sort of brutal haze that Moe and Larry probably preferred to forget. Curious fans, however, persisted in bringing back the painful memories.

"The only time I really got mad at my partner Larry was when he almost missed a show," Moe told Philadelphia television interviewer Bob Gale. "They forgot to give him a call at the hotel and wake him up. He came into the theater backstage and he didn't realize. The electrician in the back there says, 'Hey, Larry, you're on!' and Larry says, 'How am I doing?' He was clowning. Then he saw us out there and he came out. He says to me, 'You know what happened to me?' And I said, 'No, but I know what's gonna happen to you right now!' And I gave him a welt. A half hour later, you could still see the five little red fingers on his face." Larry remembered:

Our comedy speaks for itself. You have to see it to believe it. We didn't pull any punches. I say "we." *Moe* didn't pull any punches. When he hit, he hit. What you see is what we got. I mean it. Many times, we didn't even use sound effects. . . .

In *Punch Drunks,* Curly accidentally smashes Larry's violin into pieces.

We never meant to get hurt, but working rough like we were, we couldn't help it. Of course, coming into motion pictures from the stage as we did, we knew nothing about stuntmen and doubles. For the first two or three years we did our own stunts, until one day we made a football picture *(Three Little Pigskins)*. The director said, "Curly gets the ball and Moe and Larry run interference for him." As we approached the goal line the photographer said, "Hold it boys," and then he said, "The two teams will swoop down on you boys and tackle you." I said, "Tackle who? You mean football players are going to tackle us? They don't know anything about stunts. They're liable to kill us." I wouldn't do the scene, so after arguing and arguing, the director was forced to call in three doubles and when they did the scene, the doubles all went to the hospital with broken legs and arms. It was then that the producer was convinced we should have doubles. We've had them ever since but still, unfortunately, we got hurt—not seriously, but enough to lay us up, sometimes for a couple of weeks. But like everything else, nothing comes easily. If you want to dance, you pay the fiddler. Thank goodness, due to our unusual style of mayhem, nobody copied us.

Larry remembered making *Pop Goes the Easel* because of the clay. "I damned near lost an eye. In fact, there's still something in my eye yet," he told Mike Mikicel in 1973. "Plaster of Paris did it. It left a pit in my eye. It was Plaster of Paris and it had hardened. A piece caught me right in the eye and they had to send me to an eye specialist and he dug it out. When he pulled it out, it was the size of a pinhead, and I thought it'd be the size of a dime, the thing in my eye. That's how it felt."

The ever-present pies were a problem in and of themselves. The prop men or special effects technicians on the set would have a lineup of pies ready for aiming (Moe did much of the throwing), and when the pies ran out, a pile of the gooey mess was swept up off the floor—complete with nails and dust and debris—and put back in pie tins for re-sailing.

"Moe had a sadistic glee about throwing those pies," said Stooges' costar Emil Sitka, the recipient of many pastries to the face over the years. In Sitka's entree into Stooges comedies, a film called *Half-Wits Holiday,* he played a butler and was indoctrinated into the Stooges' style on his second day. "Moe was good at throwing the pies and he loved doing it. He smacked people really good and would walk away with a chuckle. I got smacked many times by him. How do you think I got this bent nose? The first time I got hit with a pie, when I got hit, I didn't know it was going to be that heavy. Like concrete. I thought it was going to be fluffy and soft like lemon meringue. When it hit me, I saw some blue light. I kept my composure, recovered and ad-libbed a line. The glass was wobbling on my tray. I balanced it and walked out and after that, I thought 'What the hell was that?' One take and that was it."

Big-eyed blonde actress Connie Cezon was one of Jules White's casting favorites and he threw her in a few of the messiest of the shorts. "One of the sequences, probably the most outstanding one I think, was the cake that was pushed over my head. That was a horrible feeling to have all of this goo fall all over your head. You couldn't see, you couldn't breathe, you couldn't do anything until they said cut," said Cezon. "They scooped out the middle of a huge cake and filled it with chocolate sauce and marshmallow and fudge and everything gooey. The top looked like a cake with frosting on it. One of the Stooges, I remember, picked it up as if he was going to throw it across the room and then the next shot was the prop man holding it in front of me, saying, 'Now take a big breath when we push this over your head.' So I was supposed to jump in front of it and say 'Stop!' It was just one take and we had to get it right."

Cezon, who died in 2004 at age seventy-eight, worked primarily in the Shemp shorts in the '50s and remembered the speed with which the Stooges put slapstick on film: "They worked so well together, there wasn't that much rehearsal. Quite often Jules White

The Stooges promote the Pillsbury/Farina "Three Stooges Moving Picture Machine" in the early 1940s.

would get together with them and say, 'How about do it this way and this way and then you go over there and pick that up and hit Moe in the head this way and then Larry, you cross over here and then when she bends over, you shoot the gun with the pellets,' and then they'd film it right away. It was that quick. They'd always have something new they thought of on the spur of the moment. It wasn't always by the script."

Props didn't always work the way they were supposed to on the Stooges' comedies. The Stooges were not ones to rush through a scene without rehearsing, they spent time studying each prop—especially the custom made utilities. Larry recalled the short *Dunked in the Deep*, which costarred Gene Roth as the Russian spy who hid secret microfilm in watermelons. ("Give me dat filum!") Said Larry: "Let me tell you something. They made those watermelons out of wood. They had seams, they put the pieces together. Gene Roth, the big guy who played the Russian, got hit right in the stomach and it broke his rib. The seams on the watermelons were wood, thick, and that did it. We threw

the watermelon, which, was on a wire, but it hit him and broke his rib."

In *Punch Drunks,* Larry was a fiddler who befriends Moe and Curly and helps prepare Curly for a big fight. One scene had the Stooges taking Curly outdoors for exercise and training while Larry accompanies with his fiddle. Larry was supposed to fall in a swamp near the road. "What I didn't know was that they had built that out of a mud hole and made it appear like a lake," said Larry. "When I dived in there, my arms went elbow deep in mud and I couldn't raise up. They just dug it out and added water and created mush. I damn near drowned before they realized."

The kicker of the gag in *Punch Drunks* was to have Larry emerge from the swamp with a frog atop his head. The prop men applied some sort of adhesive to Larry's head, which was supposed to keep the frog up there, except the overly large frog became irritated. "The thing scratched the hell out of me, right on top of my head. I never saw such a big frog. And they didn't even use the scene with the frog."

The Columbia shorts were like time capsules: If Larry viewed one of his films, he would instantly recall

Larry is the jockey steering champion racer Thunderbolt in *Playing the Ponies* (1937).

any injuries he might have suffered during filming or extraneous moments out of his home life. While watching *Playing the Ponies* in 1972 with a fan, for instance, he recalled riding the horse and the animal getting a little out of his control. The animal came too close to a high railing and brushed hard up against a wooden barrier, painfully crushing Larry's leg.

Maybe the pinnacle of pain, for Larry anyway, occurred during the filming of *Heavenly Daze*. The Stooges were trying to pawn off their invention—a fountain pen that writes under whipped cream—on a curious society couple. "We had a scene where the fountain pen goes wild and jumps out of a bowl of whipped cream and hits me right in the middle of the forehead," said Larry. It was rigged so the pen was on a wire and it would essentially be shot into Larry's forehead and stick into a little tin plate attached to Larry's forehead. "We went through all of the preparations. I said to Jules [White], 'Look, the hole they shot it in with the wire is too big. It's gonna hit me right in the skull.' He told me, 'I won't let anybody hit you, Larry.' So I see the prop man. I know what he's going to do and fast. He did and the pen went deep in my skull. I finished the scene and I pulled the pen out and ink and blood went all down my face. I let him have it. Some choice words."

Moe told an audience of college students: "Curly got nine stitches in his head in one picture. Remember the one where the gangsters mistook us for doctors? We operated on the gangster and we pressed the button and he flew out the window and then Curly took his place. Curly was so heavy, when we pushed the lever, he slid down and his head hit the edge of the windowsill. First, they shaved away the hair from the cut and put some Collodian on it and glued some false hair on top of that until he finished the scene and then they put the nine stitches in."

Larry recalled what sounds like the same injury, only in a different setting: "Curly was playing his own father, and he fell down an elevator shaft. And he was pretty heavy and all, they piled some mattresses down there for him, but when he hit the mattresses, he hit the wall with it and split his head open. Having no hair there, they put about six or eight stitches there, covered it up with tape and then put some glue on that and covered it up with some fake hair over it."

Emil Sitka happily reported that he was never injured while working with the Stooges. "Not with the Stooges," he was quick to emphasize. Sitka was no stranger to sustaining injuries and short circuits at the workplace; he broke his nose and fractured a vertebrae while filming a scene in a Billie Burke short subject.

"Now with the Stooges, I did a lot of dangerous things, but didn't get hurt. Like that tractor-submarine in *The Three Stooges in Orbit*, when it's chasing me

Larry was the only one of the team who actually played the violin, a trademark talent he performed on film with every "set" of Stooges over the decades.

80

down the airport runway. That weighs tons. They had a crane, you know, about eight stories high with a big cable that is supposed to pick it up. It didn't go up by itself, you know. I'm supposed to fall at a certain place, when they were rehearsing it, they had a big *X* mark where I'm supposed to fall. It missed it several times without me there. It went over the *X*. My heart was beating fast. When they went to film it, they told me, 'Now we think we got it.' Oh boy. I told my kids goodbye that morning. And they didn't know why I was kissing them goodbye and all. Not that I was leaving, but just that extra special something.

"The funny thing is," Sitka added, "sometimes the Stooges got hurt and it was not part of the action. Moe, one time, was doing all kinds of things, getting hit over the head, smacking and all. He was going off the set, walking out, he hit into a door with his toe. His foot was swelling up . . . oh my God, there were doctors, everything."

Although he delivered most of the abuse, Moe took home his share of war stories. Moe recalled smashing a lit cigar in Curly's mouth in the live stage act once and sparks flew all over the place. Moe laughed at the time,

continued the act, and within minutes he knew he'd seared the palm of his hand pretty well.

"In the films, I really got beat up," he told one reporter. "One picture, I was fixing the electric works in the kitchen of this place and the other guys were in another room, pulling a wire. I had the bell in my hand. They pulled my hand through the wall. Finally I tied it around my hand and they gave a pull and I went head-first right through the wall. My head was inside the wall and a big beam—a balsa beam, eight by eight, came right down on the back of my head. They didn't know about that because it was loose up there."

Maybe the most serious injury Moe sustained was during the carpenter scenes in *Pardon My Scotch*. Larry recalled the incident years later: "Once we did a scene with Moe on a table and Curly and I were sawing a piece of wood on a table and we were sawing right through the table—with the wood. It was wired so it would break away and Moe knew that, and as they pulled the wires they failed to work; the jerk of the wires made the table collapse and Moe went straight down and broke his ribs. He got up and finished the scene and then collapsed."

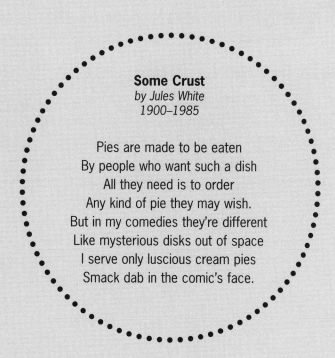

Some Crust
by Jules White
1900–1985

Pies are made to be eaten
By people who want such a dish
All they need is to order
Any kind of pie they may wish.
But in my comedies they're different
Like mysterious disks out of space
I serve only luscious cream pies
Smack dab in the comic's face.

Is On." Years later, Jules White recalled in an interview that *Sweet and Hot* was the Stooges' final short at Columbia. (They actually made two more.) Maybe White subconsciously realized that with this clunker, the Stooges were finished.

Muriel Landers belts out "The Heat Is On" with accompaniment from Larry and Joe in the finale from *Sweet and Hot* (1958).

SOUNDS LIKE . . .

Director Edward Bernds, who began his career at Columbia Pictures as a soundman, contributed these recollections to Film Fan Monthly *in 1972. Here, he reveals who the master was behind the Stooges' unique sound effects—unquestionably an integral part of the Stooges' brand, as well as the team's appeal and success.*

Two-reel comedies provided a field day for sound-effects, and an old friend of mine, Joe Henrie, was responsible for most of them at Columbia. The Three Stooges comedies were his babies. Even after he became head of the sound-effects editing department, responsible for the sound effects in all of the Columbia pictures, he continued to give the two-reelers his personal attention, making sure that every head-clunk and stomach-punch was as devastating as he could make it. This is how a sound-effects editor works: he has an immense library of recorded sound effects—dogs barking, lions roaring, mountain streams flowing, thunder pealing, horses galloping, doves cooing. You name it, he's got it. If he hasn't, he'll buy it (there are film libraries that sell sound effects) or get a sound crew and record it. Some sounds he'll fake, or perhaps I should say "manufacture."

Joe Henrie recently recalled some of the specialties he used in the Stooges comedies: "First, the temple block for fist-on-forehead, or top of the head; a violin or ukulele plunk for pulling hair from head, a plunger for pulling a tooth, or someone from a mud hole; a high-pitched plunk from a violin for cutting a hair from a head; sandpaper for shaving or rubbing Curly's nose or face. For hitting the head with a crowbar or metal pipe, we would choose a special type of plunk from the many types of metal thuds we have in the library. For a shovel on the head or back we would make the sound by hitting the flat side of a musical saw, or a regular carpenter's saw—it depended on the type wanted.

"For twisting an ear, leg, or arm, we would use different types of ratchet sounds. For cracking knuckles, we would break a stick of wood. We would use different types of Jews harp twangs for tweaking a nose or for other types of sharp, short and long twangs. A bass drum beat was used for a stomach sock. For pulling a handful of hair from the head we'd use a good short cloth rip."

Joe Henrie, in my opinion, is damn close to being a genius as a sound-effects editor. He has a lively, zany sense of humor, and in the two-reelers he was never satisfied with a sound effect until he had gotten it as startling and as funny as he could make it.

The Stooges are resuscitated by television in 1958. Photographed by Schaeffer Studio in Hollywood, this is among their first costumed publicity shots with Curly-Joe.

4

THE REVIVAL

The 1950s were a time of upheaval in the entertainment industry. For the Stooges, television at first seemed like a threat, but eventually it became their greatest ally. Larry Fine said:

> We weren't sure where we were going next. In 1958, Columbia said, "We're going to let you boys go because we put you on TV and you're through in theaters when they can see it for nothing. So they ain't gonna pay to see you anymore." I accepted it as fact. I wrote my sister, in fact I called her, and I said, "Lyla, I'm gonna sell my home, I got a few hundred thousand dollars, I'm coming to Philadelphia and I'll open a business with your husband." Because I thought I was through. She said, "Are you crazy? . . . We see your pictures on TV and all the kids know me as your sister." So it worked the opposite way. Our fee jumped from six thousand to twenty thousand, just from putting the same shorts on TV. Remember, those pictures, we started making them in 1934, and on TV, the same pictures, but everything went up three hundred percent. And Columbia, who had let us go, had to sign us up again to make six features for much more than they were ever paying us [before].

It was January 1, 1958, when the Stooges faced unemployment and actually considered the act washed up. When Columbia Pictures released the Stooges from their contract after twenty-four years—a record for the longest consecutive studio contract in held in Hollywood—Moe and Larry were confused about the future. Would this mean the end of the partnership? Neither one of them

Moe and Larry welcomed comic and former vaudevillian Joe DeRita into the act in late 1958 and he forever became known as "Curly-Joe." In this, the first portrait of the new team, DeRita had not yet buzzed his hair or created his own persona, but it didn't take long for the three to mesh.

wanted to quit working. Financially, Moe didn't have to work and he and Helen were planning on an extensive vacation tour of South America. Larry was not as solvent and needed the work. Joe Besser had no interest in continuing in the act, so the team was once again crippled and it became a duo of Moe and Larry on their own again. So, for a brief period, a haze clouded any future for the two Stooges—in films, anyway.

What happened next? Television happened. Columbia Pictures syndicated the two-reelers in a handsome package deal in the fall of 1958, which attracted nearly every major market in the United States. Stations began running the initial package of seventy-eight short subjects in their weekday afternoon schedules for kids to watch after school. They also found that the shorts worked well when they incorporated them into the programming of their own locally produced kiddie shows. It added up to a phenomenal amount of publicity the team couldn't have afforded on their own, and best of all, it was gravy from the twenty-four years they'd put in at Columbia Pictures. The clouds had lifted, and Moe and Larry knew it was the right time to cash in. Larry and Mabel remained in Hollywood, and Moe and Helen cancelled their tour of South America.

The newly rejuvenated team picked up a new partner, Joe DeRita, who was working in a Minsky's review in Las Vegas. He would be known from then on as Curly-Joe. The rotund DeRita, a former vaudeville and burlesque comic with some decent timing, had an overblown belly to fit the role as the third Stooge; he would be expected to emulate Curly to some extent, and he stood about the same height as Moe and Larry—all under 5-feet-5. Like Curly before him, he shaved his head, usually down to a crew cut (*TV Guide* likened his head to "a dirty tennis ball"). Curly-Joe rehearsed the act with Moe and Larry to get acclimated; they broke in new material geared for the kids (with less violence) and took to the road.

DeRita remembered:

It was a very odd thing. I was out of work and they were looking for some bum to work with them. Actually, I had quit my job to join them. I was under contract, but I got out of that and I joined them in June of '58. They wanted to go out on the road after their contract was up at Columbia Pictures and they wanted to make personal appearances. Joey Besser had been working with them up to the end of their contract because he replaced Shemp. Joey didn't feel like going on the road and they were asking around and somebody mentioned me and I had met the boys many, many years ago in Chicago when they were headlining the Oriental Theatre. I got word from an agent to come down and I talked with Moe and Larry and we finally got together and broke in the act in Bakersfield at a restaurant. They were going to cancel us and we begged to stay on to try to get more work and to find out what we really had. We stayed two weeks and it worked out fine. And about four or five weeks later, we went to Pittsburgh around Christmastime of '58 at the Holiday House and the boys were a big hit because their pictures had been released to television about three months ahead of that. They were on every night in Pittsburgh and naturally, they were a very hot attraction. We opened in Pittsburgh December the 22nd, 1958, and we were held over for three weeks and we didn't finish the three weeks because Steve Allen wanted us to come in to New York to do *The Steve Allen Show.* That's when he was doing the Sunday night show, a big variety show on the order of Ed Sullivan. We did three of those, two weeks apart. We did the *Ed Sullivan Show* four times. We did most all the shows.

Joe DeRita always felt lucky that he joined the Stooges—an established triumvirate—and could ride into the sunset with Moe and Larry.

Larry's sister, Lyla, remembered the resurgence clearly because when the fuse was lit, the fireworks exploded in her own backyard. "I don't think Larry was aware of how popular he was," said Budnick. "None of them were really aware of it. When they came to Pittsburgh after the shorts began showing on television, they came by train and when they got off the train and they saw all these people at the station, they wondered who the VIP was on the train, not realizing the crowds were for them. They had absolutely no idea of how popular they were."

At Pittsburgh's popular Holiday House—essentially a nightclub—where they hit big, it took no time at all to fill the seats. Less than six hours after their appearance was announced the house capacity of seven hundred seats was sold out. Management sold more hamburger (some seven tons) than ever before in the establishment's history. Kids came in with their parents and the moms and dads brought money. Bottles of pop were passed around like beer at a summer ballgame. Extra dates had to be added as the Stooges were adding to their material day by day, honing it for television appearances to come.

Within two months, the Stooges were on fire. Bookings for the trio in theatres, circuses and auditoriums went through the roof, with personal appearance dates set up to six months in advance. Coral Records signed the Stooges

A *Fleer* for Comedy
An assortment of the collectible 1965 bubblegum cards from Fleer . . . 5 cents a pack.

Canuck, Canuck, Canuck Seen here in Toronto with just a portion of the massive audience (more than eighty thousand) in attendance, the Three Stooges were the main attraction on the grandstand at the Canadian National Exhibition in the Fall of 1962. They returned the next year and broke attendance records again. A joke from their act:

> **Moe:** Why does a traffic light turn red?
> **Larry:** I don't know, why *does* a traffic light turn red?
> **Moe:** Well, wouldn't you turn red if you had to stop and go in the middle of the street?

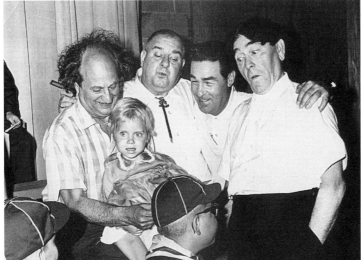

Always a sucker for the kids, Larry just couldn't help but entertain this bright-eyed tyke at a personal appearance with television host Paul Shannon.

Stooges On Parade The boys take to the streets in a parade through Pittsburgh, Pennsylvania in 1968.

to record an LP album geared at kids and Columbia Pictures was in negotiations with the team to star them in a feature film. As slapstick comedians, they were a hot commodity—and more than that: a rare one. The entertainment industry had all but run out of established comedy teams: Abbott and Costello were no more; Martin and Lewis had split; the Marx Brothers had dissolved long ago. The Stooges were almost the last of a dying breed.

Although Joe DeRita was the neophyte, ten years younger than Moe, his energy level and stage persona matched that of Moe and Larry. Moe was nearing sixty and Larry wasn't far behind. "There's one thing that mystifies me," Moe told a reporter at the time. "I play the heavy, you know, the bully. Twenty years ago, kids didn't like me because I was the villain. You could frighten some kids to death just by showing them my picture. But now they love me to death, even though I am the villain. What do you make of that?"

Moe and Larry, a little craggier than when they were slinging pies in the

1930s and '40s, appeared much the same. Moe kept his hair dyed black (since the 1950s) and Larry's reddish brown frizz featured just a speckling of gray on the sides by now, but more importantly, both men still *had* hair to pull. Their facial features were now more exaggerated and cartoonish than ever, bags under Moe's eyes like suitcases and Larry's pate as inviting of smacks as ever. *Time* magazine pinned Larry as the one with the "tuber-nose." Kids could see these guys were older, but it was *them*! And they were now rolling in the dough, rather than tossing it across the room.

A Fine Mess While filming *The Three Stooges in Orbit* at the Air National Guard Base (Van Nuys, California Airport), the boys take time out for some chow; Larry makes it known he's no fan of lima beans.

Based on current booking projects, reported *Broadcasting* magazine in February 1959, "the team expects to gross $350,000 this year, as compared with an average $80,000 annually for the past ten. Not one dime comes from the two-reelers themselves. Those on the market now are all pre-1948, and the Stooges have no ownership interest in them."

Moe was no lamebrain. He kept track of the money for the team and negotiated deals in concert with their new agency, the most shrewd and most

The Stooges are about to make a bang in the headlines when they appear at the Steel Pier in Atlantic City, New Jersey, August 1959.

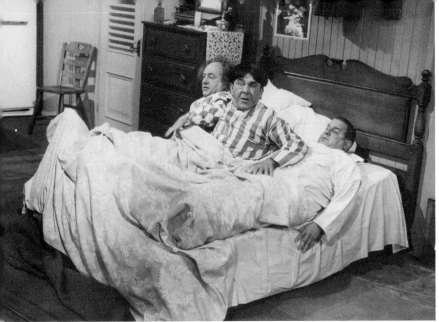

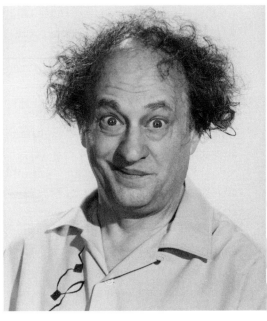

Bet Curly-Joe wasn't prepared for this sort of physical comedy when he signed on with the boys.

Sock it to Moe! The Stooges stage a laugh-in on *The Frances Langford Show* in May 1960 on NBC-TV.

The Stooges clown onstage in March 1965.

92

prestigious in show business—the William Morris Agency. Moe always knew the worth of the Stooges, although even he might've underestimated it. In 1954, he attempted to purchase the shorts from Columbia Pictures, but his $1.25 million bid was "laughed out of the office," he remembered. When asked in 1959 if he regretted seeing Columbia Pictures reaping all of the profits from the shorts, he recounted a family business axiom: "My mother, bless her, was a successful real estate operator. She left me with this thought that I've always remembered: 'If you want to make a success in business, always leave room for profit for the other man.'"

Moe, in his customary fashion, explained years later to Stooge fan Mike Mikicel—in financial terms—just what television meant to the Three Stooges in the late 1950s. "You can't cry with a loaf of bread under your arm," as he put it. "It was the exposure of the characters on TV that made everything else possible. It doubled, tripled, and quadrupled our salaries on personal appearances.

"Originally all those comedies were made for exhibition in theaters," Moe explained, "so that the four, five, six, seven, eight-year-olds never got into the theaters to see those things. Suddenly those films were dumped on TV, where the little kid would sit in his room and see the Three Stooges and became familiar with us. Now, those kids who were little in 1936 are now forty-six." (It's interesting to note Moe Howard's choice of words here. He mentions a "little kid" in general terms, but then says the kid would sit in "*his* room." Clearly Moe knew that frankly most of the fans of the Stooges were boys and men, a trend that bears out even today.)

"Fact is," Moe continued, "we made hundreds of personal appearances in our lifetime in the picture industry. Our contract called for forty weeks and twelve weeks of layoff period at which time we could do anything we wanted in the way of personal appearances. That money, we kept. The money from personal appearances was far in excess of the studio salary. Sometimes we appeared as long as twenty weeks when we were ahead on comedies. We had a good deal.

"You have to understand," Moe concluded, "the interest in theaters passed out in 1958 when they issued the first shorts to TV. I heard once how many millions of dollars they made on our comedies through the TV system."

On Top of Old Larry
By the early 1960s, the Stooges' success was unparalleled; they outlasted every other comedy team in the history of motion pictures, still churning out the celluloid after thirty years as an act.

A *Broadcasting* magazine story in February 1959 described their resurgence in terms of Arbitron television ratings, a standard measurement employed in the day: "The package has been sold in 75 markets (largely in major cities) and is virtually sold out in each. . . . Screen Gems reports ratings have been 'Phenomenal' putting the Stooges in first place for their time period in many markets. These examples are cited as typical: WGN-TV Chicago opened in October with a 3.3 ARB, went up to 10.7 in November, up to 19.0 in December; WPIX-TV New York opened with 2.4 in October, up to 11.3 in November and 15.1 in December; KFJZ-TV Dallas-Ft. Worth had 6.7 in October, 11.5 in November, 19.9 in December."

No wonder Larry wasn't fond of flying.

• • •

The Fines were now back at the Knickerbocker Hotel in Hollywood where they would again rent a spacious five-room apartment as they had done years before. They enjoyed the full amenities offered within the hotel: maid service, room service, a restaurant or coffee shop within steps of their apartment, secure parking, and the like. With their children grown and living on their own, they could relax a little more, relinquishing the responsibilities of the formal upkeep of a large home with a yard. Most of all, perhaps, Larry felt comfortable traveling extensively with the act and leaving Mabel behind as long as she had assistance keeping the apartment clean and food services within reach twenty-four hours a day. Mabel's depression escalated, as did her drinking. Larry and the immediate family attempted to keep the matter private as their concern grew. Although he was nervous about her continued binges with alcohol, he felt she would be in better hands at the apartment with neighbors and friends nearby when needed.

• • •

Time magazine in May 1959 dubbed these comeback kids "Brillo-headed knockabouts" in the midst of the most startling resurgence in entertainment history. On the comeback trail, they were indeed. Kids, they were not.

Parade magazine put the Stooges, as big as life, on the cover of their Sunday supplement in gorgeous, full-blown Kodachrome colors—something almost unseen by anyone accustomed to seeing them only in black and white. In the November 1959 *Parade* issue, writer Lloyd Shearer reported on their smashing success: "Surprise of surprises! The two-reelers were gobbled up by

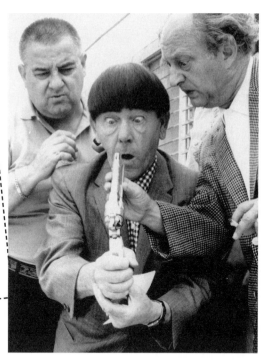

Concerns about violence poured in from parents. The tone of Three Stooges comedy was altered in the '60s, believe it or not, to feature less violence.

comedy-hungry video stations from Portland to Peoria. Of the 240 leading markets in the U.S., the Three Stooges are being seen in 200 by more than 25 million people watching 280 TV stations. . . . Their popularity has zoomed to such heights that in the past seven months, they have granted 29 licenses to various manufacturers who are turning out 52 different items bearing a Three Stooges tag." The boys were being rediscovered by new generations of fans and their faces were being splashed on everything from bubble gum trading cards and board games to comic books and finger puppets. You name it, the Stooges' mugs were on it: coloring books, flicker rings, punching bags, dolls, jigsaw puzzles, hats, a Colorforms kit, and a host of other delights to purchase. A massive merchandising launch was under way, and the Stooges' overwhelming success was evident not just on television and in the theatres, but in the dime stores and novelty shops as well.

In early 1959, Steve Allen introduced the team on his live variety program with obvious pride: "Among the great comedy names of our time are three men who, for many years, convulsed the motion picture and vaudeville audiences of this country with their hilarious knock-'em-about style of comedy. It took the medium of television and the perceptive minds of today's youngsters to rediscover their greatness. So here from three record-breaking weeks at the Holiday House in Pittsburgh are—let's welcome them—the Three Stooges!" Larry came trotting out first with Curly-Joe and Moe bring-

Stoopendous The team was all over the tube in the 1960s, making guest appearances with Johnny Carson, Frances Langford, Steve Allen, Joey Bishop, Ed Sullivan, and many other variety shows over their decade-long career finale.

ing up the rear as they stopped, knocked into one another, and sang, "Back again, back again . . . it's great to say hello! Hello! Hello! Hello!" The bops and bangs started almost immediately as an agitated Moe took aim at Curly-Joe. Their timing proved fast and the craving audience went wild. Immediately, the Stooges went into a hilarious routine that took place in a hospital operating room featuring Curly-Joe in drag as a myopic nurse (with google-eye glasses), Larry the patient, and Moe the wacky surgeon. There was no shortage of slaps and swinging sticks.

The blend of the newly formed team was smooth and Joe DeRita proved himself an appropriate choice on his national television debut as the third Stooge. For the trio, it was a graceful transition and all was well with these guys as they wowed national audiences and they accepted Steve Allen's invitations to return to NBC for more guest shots.

And then the complaints from parents' groups and teachers began to trickle in. Reports that kids were hitting each other and injuring their siblings began to surface. The Three Stooges were simply too violent for audiences, they claimed; it was rude and objectionable comedy. Parents were frozen in their fear that children would begin to emulate the Stooges and begin poking each other's eyes out or slamming wicker chairs over heads to get a laugh. And it did happen, there's no question about that. The concerns were valid.

Initially, the Stooges themselves stood up and defended their comedy, stating that no one ever died in their short subject comedies and compared themselves to animated cartoon characters. The Stooges urged the parents to take some responsibility in the matter as well and educate their children as to what was fantasy and what was reality on television and in the movies. The boys, however, were confronted with making a necessary change in style: The comedy was being brought directly into people's homes now, more concentrated, more memorable, more frequently. They needed to get rid of the cutting edge—quite literally.

Mainstays Moe and Larry in their sixties.

They soon realized they needed to eliminate—or at least, tone down considerably—the violent shenanigans. Moe explained to reporters that the violence found in their old films actually "grew out of the belief of some of their directors over the years that if getting slugged by an opening door was funny, shoving someone out of a ten-story building was hilarious. It just sort of crept in," he said, quietly referring to the dictatorial direction style of Jules White. "If we'd had something to say about it, we wouldn't have done so much of it, but we didn't. I don't mean our association with Columbia wasn't a happy one. It was. But they owned every other breath we took and we couldn't say 'we won't do this or that.'"

The Stooges of the new era adopted a policy of toning down the smacks and punches unless it really came out of the comedy or routine. Props will still fall, pies will fly, and accidental slips on a wet floor will still occur, but "a poke for the sake of a poke isn't funny any more," said Moe in a 1960 *Los Angeles Examiner* interview. "In our Three Stooges [fan club] kit we include a letter, signed by us, telling the kids that we're only making fun in the pictures and they could hurt themselves trying to copy what we do. We even hurt ourselves sometimes."

Boy, did Larry know *that* all too well. On the set of their first motion picture with Curly-Joe, a cute low-budget quickie called *Have Rocket, Will Travel* that was filmed and released in 1959, Larry fell into one of those all-too-often traps of his trade. He explained:

In *Have Rocket, Will Travel,* we were dressed in these space suits and in the scene we were all running. We were wearing these large round space helmets, so it was hard to see anything

Houston, We Have a Problem It was while wearing this precarious helmet that Larry split his lip open during the filming of *Have Rocket, Will Travel.*

unless directly in front of you. Joe was behind me and tripped and he hit me in the back with his head and down I went. The space helmet crushed my lips and teeth. Luckily it didn't break them. I must have been unconscious for a few minutes because the next thing I knew a doctor was examining me and seeing I had a space helmet on, they bandaged me up and I finished working that day. There was blood all inside my helmet. My face was swollen and sore for a week or so and they fixed me up with makeup under the space helmet. I've got a little scar on my lip that formed from that and it's never gone away.

The Kiddie Show Years

Early in 1960, *Variety* dubbed the Three Stooges the "hottest comedy team on television." Actually, they were just about the *only* comedy team on television. (New teams were only beginning to emerge: Rowan & Martin, Allen & Rossi, etc.)

The seasoned Stooges were now targeting a "family audience," with a new television pilot, *The Three Stooges Scrapbook,* filmed entirely in color with a laugh track and featuring some animated segments in between the

The boys shoot a color scene, a parachute drop, outside the landmark Chaplin Studios in Hollywood (on La Brea Avenue) for the television pilot *The Three Stooges Scrapbook.*

Should they move to Lompoc? A decision must be made and Moe is not happy about it.

Director Sidney Miller walks through the scene with the boys during production of *The Three Stooges Scrapbook.* Much of this bedroom scene was transferred to black and white and reused in *The Three Stooges in Orbit.*

THE REVIVAL   99

Emil Sitka revisits his eccentric scientist role in the color television pilot *The Three Stooges Scrapbook* . . .

Later, some scenes were restaged and reshot in black and white for *The Three Stooges in Orbit.*

team's live antics. It was proposed as a half-hour weekly TV series for prime time. The animation was to be handled by TV Spots, the studio that was also busy producing the television cartoon *Crusader Rabbit.* This new phase of their career being steered by Moe's son-in-law, Norman Maurer, who served as a manager, producer, and sometimes writer.

Director Ed Bernds remembered, "In 1959 or '60, Norman Maurer and the Stooges made this pilot. Elwood Ullman wrote the script, tried and true material featuring scare sequences," Bernds said. "Norman wanted me to direct it, but I was busy as a writer-producer on a TV series, *Assignment Underwater,* so he hired Sidney Miller. The pilot did not sell, and Norman, to recoup the cost of the pilot, had Elwood incorporate the material into the script of *The Three Stooges in Orbit* a year later and Columbia accepted the idea, paying Normandy Productions (the Stooges' producing entity) the full cost of the pilot for use of the film. So, Sidney Miller actually directed part of *Orbit.* Just how much I can't recall. I would guess about one tenth or less of the final footage. He would have been entitled to share directorial credit, but perhaps he didn't ask for it or want it."

In *Scrapbook,* the Stooges portray actors who are kicked out of their rooming house when a nosy landlord catches them cooking up a feast in their apartment. While hunting for new living quarters, they meet a creepy eccentric, Professor Doolottle (Emil Sitka), and move into his spacious mansion. The professor is in the process of inventing a new secret weapon: a tank-helicopter-submarine, which he plans to use against alien forces who he is convinced are going to invade.

Larry was fond of one scene in particular, in which he lies in bed asleep in his striped long nightshirt and unknowingly gets carted away by a monster alien. Cradled in the arms of the monster and still dreaming, he mumbles: "Oh Mabel, you're here at last . . . you swept me off my feet . . . I'm safe in your arms."

Moe explained the television show's premise to a reporter from the *St. Louis Post-Dispatch* in 1960: "The difference in this

That's actually Emil Sitka in the costume as the hooded goon, hauling a slumbering Larry off into the secret passage.

new series will be the presentation. In these, we are very successful people who host a TV show—but we show the messes we get into during the day. The Stooges at home, before they get into the studio. That will be us, in the flesh, for twenty minutes. Then we'll have a five and a half minute cartoon with the characters drawn on us, the Three Stooges."

Moe also characterized the cartoon as "educational television." For example, the first cartoon concerned the discovery of America by the Three Stooges and Christopher Columbus. The great Mel Blanc contributed his voice-over talents in the pilot as a talking parrot, among other characters. The second cartoon (never produced) was going to present the true story of Paul Revere's ride. "Revere almost didn't make the ride," Moe furthered, "nobody had a match to light the lamp in the church steeple. Larry comes to the rescue with a cigarette lighter."

The pilot never sold to the networks. However, Moe's son-in-law, Norman Maurer, eventually made use of it. Some footage was transferred to black and white for reusing, and these bits were fleshed out into a full-length feature film that became *The Three Stooges in Orbit,* released in 1962. Changes were made: sets such as the professor's study and living room were rebuilt on a grander level, the butler was recast, the laugh track was removed, and the small scale model of the tank-helicopter-submarine was redesigned. Ultimately the TV pilot was shelved as the Stooges pursued other film projects and many more live appearance tours across the country.

Nepotism did not run exclusively in the Howard strain of the Stooges. In the '60s, Larry hired his brother-in-law, Nate Budnick (married to Lyla

The Stooges goof around for photographers at an impromptu press conference in their Cleveland, Ohio hotel suite (August 1960). *Below,* Cleveland Airport's Avis Rent-a-Car attendant Pat Hodous attempts to push things along and have the Stooges sign in triplicate— insisting they take out the extra insurance.

Moe demonstrates the hand-to-palm snapping bit for the kids while Curly-Joe sits this one out. (1963)

Feinberg), as the team's road manager and soundman. Because Budnick had been around the Stooges enough over the years and had seen their relatively unaltered act so many times, he knew the routines and how precise the sound effects needed to be. Budnick traveled with the team and handled some finances, some trip planning, and even some publicity chores when needed. Just offstage, Budnick handled the ever-important sound effects, which always improved the live act, but he never replicated the unique punches and slaps that echoed in all of the Stooges' Columbia shorts.

"Without the sound effects, they got no laughs," Budnick pointed out. "I want you to know that."

Budnick lived in Philadelphia and flew from city to city with the Stooges or drove with the team from one engagement to the next. The Stooges were booked into fairgrounds, mall openings, theaters, summer-fests, circus appearances . . . you name it. Twice they were the featured act at the Canadian National Exposition and played to their largest audiences—nearly a hundred thousand spectators in the stands. Each of their live performances were essentially the same: some songs, some mild slapstick routines, banter and bangs to the head. Sometimes Larry played the fiddle. Kids went wild over these old Stooges and their well-timed antics alive and misbehaving, right in front of them.

Occasionally, the Stooges included audience participation in their live act. Larry Brown, a Stooges fan who grew up in Massachusetts, recently recalled seeing the Stooges live on stage at Pleasure Island's Show Bowl the-atre in 1959 or 1960 and divulging this bit of notoriety to his young son. "My eleven-year-old son had just received his first Three Stooges video, and as we watched it I proudly told him that I had appeared onstage with the trio. The Stooges invited three kids onstage, dressed us as babies, and conducted a contest to see who among us could empty a baby bottle full of milk through a rubber nipple. Fortunately, I discovered that if you just let the milk slide out through the enlarged hole, you could avoid constricting the flow by sucking on it. My prize was a plastic model of a knight in arms—and the short-lived awe of my son."

Writer Laurie Jacobson was just six years old when she got to meet the Stooges in St. Louis during one of their personal appearances.

I remember shaking hands with them and thinking, "Whoa, you guys don't look anything like you do on TV." Of course, they were old, and it wasn't Curly. I wondered, "What happened here?" I vividly recall that.

I was at home with my girlfriend and she said the Three Stooges

The Stooges were the season's opening attraction at Pleasure Island, a "family fun park" in Wakefield, Massachusetts, in June 1960. The comedians christened the stage at the park's new five-thousand-seat Outdoor Show Bowl.

are going to be somewhere in a half hour and asked me if I wanted to go. I said yes and my mom came running home and got us and we went to some field somewhere. There was a lot of grass and ground. I don't remember anything they said, but as they walked toward the crowd, they reached out to shake hands with people. It was Moe, Larry, and Curly-Joe, in that order. I remember vividly them coming toward me and I couldn't believe how wrinkled Moe's face was. I was six. I'd seen them the day before in a 1940 short and suddenly here he was twenty-five years later in front of me, and that was shocking to me.

ONE FiNE STOOGE

"Larry looked pretty much like Larry," Jacobson recalls. "Moe had aged. Deep face wrinkles, but the hair was there, it was the same. And it wasn't Curly. It was Curly-Joe. He was kind of mean-looking and that frightened me a little, I wondered 'What have they done with Curly?' I drew back from Curly-Joe. I always thought Curly-Joe's eyebrows gave him a little bit of a mean look."

• • •

When traveling, the Stooges adjourned to their individual hotel rooms, although occasionally Budnick stayed with Larry. Moe calmed his nerves by reading or knitting and hooking rugs to pass time, mostly keeping to himself. Larry would run around and meet people in the lobby, try to arrange tickets to the fights, or meet with friends in each city. "In every town, Larry knew people who owned restaurants," Budnick said. The Stooges traveled together, often ate together, and when they could, they hit the nearest baseball stadium during summers to see the games around the country and meet the players nearly any time they wanted.

"Offstage, they all had their own thing to do, some responsibilities," Budnick explained of their free time. "Moe would do some of the managing, Larry would make sure of the music, make sure the musicians would come in at the right time. Joe took care of the clothing, wardrobe, and props, and made sure they arrived at the different places. And Joe wrote the checks for the expenses. And that's the way it would work."

Budnick recalled more of the "downtime" than any of their performances. He says he spent more time getting to know Curly-Joe DeRita than spending time with his own brother-in-law. "Joe was a very funny guy, an instigator," Budnick said. "Nobody realizes his sense of humor. He loved to set up Moe and Larry into an argument.

"I'd be playing gin and Larry would be looking over my shoulder. I'd make a dumb move. I did it purposely. Then Moe would go over to Joe's shoulder, peek over, and take a look at his cards. He'd say, 'Joe, you stupid ass, don't you know how to play gin?' Then they'd take over the card game. Then the two of them would start fighting each other and they would argue and Joe and I would stand in the other room and laugh like hell.

"Joe was also a big eater," Budnick added. "That sticks out in my mind very well. They never ate before showtime. After the show, about 11:30, Larry and Joe and I went to a diner and we sat down. After dinner, he'd say he wanted dessert. He'd eat an entire pie . . . the whole thing.

"Or if I said I'm going out to get a sandwich at some fairgrounds they were playing, Joe would say, 'Nate, are there hotdogs at the stands? You

FANS, ROMANS, AND COUNTRYMEN!

In the throes of a hot comeback with young audiences across the nation, the Stooges toured with the RKO Theatre chain in early 1962 promoting their feature film *The Three Stooges Meet Hercules.* Imagine: Moe and Larry were in their sixties and Curly-Joe, a cueball of a baby still in his fifties. Here these old men—throwbacks from vaudeville, yet masters at creating laughs—were dressing up in togas and long johns, slapping each other in madcap mayhem onstage for screaming crowds. The Stooges warned the kids not to practice the slapstick themselves—that was important to Moe, who didn't want to be responsible for kids getting injured. Lots of lucky fans got to meet their idols during that hectic tour, taking pictures, getting autographs, and even asking Moe to show them the eye-poke. But most enthralled possibly were the Stooges themselves, always driven by the enthusiasm and rush of a live crowd.

An unnamed reporter who traveled with the junket along with the Stooges, Norman Maurer, and some security personnel in a bus, described the East Coast experience like this: "The reception the Stooges received was always the same: at least three thousand screaming kids outside the theatres (rain or shine); a blaring brass band with two or three satin-clad majorettes doing a rhythmic, pelvic twist; and then backstage, in a dimly lit area, some little old cleaning lady served cookies and Coke amidst the theatre's dangling ropes, curtains, and props. The Stooges would wait backstage: Curly-Joe adjusting his cigar, Moe combing his hair over his forehead, Larry fluffing up his tousled mop and nursing a finger that had been scratched or bitten in the chaos outside. The children lucky enough to get in were out front watching the feature. They sat enraptured. When the screen finally dimmed at the end and the lights went up, a shrill cheer filled the auditorium and the Stooges entered. Their routine was short and on the surface nonsensical. . . . This was twelve minutes of theater at its most absurd. Why not? This was the Three Stooges."

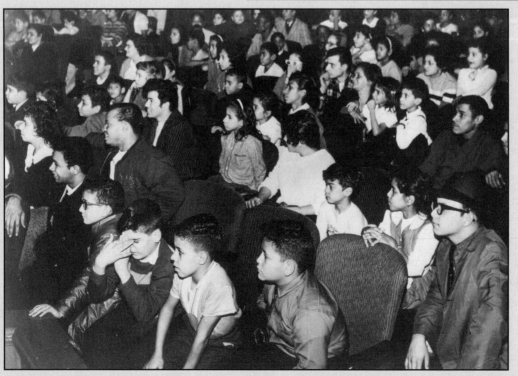

know what to get me!' Larry would say 'Get me a hotdog,' and Moe would want a hotdog and a soda. I'd bring back for Joe six hot dogs, a few sodas, and about four pieces of pie or whatever goodies they had. He was ashamed to say 'Bring me six hot dogs' in front of everybody, but I knew what he wanted."

Joe was a "very charitable man," added Budnick. "You see, the corporation the Stooges set up, Comedy III, paid for their cars. Larry had a big Lincoln; Moe had a sports car, a Porsche; and Joe would maybe have a Dodge or Chevy station wagon. Everybody would wonder why. He had told me why. They used to trade in the cars every two years and he would buy the station wagon back and give it to his sister in Baltimore and she had a few children and gave it to them. He also took care of his mother."

Budnick remembered Moe being not quite as charitable. "He was cheap." Choosing his words more carefully, he added, "Well, I like to say 'thrifty.' *Very* thrifty!"

One example leapt to mind: "We were playing the Latin Casino in Philadelphia," recalled Budnick. "The owner sent up a ten-pound box of candy to the dressing room. It was enormous. They were there about four or five days and about the second day, it wasn't even opened. So, Joe says to me, 'Nate, you got a bunch of kids, take the box of candy home to the kids.' Just then, Moe said: 'Now hold it, Joe. One third of that is mine. If you want to give away yours and Larry wants to give away his, that's their business.' He counted out the pieces and took one third."

According to Budnick, at the beginning, Curly-Joe was not receiving an equal share of the profits. "Moe and Larry were partners and they discussed everything," Budnick recalled. "Then after Joe joined them, he was like a junior partner, let's put it that way. After a couple of years, Larry said to Moe, 'Let's make him an even partner.' I'm not sure what the split was, maybe 40, 40, and 20. Moe questioned it, but Larry forced it on Moe. I told you, Moe was thrifty."

The extensive traveling wasn't without its problems. Moe and Larry argued, "but it was friendly arguing," Budnick pointed out. "That's the way

COURTESY OF EBERENZ FAMILY

The Stooges pose with Raymond Eberenz and his two sons, Rickey and Randy, backstage at the St. Louis Police Circus in 1967.

they were. Or if Moe kept it in and he was still angry, he would go out on stage and put his ring on and when he slapped Larry he'd hit him with that ring and later Larry would say, 'You sonofabitch! . . . You did that on purpose! You're taking it out on me.' Moe would sometimes forget. He had a big ring, it was a turtle or something, and it would stick out. He'd forget every once in a while and Larry would get cracked across the face. Sometimes, by accident, Moe would poke him in the eyes. He got poked many times."

"Larry would get him back," Budnick remembered, smiling big. There were times when Moe would simply zone out on stage and become blank. It wasn't often, but when Larry recognized that Moe was in this nebulous state or distracted by something, he found his chance to take sweet revenge. The revenge wasn't altogether innocuous. "I saw this happen: Moe went up to the microphone and was in a fog and was going to say something, but Larry ran up to it and said, 'Hey kids . . . you want to see something different?' And the kids would all yell 'Yeahhh!' Then Larry would take his hand and *crack!* Right across Moe's face."

What really energized the Stooges during those years and those live performances were the laughs, the out-loud yuks from the revved-up kids. This

Larry walked his little white poodle, "Angel Boy," around the Columbia Ranch in between scenes during the production of *The Outlaws IS Coming!* Mort Mills ("Trigger Mortis") and Larry's son-in-law Don Lamond ("Rance Roden"), take a minute to play with the pooch, too.

was fresh territory for the Stooges, who had played to adult live audiences mostly during their career. The admiration was purely reciprocal: The kiddies fell in love with the Stooges—these grandfatherly kooks who whacked each other on the head. And the Stooges cherished every smile of amazement that the kids and teenagers went home wearing. For years, a rumor circulated that Moe Howard detested children in much the same way W. C. Fields was known to. Nothing could have been further from the truth. In fact, Moe was confounded by this adulation. He had played the "heavy" Stooge, the villain, who delivered the pokes and slaps, for decades—and suddenly the young Stooge fans adored him for his meanness. Larry told *TV Guide* in 1959, "The kids paint our faces on eggs and electric light bulbs now. They used to throw those things at us."

Larry was a softie, melting around most kids. He had grandchildren of his own whom he loved to spoil and show off for, but there was something about reaching out to the young fans and meeting them in person that he craved.

ONE FINE STOOGE

He never refused an autograph seeker or someone wanting to take a snapshot with him. Even in airports, when his hair was combed back, he'd occasionally muss it up for a fan just to please them, then comb it back. Especially in the later years, when the Stooges themselves became oddly cartoonish in appearance, Larry seemed even more approachable with that wonderful jowly face, always with a genuine smile and a gentle manner; his euphonic nasal voice was instantly recognizable even if his face went unnoticed. Kids warmed up to Larry immediately. What youngster didn't want to reach up and touch that wild frizzy hair? Was it for real?

"There was one thing that really got to Larry once," revealed his son-in-law, Don Lamond:

> The Stooges went back to Philadelphia and they did a show in a night-club, but they did it on weekends for kids only, and they served Coca-Cola and popcorn. And the guys did their show and it did fantastic business. But the thing that got Larry was this: The manager brought backstage a blind kid who wanted to meet the Stooges. And while he was feeling Larry's face, he said, 'I watch you guys all the time.'
>
> Larry had to get up. He had tears and it broke him up. He just went. That really got to him, because he was an old softy. He talked about that for quite a while.

• • •

Don Lamond, who married Larry's daughter Phyllis in 1948, was a budding television actor and broadcaster when he joined the Fine family. Lamond had come from a show business family, his father being an accomplished musician, pianist, and arranger/conductor, he says. By the early 1960s, Lamond was hosting a children's television show on KTTV, Channel 11, Los Angeles's local independent station. Lamond had the great advantage of featuring the Stooges in guest appearances and, as usual, pies were flung.

Lamond was less gimmicky than the usual kiddie show hosts around the country: he wasn't playing a pirate or a clown or a Western sheriff or an astronaut hosting the show. No costumed character. "The set had pictures of the Stooges in the background and I had a tall desk," Lamond says. "People made sock puppets of the Stooges and we had a funny-looking crow that I interacted with . . . the ugliest thing you

In this rare photo the Stooges cheer up the kiddies at a children's hospital in Los Angeles. "We don't entertain sick children for publicity purposes," Moe told a grateful parent. The Stooges rarely allowed exploitation of their charity.

ever saw. It was a nonsense set with lots of bright colors, a live show with two cameras.

"For six years I hosted a half-hour Stooges show at 7 o'clock at night, prime time, Monday through Friday, five nights a week, and we kicked ass with the ratings in Los Angeles. It was a kids' show, but in prime time. Normally, we did a little intro and [then we'd] get right into the shorts. No cartoons, just the shorts. The show was called *The Three Stooges*."

During one week's shows, Lamond recalls a contest that was held on the show and the winner was treated to a dinner out at a nice restaurant. "It was a little girl who won the contest and I took her and her parents to dinner,"

In the sixties, they were swarmed.

The Stooges and a pack of funny friends rally backstage at a Pittsburgh appearance in 1968.

Harry Fender, of KPLR-TV channel 11 in St. Louis, played a popular old riverboat sage known as "Captain 11" and introduced Midwest kiddies to the Stooges throughout the Sixties. When the Stooges passed through the gateway city, they would eagerly stow away aboard *Captain 11's Showboat* for some antics on live television.

Lamond recalls. "Then I got up and quietly made a phone call. A little later, Larry showed up and he came over and he just sat down beside her and she did a double take . . . it was just marvelous. She was amazed."

Neither Lamond nor the West Coast had the market cornered on Stoogemania in the early '60s. New programming for kids featuring Stooges shorts sprouted up all over the country in local markets, amplified by the boys' live appearance tours and prime-time television guest shots. The Stooges were everywhere, praised by children from all corners of TV Land, black and white or color: It was the decade of the Stooge.

● ● ●

Anyone who grew up watching television probably formed a strong attachment to the local TV kids' show and host who guided them through afternoons in cartoonland or Saturday nights in frightville. Long before Pee-wee Herman, there were Pinky Lee and Soupy Sales. And long before *Blues Clues*, there were Shari Lewis and Captain Kangaroo. In the mid-1950s and '60s, a flood of children's shows filled the network schedules—*Beany and Cecil*, *Howdy Doody*, *Kukla Fran & Ollie*, *Andy's Gang*, *Romper Room*, and *Bozo the Clown*. There was no shortage of puppets and over-the-top live characters to feed the unquenchable minds and viewing habits of children and, of course, sell merchandise and toys. And in the early '60s, with the advent of color television, the world of animated cartoons took on a whole new importance as the studios began dispatching their film libraries to local markets: *Popeye, Heckle & Jeckle, Crusader Rabbit*. An endless parade of cartoon characters debuted on Saturday morning television as well as in the early prime-time hours. Eventually, in 1960, cartoons hit the adult hours, with Fred and Wilma Flintstone carving out rock solid ratings in prime time.

Television was still in its infancy in the late '50s and early '60s, but the medium began evolving, taking on a creative twist, not only in educational styled children's shows, but with local programming becoming more popular than network fare. It was a period of bizarre and wonderful television magic that came and went, an era never to be repeated. And if you grew up during these explosive years, latching onto a local TV kiddie show in your own city, you tucked away those sweet memories forever.

It was a fad that lasted until the mid 1970s: Major television markets across the country introduced their own stylized children's shows, complete with a unique on-air personality to befriend the kiddies, even inviting kids in to be a part of the live studio audience—a thrill like no other. It was Howdy Doody's Peanut Gallery in your own hometown and kids went nuts for the opportunity to visit an actual television station and maybe get on camera.

ONE FINE STOOGE

Hometown affiliates saw a great future in the kids' television market and late-afternoon programs began sweeping the nation.

The varied hosts taught and entertained—but more importantly, they sold product. Western shows with cowboy hosts outdrew any other themed kids shows across America, on the average, and clown hosts who sprang from clubhouses came in a close second in popularity. Every major city had a kiddie show or two, and the hosts were as varied as the landscape they covered: fire chiefs and funky uncles, Indians and train conductors, milkmen and mailmen, wacky grandpappys, sailors and skippers, puppeteers and pirates, magicians and space travelers—all became local icons in the minds and hearts of the young viewers. Some of the hosts' monikers were simply fantastic: Minneapolis had "Clancy the Cop" and his co-host "Willie Ketchem"; "Captain Zoomar" and his lovely assistant "Saturna" landed safely on the airwaves of Montgomery, Alabama; "Icky Twerp," an eccentric nerd, led the eager audiences in Dallas and Fort Worth, Texas; Cleveland had a pointy-eared leprechaun named "Barnaby"; quite appropriately, St. Louis—situated on the Mississippi River—boasted a friendly riverboat host known as "Captain 11."

Writer Gary Grossman, in his book *Saturday Morning TV,* noted, "Whether they were wearing uniforms, civvies, six-guns, or open shirts; whether they spoke directly into the camera or to the studio audience; whether they were network stars or local facsimiles, they helped shape the early picture of TV."

The Stooges landed directly in the middle of this early television trend and rode that wave, which helped instill them permanently into the hearts of young viewers. The Three Stooges were as loony as the local hosts, a good pairing without a doubt, and the timing was perfect for the comedy team's comeback. And because of this timing, the Stooges became a sweet memory, even an important visual for so many—with much credit going to these local television programs.

Time magazine described the Stooges' turnaround as "from quickie flickies to cornea corn," in May 1959. "The trio considered breaking up the act—until TV, that supposed wrecker of old-style comedians, turned out to be their salvation. The kiddy population roared at the antique routines. By last week, the reruns were running ahead of such competition as Popeye and Mickey Mouse among the romper set, and the rejuvenated Three Stooges were swinging cross-country in a highly profitable nightclub and theater tour."

Major studios began syndicating their animated cartoons, and local stations gobbled up shows like *Popeye the Sailor, Mighty Mouse,* and *Mr. Magoo,* to name just a few. Eventually, short-subject comedies with stars like

Laurel and Hardy, the Little Rascals, and the Three Stooges were added to those syndicated film packages, and many local shows built programming around them. The kiddie show hosts would do some shtick and then segue into a black and white comedy. And as *Time* pointed out, the Three Stooges began touring the country extensively and meeting the public. They were retracing miles they'd traveled before, hitting the same major cities they'd played in vaudeville, as well as nightclubs in the 1940s and '50s. Only now, they were playing to the children and grandchildren of audiences they'd entertained for decades. It was a built-in support system because the parents themselves loved the Stooges and, for the most part, highly recommended them for wholesome afternoon television viewing.

St. Louis, long known as a loyal "Stooges town" with Midwest television viewers, was one of the first of the major markets to host the Stooges in

Captain 11, St. Louis's favorite riverboat captain, hosts the Stooges.

1958. The city's local independent station, KPLR-TV Channel 11 (owned and operated by Harold Koplar), not only welcomed the Stooges to the Gateway City many times for personal appearances, but created a kiddie show to exploit the team's comedy films. KPLR repeatedly renewed their license with Columbia Pictures over the decades and broadcast the Three Stooges shorts in one form or another, almost continuously on their schedules, until the early 1990s.

In most respects, the Three Stooges and their St. Louis kiddie show relationship with KPLR typified what was occurring across the nation. The midwestern TV station created an immensely popular live children's show called *Captain 11's Showboat,* which starred former Broadway and stage actor Harry Fender, who was then a local personality in the Show Me State. Fender, who was also a radio broadcaster with a beautiful deep and resonant voice, patterned his kiddie show persona after Mark Twain. The mustachioed grandpappy-like riverboat captain donned a white shaggy wig and steel-rimmed spectacles and endeared himself to children—not to mention charming the hell out of the parents. Fender had the great skill of being able to handle any audience. He entertained, educated, and introduced cartoons and Three Stooges comedies on his show.

Aboard the bridge of his mock riverboat, Captain 11 and his co-host, JoJo the Cook (played by Joe Cusanelli), would toot the horn and swing the ship's giant wheel, which would take them "off to Stoogeville," with a crew of as many as forty screaming kids in the live studio audience each day. They kept the kids going with conversation, skits, contests, special guests, and birthday parties. The average age of the kids in the studio was between ten and twelve, and the overwhelming requests for tickets to the show ensured capacity crowds scheduled months in advance. Every grade-school classroom, every Cub Scout den and Girl Scout troop in St. Louis, southern Illinois, and the outlying areas wanted to be a part of the excursion on live TV with the Captain.

Fender explained to the *St. Louis Globe-Democrat* in 1960 how he created the character: "I went to the Jefferson Memorial to look at pictures of old riverboat captains to get an idea of how I should dress. The pictures of most of them I considered a little too frightening. I didn't want to scare the children." Fender eventually leaned toward a Mark Twain appearance which he felt would appeal to the kids. In the beginning, Fender wore a false mustache, but after a few mishaps with curious kids pulling it off live on camera, he decided to grow his own. "I'm still amazed at the way these little kids believe in things. One of them got so carried away one day, she asked me, 'Does the boat stop at Jefferson Barracks? I live in Lemay and I'll get off there.'"

The high spot during the show was always the sugary treat: Banana flips and soda all around. Sticky hands and ice cream bars were all a part of the studio experience. Naturally, there would be a frenzy as production assistants helped clean up the spills before the commercial break was over.

During the Stooges' frequent Midwest tours and appearances at the St. Louis Police Circus benefit show, they would take time to clown with Captain 11 live on the air, hand out popsicles to the kids in the audience, and plug their current gig or movie at the local theater. Long gone are most of the clips of the Stooges and Captain 11—just precious few bits and pieces of film kinescope survive to mark those magical moments. Captain 11 became a St. Louis television mainstay for more than a decade as the whiskery character steered young audiences down the "ol' Mississloppy." This memorable character was beloved by children—but not because the captain was that intense or intriguing. Most fans who grew up with Captain 11 would be hard-pressed today to recall any famous lines or sketches from his show. They kept him in their heart because he was *their* TV host. He was the one *they* grew up with

The Stooges appeared many times on the WTAE-TV kids' show *Paul Shannon's Adventure Time* in Pittsburgh, Pennsylvania.

and admired, and every city had a Captain 11 . . . or a Corky the Clown . . . or a Cookie the Sailor. So when Fender died in 1995 at the grand age of ninety-eight, the rest of his lengthy career in show business seemed to have vanished because most in his city lovingly remembered him for just one thing: Captain 11 and the Three Stooges.

In the Big Apple, sportscaster turned kids show host Joe Bolton amused audiences as the towering Officer Joe, a make-believe policeman on WPIX-TV Channel 11's popular *Three Stooges Fun House* show, which took to the airwaves in 1958. He was one of the good cops, a friendly officer in a black uniform who made sure to warn the kids not to attempt to duplicate the Stooges' antics because somebody might get injured. Bolton stressed the Stooges were like cartoons and they didn't get hurt. Naturally, when the Stooges were in New York, they stopped by to make an appearance with Officer Joe and the lucky group of kids in the studio that day got to shake hands with Moe, Larry, and Curly-Joe. Bolton was as revered by the children of New York City as much as Sally Starr, the smiling blonde cowgirl from Philadelphia, was in her territory. Larry Fine, also being from Philadelphia, gave special attention to Starr's show and made sure the boys moseyed over to Sally's show to join her live and thrill the youngsters.

Paul Shannon took on a similarly iconoclastic existence in Pittsburgh when he began hosting WTAE-TV Channel 4's *Adventure Time* in 1958. Shannon, a soft spoken former radio announcer with a kindly face resembling Roy Rogers, hosted a kids' show as himself. He wasn't Uncle Paul or Sheriff Paul . . . just himself, although occasionally Shannon changed into costumes to portray guest characters such as Randy Rocket or Nozmo King (named for a sign which read: "No Smoking"). Shannon, like most of the kiddie show hosts, wrote and created his own material each day and invented innumerable ways of educating the little ones on camera. Shannon welcomed the Three Stooges live in his studio often during his reign as Pittsburgh's top children's show personality and appeared alongside the team in local parades. Occasionally, the Stooges helped Shannon promote Muscular Dystrophy's Backyard Carnival campaign, urging kids to organize their own carnivals and raise funds to aid Jerry Lewis in the fight against the disease.

ONE FiNE STOOGE

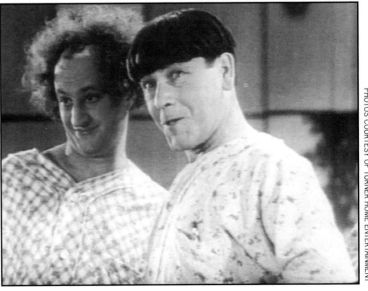

Just Kids They began with the advent of talking motion picures. From 1930 to 1934, Ted Healy and his Stooges appeared in seven features and six short films, including an experimental two-strip Technicolor short, *Nertsery Rhymes. Above right,* The original poster art for *The Big Idea* featured the mastery of Al Hirschfeld with some of his earliest published caricatures.

Clockwise from right: A rare unretouched color photo of Shemp, Larry, and Moe testing some wardrobe outside a Columbia Studios soundstage in 1949. Joe Besser and his wife, "Ernie," at home not long after his departure from Stoogedom. An unusual color publicity photo of the Stooges, circa 1947.

Stereophonic Stooges Moe and Larry made a huge comeback with Curly Joe DeRita in 1959; the trio began appearing in clubs, performing on live television, and marketing a wide range of kiddie merchandise.

Officer Joe Bolton welcomed the Stooges on his New York City kids' show on WPIX-TV.

COURTESY OF TRENT REEVE

The Three Stooges and color television were meant for each other. The boys and comedienne Martha Raye were guest stars on the NBC-TV special *Danny Thomas Presents the Comics,* broadcast November 8, 1965.

Snow White and The Three Stooges, the trio's most expensive feature film and the only one produced in color, costarred champion ice skater Carol Heiss in the lead and handsome Edson Stroll as her Prince Charming.

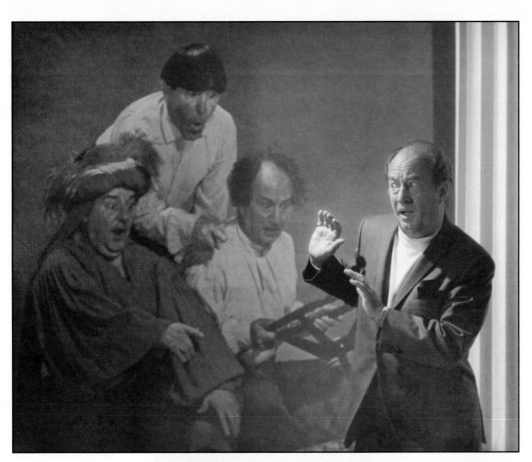

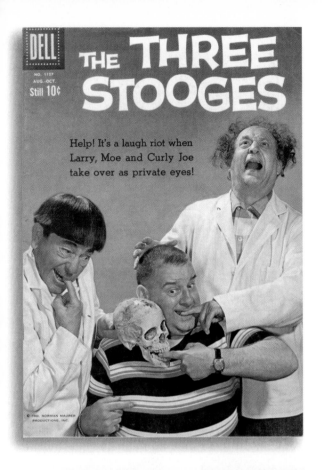

Numbskulls The sixties became the most colorful period in the team's career with comic books, a cartoon series, and a rare television pilot called *The Three Stooges Scrapbook* (never broadcast).

Pulp Friction The Stooges were the stars of an immensely popular series of Dell and Gold Key comic books throughout the sixties. The wacky comic book covers were created in excruciatingly long studio photography sessions; they spent countless hours posing, causing general mayhem for the camera by changing costumes, props, and vibrant backgrounds. It was grown men playing . . . and they loved it.

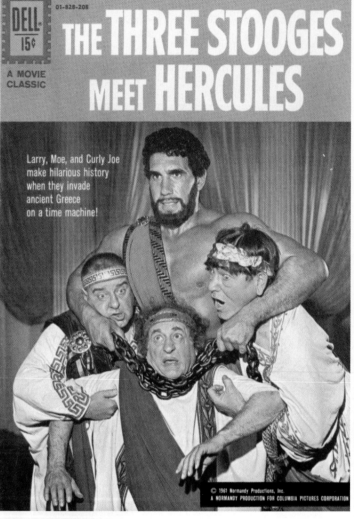

TOP COMICS
THE THREE STOOGES

The Stooges make hysterical history when they crash a tea party in Boston!
THE YANKEE DOODLE DUMMIES

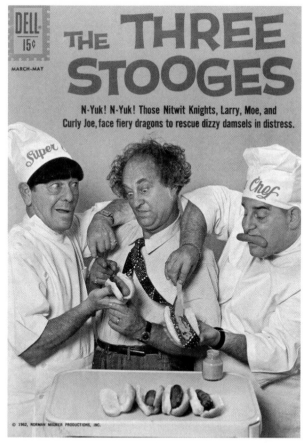

DELL 15¢
MARCH-MAY

THE THREE STOOGES

N-Yuk! N-Yuk! Those Nitwit Knights, Larry, Moe, and Curly Joe, face fiery dragons to rescue dizzy damsels in distress.

© 1962, NORMAN MAURER PRODUCTIONS, INC.

GOLD KEY
10005-906
JUNE

THREE STOOGES
the Three Stooges

15¢
FUN-NEE!
LARRY,
MOE and
CURLY-
JOE

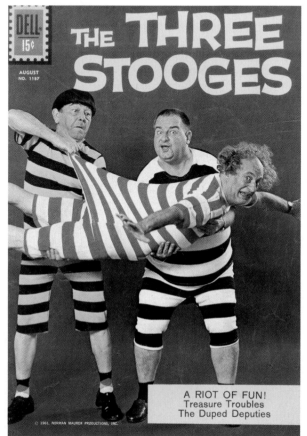

DELL 15¢
AUGUST
NO. 1187

THE THREE STOOGES

A RIOT OF FUN!
Treasure Troubles
The Duped Deputies

© 1961, NORMAN MAURER PRODUCTIONS, INC.

Above, The follicly challenged trio in 1967. *Right,* Larry and Mabel celebrated forty years of marriage in 1966. *Below,* This large portrait of Larry, which was displayed prominently in his Hollywood apartment, was painted by a sixteen-year-old artist named Belita Provenza William.

Above, The Stooges go nutsy-cuckoo on a Danny Thomas television special in 1965. *Below,* Publicity for *The Three Stooges Meet Hercules* featured designs and artwork by Norman Maurer.

MORE FUN THAN A ROMAN CIRCUS!

THREE STOOGES MEET HERCULES

WITH VICKI TRICKETT

Screenplay by ELWOOD ULLMAN · Based on a story by NORMAN MAURER · Produced by NORMAN MAURER · Directed by EDWARD BERNDS · A NORMANDY PRODUCTION · A COLUMBIA PICTURE

Above, Tom Snyder interviewed Larry on KNBC-TV's *The Sunday Show* at the Motion Picture Country Home, in March 1973. Larry kept busy during his retirement doing interviews, visiting fans, charming the ladies, and appearing regularly in the Country Home's resident productions such as the "Ding-a-Lings" show.

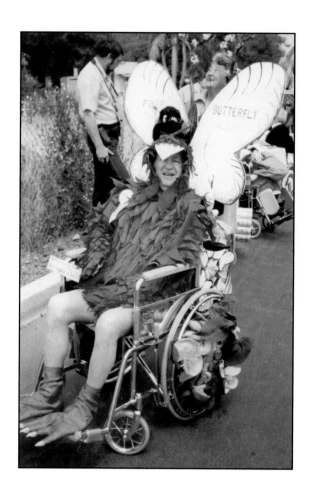

In some wildly imaginative costumes, Larry participated in the Motion Picture Country Home's annual Wheelchair Parade. One year, he took the competition's top honor for Most Original with his *Whatever Happened to Baby Jane?* entry.

COURTESY OF GARY LASSIN

Clockwise from above: Larry with his sister, Lyla Budnick, and her husband, Nate, in 1973. Moe frequently visited his old friend and comedy partner at the Country Home. Larry displayed his own artwork in this photo taken by Scott Reboul on April 16, 1974.

A fan caught the old Stooges in a snapshot during the filming of their final effort, *Kook's Tour,* in Idaho, 1969. *Kook's Tour* was released on Super 8 mm for home usage in the early 1970s.

Above, Larry reminisced with Milton Berle at the Friar's Club in Beverly Hills in 1973. *Left,* Larry's personal appearances ran the gamut—from college auditoriums to classrooms full of school children.

Above left, Emil Sitka's last visit with Curly-Joe in 1979. *Above right,* Phyllis Fine Lamond, Joe Besser, and Joan Howard Maurer appeared together at a National Film Society convention honoring the Stooges in October 1982. *Below,* A coveted star for the Three Stooges on the legendary Hollywood Walk of Fame was unveiled by Joe Besser (along with many Stooge relatives) on August 30, 1983.

Milwaukee's Tommy Richards welcomed the Stooges on his WISN-TV Channel 12 daily kids' show, *Pops' Theater,* in the early 1960s. Richards, a former stand-up comedian, portrayed a theater usher, cantankerous and kooky, who burst onto the set in a red jacket "with a little monkey hat," Richards said in 2004. "I would mumble like Charley Weaver. I patterned the voice after him and I'd come out with a feather duster or a mop and I'd be cleaning the theater lobby." His set was extremely simple: a desk, phone, and an all-important counter-top to sell Double Cola, cookies, and cereals on the program. When it was time to start the cartoon or the Three Stooges short, he'd yell to the projectionist—whom no one ever saw—"Roll 'em, Lester!"

The boys clown around with Tommy "Pops" Richards on Milwaukee's kiddie show, *Pop's Theater,* on WISN-TV, channel 12 in the early 1960s.

"The name 'Pops' comes from Burlesque," explained Richards. "Pops was the guy who used to keep the Johns away from the women and the dancers in the back of the theater. It's kind of an old showbiz title. But of course, on the kids show, I was Pops to the kids, more like an uncle or a friend. I'd mumble and ad lib, and always kept it clean, but there were some really funny things that happened with the kids. Remember, this was live television . . . anything could happen.

"A little kid once asked me on the show, 'What goes in hard and comes out soft?' He looked at me for half a minute and my mouth was gaping open. The camera, the red light was on me. I know I looked like I'd just gotten a pie in the face. I said, 'I don't know.' He answered: 'Chewing gum!'"

Richards pointed out that any host of a children's show must have one basic trait above all—a genuine love for children. In addition to his television duties, Richards took time to make regular appearances at children's hospitals in the Milwaukee area dressed as Pops and ready to play. "If you don't like children, they know it. You can't hide it," he said. "It's almost like playing Santa Claus. The kids look at you as somebody who loves them. It goes right through that TV tube, believe me."

Richards laughed as he recalled demonstrating a product in a closeup shot on camera one day. Realizing from the monitor that his fingernails were dirty, and rather than try to hide it, he asked the kids out loud, "What am I gonna do?

"It was right after Christmas," he said, "and a little girl stepped up to give me a little fingernail kit she had with her that she'd gotten for Christmas. Just then, the floor director gave me a 'stretch . . . stretch' signal, so I sat there and the little girl just sat there with me and talked and she did my fingernails. I had fingernail polish all the way up to my knuckles. The little chatterbox just went on and on, just like a little manicurist."

In 1964, when the Stooges filmed what would be their final motion picture for theaters, *The Outlaws IS Coming!*, they came up with an inspired idea for the cast, which was composed of a gang of emcees from local children's shows. The Stooges, along with producer/director Norman Maurer, created roles for ten of the country's leading hosts. They sent out personal invitations to a select group of these kiddie show personalities, with the offer to portray an outlaw in a comedy western spoof. The concept had two major benefits: The Stooges felt that this was not only a way of thanking the hosts for promoting their comedy films over the years and welcoming them in their respective cities, but they were certain it would result in an excellent publicity scheme to promote the film.

As the individual television personalities returned to their respective cities, they had the opportunity to uniquely promote *The Outlaws IS Coming!* on their television show with specially shot behind-the-scenes footage, photos, clips from the actual movie, and personal stories to share about working with the Three Stooges in Hollywood. (Following the film's completion, Moe Howard hosted a barbeque/wrap party at his home for the entire cast and filmed the event like a home movie—complete with gags and food flinging. The 16mm black and white footage was duplicated and provided to the cast members to take home for exploitation in their individual cities.) Naturally, newspapers in each market featured stories about the local TV personalities costarring in a film. This was all topped off by Columbia Pictures' national publicity campaign and some personal appearances from the Stooges themselves. It was Stooge synergy. Even with a mediocre script, the marketing paid off.

The group of hosts hired to portray the Wild West's most ornery gunslingers in *The Outlaws IS Coming!* included "Officer Joe" Bolton (New York City), who portrayed Rob Dalton, one of the

The Stooges join Paul Shannon on Pittsburgh television to promote the backyard carnivals benefiting the Muscular Dystrophy Association (1967).

ONE FINE STOOGE

The cast of notorious heavies done arrived . . . in *The Outlaws IS Coming!* The sappy western featured television kiddie show hosts from around the country portraying the infamous gunslingers. *Seated:* Moe, Paul Shannon (as Wild Bill Hickock), and Sally Starr (Belle Starr). *Standing:* Bruce Sedley (Cole Younger), Curly-Joe, Bill Camfield (Wyatt Earp), Wayne Mack (Jesse James), Ed T. McDonnell (Bat Masterson), Larry, Hal Fryer (Johnny Ringo), and Joe Bolton (as Bob, one of the Dalton Gang).

A publicity still from the Stooges' final feature film, *The Outlaws IS Coming!*

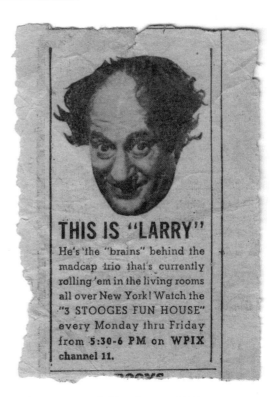

THIS IS "LARRY"

He's the "brains" behind the madcap trio that's currently rolling 'em in the living rooms all over New York! Watch the "3 STOOGES FUN HOUSE" every Monday thru Friday from 5:30-6 PM on WPIX channel 11.

Larry savored this clipping. While in New York, he tore this gem out of the newspaper himself and took it home to place in his scrapbook.

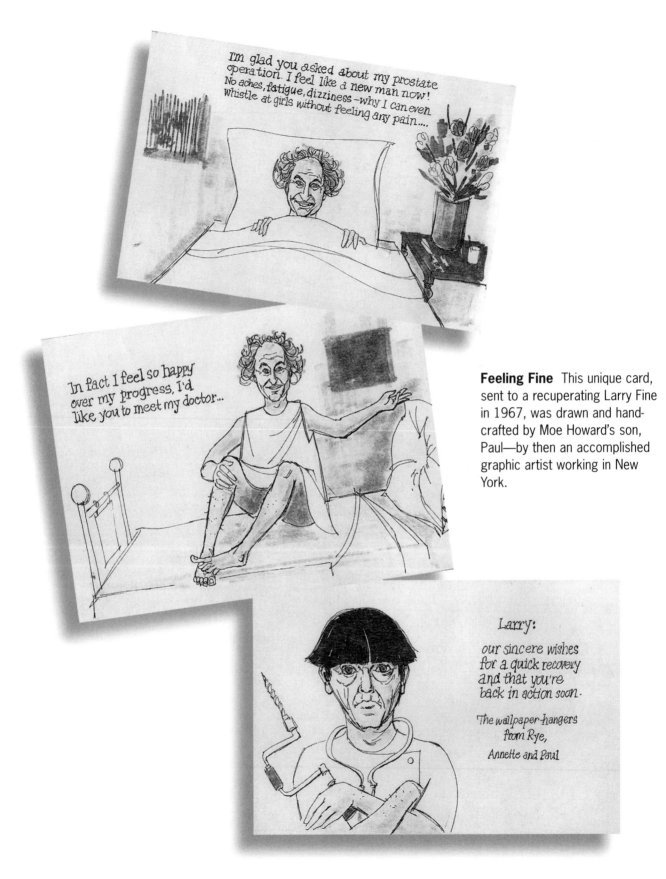

Feeling Fine This unique card, sent to a recuperating Larry Fine in 1967, was drawn and hand-crafted by Moe Howard's son, Paul—by then an accomplished graphic artist working in New York.

ONE FINE STOOGE

Dalton Gang; Bill "Icky Twerp" Camfield (Dallas/Ft. Worth) as Wyatt Earp; Hal "Harlow Hickenlooper" Fryar (Indianapolis) as Johnny Ringo; Johnny Ginger (Detroit) as Billy the Kid; Wayne "The Great McNutt" Mack (New Orleans) as Jesse James; Ed "Major Mudd" McDonnell (Boston) as Bat Masterson; Bruce Sedley (San Francisco) as Cole Younger; Paul Shannon (Pittsburgh) as Wild Bill Hickok; and Sally Starr (Philadelphia) portrayed Belle Starr. Harry "Captain 11" Fender, who also hosted a CBS radio show from St. Louis, was supposed to appear in the film as Doc Holliday, but he was forced to decline due to a scheduling conflict.

• • •

As the Stooges broke in Curly-Joe DeRita as their roly-poly partner, Columbia Pictures invited them back with outstretched arms. This time, the team was making feature films, something they had longed to do, according to Larry. They were also sharing in the profits with a nice 25 percent chunk in their new contract with Columbia. DeRita made his film debut with Moe and Larry in *Have Rocket, Will Travel.* The film cost a mere $375,000 (which is apparent), was made in eleven days, was released in August 1959, and grossed $2.5 million. It was more than a proper launch for the new team.

The team signed on with 20th Century Fox for a one-picture deal in 1960 and production began in December of that year for their first—and only—Technicolor CinemaScope feature film, *Snow White and the Three Stooges.* Designed to be a splashy showcase for world champion women's figure skater Carol Heiss (an Olympic gold medalist), the film was a great departure for the Stooges. Not only was the production a lavish musical shot in gorgeous, rich Technicolor, but the team hadn't worked at Fox since their debut in films in 1930 with *Soup to Nuts.* As the Stooges filmed at Fox, contracts were already signed at Columbia for them to begin their next feature, *The Three Stooges Meet Hercules.*

The Stooges serenade Snow White (Carol Heiss), Quinto the Puppet, and Prince Charming (Edson Stroll) in *Snow White and the Three Stooges.* The voice of Quinto was supplied by legendary cartoon master, Mel Blanc.

Today, Carol Heiss says one of her most vivid memories of working on *Snow White* with the Stooges was the day she celebrated her twenty-first birthday on the set. "I have a big picture with the company presenting me with a cake and blowing out the candles with the Stooges and Edson Stroll;

Charlie Wick, who was the producer; and Walter Lang, the director; and all the people on the set, the makeup ladies, all celebrating my birthday.

"Everyone wants to know what they were like," she says. "They were very much family men, Moe and Larry, who both gave me a lot of advice. Their wives would come over and visit them on the set. They were grandfathers when I made the movie. On the skates I looked a little taller, but actually we were about the same height. A bunch of short people and I had a ball."

Larry, she says, was warmest toward her. "I liked the other two, but Larry always made me laugh," Heiss says. "He was just a very funny man offstage. Moe was very serious, but Larry had a quick wit. We'd sit at lunch in the commissary and talk. This was all so new to me, so it was nice to have a friend like that.

"I remember the scene where I'm laying on the slab, supposed to be dead. I tried to be so serious during that and Larry was always the one saying, 'I can see you breathing . . . you gotta stop breathing. Hold your breath.' And then we'd start laughing. And Larry would say, 'Don't fall asleep.' I'd get to the point where I'd just laugh so hard, especially in rehearsals."

The film employed the old Sonja Henie ice rink on one stage, and with an Olympic gold medalist on the lot visitors were plenty. "The pipes were all still there and they'd just rejuvenated the rink," Heiss recalls. "We would all joke about teaching the Stooges to ice skate, but they'd say 'Oh no! We've got doubles for that!' It was a huge set and lots of celebrities would come by. I have a picture of myself with Elvis Presley and Colonel Parker. They stopped by. Word got around and all the stars at Fox making movies would want to come over and see the rink because it was so unique and see the Stooges working."

Edson Stroll, the film's Prince Charming, was Marilyn Monroe's "next door neighbor" at Fox during production of *Snow White*. "Her dressing room was next to mine and we were very friendly. I remember her stopping by the stage and watching the Stooges on the set. They really liked her," he says.

"Moe was much more businesslike, but Larry was more approachable. Larry used to like to go to the track and bet the horses," says Stroll, "and I talked to Larry a great deal about the races during downtime on the set. We'd go to lunch and talk about the track and I had devised a system on betting and shared some of this with him. He used it the next time he went to the track and thanked me later."

By the end of June 1961, the Stooges had completed their third feature film with Curly-Joe, and possibly the one fans favor most: *The Three Stooges Meet Hercules.* Filmed "in glorious black and white," as the credits boast, the Stooges trek back centuries with the aid of a time machine and are let loose

Patricia Medina was fairly wicked as the Evil Queen in *Snow White and The Three Stooges.*

Too Many Cooks In *Snow White and The Three Stooges*, respected British actor Guy Rolfe portrayed the menacing Count Oga—a role that future Oscar winner Martin Landau tested for.

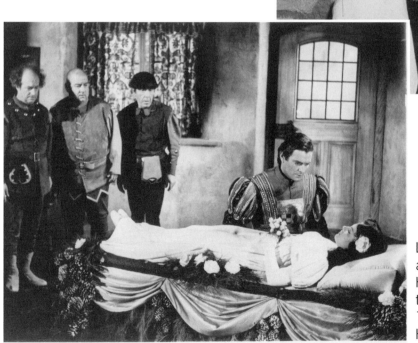

Larry and Moe relax with cigarettes and watch while Edson Stroll and Carol Heiss get the solemn shot ready for the cameras in *Snow White and The Three Stooges.* Larry kept teasing Heiss: "I can see you breathing."

THE REVIVAL

Carol Christensen, who costarred with the boys in *The Three Stooges in Orbit,* admitted Larry was her favorite: "He was so real and warm and funny. I adored him and thought the world of him."

in Ithaca, Greece, around 961 B.C., where they meet Hercules and battle a two-headed Siamese Cyclops in this mixed-up historical romp.

The Stooges were generous comedians, rarely in the practice of hoarding the laughs in their films or trying to dominate. They relished the great stock company of performers surrounding them, performers like Emil Sitka, a standout in virtually every scene he played with the Stooges. His confrontations with the boys are amongst the best on film, most notably stealing the scene right out from under them in his two-minute role as a confused old shepherd in *The Three Stooges Meet Hercules.* "I liked the part in *Hercules,* the hermit," Sitka said in 1979. "That was an interesting part. It wasn't written to be that way, it was just an ordinary speech where I'm supposed to give them directions and I added most of the goofy directions in there, my own way, like an old guy, and then I added the line about the shortcut. I ad-libbed that speech in such a way, they were all howling when I was doing it there and it seemed very funny. An interesting little bit. For an old man like that, or in *All Gummed Up,* where I'm an old fussbudget, is my favorite type. Some fans say they like me as Uncle Phineas with Shemp."

Hercules came in at a budget of $420,000, and although most reviews later relegated this comedy strictly to "the moppets," the story appealed to a wide range of fans and offered some of the team's sharpest timing of any of their '60s films. This, in part, was due to the fact that longtime Stooges director Edward Bernds had been brought in to help recreate some of the comedy they had made in the shorts.

"I came back to Columbia after several years' absence to direct *Hercules,*" Bernds said. "The team wasn't the same. They were older and I had to remind myself to be careful with them. Not to run 'em. I didn't want them to have a heart attack in the middle of a scene. If they had to run up a flight of stairs, I'd cut to something and jump to them at the top of the stairs.

"Joe DeRita wasn't quite the typical Stooge, he wasn't quite as willing to be hurt as Curly was or even Shemp," Bernds explained. "And Moe was very considerate of him and he knew that Joe DeRita was a little temperamental and didn't like to be hurt. Moe took pains to make sure that Joe wasn't hurt the way Larry was, for instance, or the way Shemp used to be. He didn't get slapped as much. We had to use doubles more for Joe DeRita than we did

Shemp or Curly, but it's a good practice to use a double rather than risk an actor getting hurt."

Larry didn't mind taking a few extra punches to compensate for Curly-Joe, but he drew the line at visits to the hospital. Larry remembered filming one scene in particular, because of a mishap that landed him in an ambulance headed to the emergency room. There were sirens and a slight panic racing through the production company. "The only time we had to stop production [for an injury] was in *Hercules*. I fell out of the chariot onto the ground, and Curly-Joe fell right on top of me. He landed on me, hitting me right in the chest. Three hundred pounds. I thought for sure he crushed my chest. They took me to Cedars of Lebanon and fortunately I was okay. I'm stronger than I thought I was. I went right back to work. The assistant director called and asked, 'Is Larry all right? Bring him right back!'"

● ● ●

The crushing blow Larry felt while filming the chariot scene in *Hercules* was nothing compared to the events he would have to face in the coming months.

Following the wrap of *Hercules,* the Stooges went on tour in the Midwest, hitting multiple cities and states, selling out at state fair appearances and theater engagements along the way. They were enjoying the renewed popularity with the younger crowd, and Curly-Joe was experiencing something entirely new with such worship. As the half-baked Stooge, he was almost embarrassed by the unearned popularity he was receiving along with veterans Moe and

Notice the boys' leather slip-ons (sometimes known as "slides" or "zenos"), the same type of functional brown shoe they wore in films for thirty years. One of the young ladies from the bathhouse scene in *Hercules* preferred the sensible approach to ancient footwear.

Larry. "I was riding the gravy train," he'd admit with candor in later years.

As their schedules, rehearsals and filming increased, Larry was working more and away from home more than he preferred. He knew that Mabel's drinking was escalating and that it was becoming increasingly difficult to control her during binges, so he felt it was best to keep an eye on her while the Stooges were on the road.

"Mabel was marvelous, she really was," explains Don Lamond, "and she could be a lot of fun, but there were times when she was drinking that she was not fun. And she was loud. She could be obnoxious.

"We were at a party one night at their home and there were about sixty people there and she disappeared, which she would do," Lamond remembered. "She would go upstairs and she would sit there and start drinking. The party's going on and all of a sudden at the top of the steps, we heard: 'Larry . . . you little sonofabitch!' In thirty seconds, everybody was out the door. I was the last one out and Larry said, 'Don't leave me here.' I said, 'Forget it!'"

Poor Larry suffered some mild physical abuse and major verbal abuse at the hands of his wife when she was drinking her Old Smuggler scotch, her

Larry and Mabel having dinner aboard the S.S. *Lurline,* sailing toward Hawaii in 1964.

ONE FINE STOOGE

favored spirits consumed straight or occasionally on the rocks if she felt the mood. Her behavior was one of the reasons Larry almost never consumed alcohol. Mabel had begun drinking during Prohibition and at that same time Larry had quit. He was the type who hardly even took a sip of champagne on New Year's Eve.

No matter what, Larry stood by Mabel and continued to call her his "Angel." He lovingly referred to her as "Angel Mother" or "Angel Honey" and he meant it. Mabel was the love of his life, booze or no booze, and he was there to support her and pamper her in any way he could. And yet, it was a sad parallel in his life: Larry went to work each day and took punches and slaps from Moe. When he returned home, there were times when Mabel delivered some of the same punishment—only this was reality and there were no wacky sound effects or a director to call "cut." Outside of the family, most were unaware of Mabel's alcoholism and the humiliation Larry endured privately.

You could say Larry was, in fact, a great actor—both onscreen and in life. He was guarded around most, rarely divulging his pressing domestic worries to anyone. At work and at home, and even in Mabel's presence, he masked his feelings of pain and disappointment that came from her excessive drinking. He remained affectionate toward Mabel in spite of her indulgences; if anything, he acted even more devoted because of her problems. Trying to remain positive throughout the years he dealt with this, he handled it all by welcoming any distractions from home life that came his way.

"That had to be one the great love stories of all time," says Don Lamond of his in-laws. "Larry *had* to have loved her deeply to put up with so much. Had to. What she would say and do to him sometimes is almost too embarrassing to say, and he put up with it all. I saved his life one night. She threw an ashtray at him and it weighed about five pounds. I knocked it away just before it would have hit him in the head.

"I never saw Larry get angry at Mabel," Lamond stresses. "He would get angry with Moe, but I never saw it with Mabel. It's got to be one of the great love stories of all time.

"I'll tell you how much he loved her," Lamond continued. "She would drink maybe nine, ten, eleven, or twelve days in a row. A long binge and then she'd get sober for three or four and then do it all over again. This went on for years and years. And this guy put up with this constantly. Sometimes, three o'clock in the morning, she'd say, 'Goddammit, I want Chinese food!' and he'd get up and get dressed and find Chinese food.

"Larry's son Johnny had a great line when he was little. He said to his

Curly-Joe, Larry, and Moe pose with producer Norman Maurer (behind Larry) and executives from Columbia Pictures.

father, 'Dad, what do Chinamen eat when they get a hangover?' It was a wonderful line for a little kid."

• • •

Traveling with Mabel was not the easiest thing for poor Larry, so most of the team's out-of-town engagements were solo for him; the brief separations from Mabel during these trips allowed him to regain some inner strength in dealing with his wife, no doubt. Larry was an optimist, and he rarely wore his emotions on his sleeve. He may have closed his eyes to his problems at home, but he dealt with them the best way he knew how and never reached out in any measure of desperation. After the kids were gone and made families of their own, Larry took great care of his Mabel in their later years together.

Out of necessity, Larry did some light cooking at home: bagels and cream cheese and lox, breakfasts, light lunches. There was a dining room and a café in the Knickerbocker, but they sometimes prepared their own meals in their kitchenette. Although Larry and Mabel had maid service at their disposal, he did some of the light cleaning, and even ironed clothes when necessary. When he prepared for a trip, he packed his own bags and left a meticulously detailed written schedule for Mabel so she knew where he would be at all times. Larry's phone bills were enormous. He called home once or twice a day while out of town, mainly to make sure Mabel was taking care of herself. Larry was not fond of flying. ("I'm not afraid of flying," he would tell people, "I'm afraid of *crashing.*") Mabel refused to fly, nor did she ever drive a car. Larry routinely drove their big Lincoln while Mabel sat in the back seat snapping orders at him, telling him to slow down, chauffeur-driven by her own husband.

Whenever possible, Larry traveled by train, and though it was not easy to go on the road with Mabel, at this point in time he felt an excursion to the Midwest aboard a superliner would be a good way to keep an eye on her and spend some time with her seeing countryside they hadn't seen in a while. It was the fall, and the months were slipping into the bitter winter season in the Midwest. The Stooges were appearing at near-sell-out engagements on the road. In mid-November they were in St. Louis, and then on to Kansas City, where they would be staying at the Hotel Muehlebach for several nights during their engagement.

On the evening of Friday, November 17, 1961, Larry and Mabel's son, Johnny, was heading home from his job at a radio station around ten o'clock. He was driving in Claremont, about thirty miles outside of Los Angeles, a city well known for its tree-lined streets. Johnny lost control of his car and struck a large tree in a front yard at 339 South Mills Avenue. He was just a few blocks from home, and the family suspected that he'd fallen asleep at the wheel. Johnny suffered internal injuries and died a few hours later in the Pomona Valley Hospital. He was just twenty-five years old.

"It was one of those strange things," says Don Lamond. "If he had *not* had his seatbelt on, he might have lived. He'd have been thrown out of the car and maybe lived. His body was not battered and bloodied, just internal injuries."

Johnny's widow, Christy Fine Kraus, recalls the night of the accident:

Johnny was working late and he was on his way home. He got about two blocks away when we think he fell asleep. There's a curve to go around and he hit a tree; he ended up in my mother's neighbor's yard. The neighbor came over and got to me before the police. He was very close to getting home. I think my sister babysat at home with the kids. Somebody took me down to the hospital and when I got down there I called Don and Phyllis and they came out and stayed until he died. It was about three hours that he lived. I went up to his room to see him. I couldn't accept the fact. I was not thinking he was going to die. I thought he'd get better. I was in complete denial. He had head injuries and internal injuries. My mother showed up at the hospital and I was downstairs, always thinking he'd get better. The doctor came down and told me he hadn't made it.

Don Lamond was at the studio working late when he got the call and rushed home to pick up his wife, Phyllis, and the two of them headed to the hospital. "When we went in to see Johnny, he was packed in ice," he recalls. "Phyllis turned white. We went outside and Phyllis looked up in the sky and all of a sudden, she just knew. She turned to me and said, 'Johnny's dead.' Then the doctor came down and told us they did all that they could, but he had died."

Don knew the next thing to do was to call Larry and Mabel in Kansas City. It was early in the morning in Kansas when he reached them.

"It was a call I didn't want to make," he says. "I got Larry on the phone and I delivered this awful news the best way I knew how.

"Now Larry, I want you to sit down. I've got to talk to you," Lamond told him.

"What's the matter? Some-thing's wrong." Larry stammered.

"Sit down and I'm going to give it to you absolutely straight. Johnny was in an accident in his automobile and he's dead."

"Johnny's dead?" Larry asked.

"Right then I heard a scream in the background," Lamond says. "Mabel was hysterical and Larry had to calm her down."

After he and Mabel gained some composure, Larry called Moe and Joe to explain and make arrangements to return to Los Angeles. Since Mabel refused to fly, they took the first train they could book and immediately departed Kansas City. "That was a sobering trip for Mabel, I know that," says Lamond. "I picked them up at the train station. They were doing okay, but they were in a stupor. Larry was talking and doing okay, but Mabel was just looking straight ahead. Moe and Curly-Joe stayed back and finished the show."

Christy says the next few days were a haze to her. She doesn't recall the details with any clarity, but remembers that the funeral for her husband was devastating to Larry and Mabel as well. Don and Phyllis Lamond took over much of the arrangements and had Johnny interred at Forest Lawn Glendale in one of the crypts Larry and Mabel had purchased for the family.

Nate and Lyla Budnick pose with Larry in the 1950s in Los Angeles. Lyla loved Larry and was always proud of their amazing resemblance. Lyla comforted her brother during his darkest hours.

"I remember Johnny's funeral was big and it was raining," recalls Christy. "There were a lot of people. John had been involved with the Kiwanis Club in Claremont, so a lot of those friends showed up for that. The night before they had the viewing, I remember I was still in denial. I'll never forget them making me go in and look at the casket. It was an open casket. I'll never get over that. I remember whatever the minister had said made me feel good. I didn't cry that much, but afterwards it hits you. The nightmare was, 'Why did he leave me?'"

Don Lamond recalls that Larry held up pretty well, but Mabel slipped into a depression. "Larry cried at the service and so did she. It was a normal reaction. That was the lowest I've ever seen Larry.

"About two weeks afterward, I went out to lunch with him. And we sat there and he looked across the room and he said, 'There's a kid over there that looks like Johnny.' I said, 'Larry, I'll tell you what you need to keep in mind. . . . I realize it's none of my business; well, yes, *it is* my business because I'm part of the family. Look, if Johnny had lived, he would have been an absolute vegetable. You know the doctor told us that. So you've got to realize that because of what happened, fortunately he's really now in a much better place.' He thought about it a while and said, 'Yeah, I guess you're right.' And he never really brought it up again.

"Later on, Larry would mention it in passing, but he handled it. God knows how he really felt inside, there's no way of telling. But outwardly, he handled it. Mabel went right back to her normal thing . . . drinking. I think it got the better of her."

• • •

At the time of Johnny's death, his wife Christy was unaware that she was pregnant with their third child. Months later, she had a little boy that she named Johnny, in honor of her late husband.

"After John died, Larry was really great to me. He didn't abandon me at all," Christy says. "Eventually I remarried—and had another daughter, Siobhan, in 1964—but even before that, Larry took over the house payments until I could get on my feet. I had the three kids and it was really tough for a while. I think the house payments alone were over a hundred dollars a month and that was a lot of money back then. Larry really helped. He just volunteered to do that. He religiously remembered all his grandkids' birthdays, and he and Mabel sent checks and gifts."

Larry went back to work almost immediately and immersed himself in his duties with Moe and Curly-Joe. *The Three Stooges Meet Hercules* was released in January 1962, and the boys traveled to the East coast to spring an extensive publicity tour promoting the film. Donning the very Greek togas they wore in the film, the Stooges appeared live at theaters and introduced the movie to throngs of screaming kids. The hectic travel schedule was just what Larry needed to get his mind off his son's sudden death.

Even in reviews, the Stooges were continually haunted by criticism of the violence inherent in their comedy. Of *The Three Stooges Meet Hercules,* a reviewer for *Variety* wrote: "The comic style of the Three Stooges bears a striking resemblance to the technique of the animated cartoon. Violence is heaped upon violence, yet not an ounce of blood is shed, nary a feature truly

Left, Not to let Abbott and Costello corner the *Meet* market, the Stooges trek back in time to ancient Greece and encounter a giant two-headed Siamese cyclops in *The Three Stooges Meet Hercules. Below right,* Vicki Trickett, Samson Burke, and Quinn Redeker costar with the boys in *Hercules. Below left,* USC football players the McKeever Twins are centurions surrounding the prisoners.

disfigured, with immediate recovery a foregone conclusion even in the face of apparent disaster. The natural audience, then, is precisely the one for whom the traditional cartoon short is designed—a group thoroughly dominated by children, but containing scattered easygoing adults. The nature of such comedy, however, makes it ideal for the brisk pace of a short subject. The sustained force of the slapstick is bound to be diffused over the feature length course, and this inevitably puts a strain on comic invention and limits appeal and response."

If the press continued to compare them to cartoon characters, the Stooges thought, why not *give* them cartoon characters? Norman Maurer concurred and began making rough sketches for a proposed animated TV series starring the Three Stooges, voiced by the guys themselves. It was a few years before the project saw fruition, and in the meantime the team went back in front of the cameras to film *The Three Stooges in Orbit* at Columbia, released in 1962.

So kids were their audience, and the Stooges played to them in everything they did. Emil Sitka recalls one instance, however, when the team wished that kids weren't around. "We were filming and this was on the set of *Orbit,*" he said. "The lights on the stage were dark except a few lights near where the boys were filming, so most of the stage was dark. All of a sudden, an argument erupts between Moe and Larry about something or other. I think Curly-Joe was in on it too. And I mean they were using the saltiest language you ever heard! Then, the stage lights went up! Over in the corner, we could all see gathered there was a teacher with a group of grade school kids who were on the set visiting. They all stood there with their mouths wide open and the Stooges were terribly embarrassed. They had no idea a group of children were visiting, and they apologized and hemmed

The Professor (Emil Sitka) assures the boys he has something to improve their television show. Notice the boxes of N'Yuk-N'Yuks cereal in the background . . . the prop men simply covered the front of Kellogg's Corn Flakes boxes.

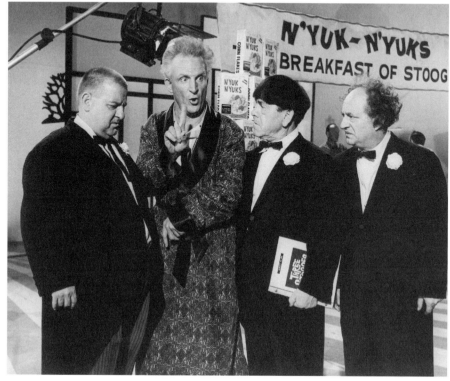

Larry and a pal take a picture together on the set of *The Three Stooges in Orbit*.

and hawed with their heads hung low. We all tried to quickly change the subject and make them feel at home, take pictures, autographs, and whatnot."

Carol Christensen, who costarred in *Orbit* with the Stooges, remembers Larry at this time as fairly well-adjusted following his son's death. Married to actor Dwayne Hickman at the time, Christensen portrayed Carol Danforth, the daughter of the eccentric Professor (Emil Sitka) in the film. "Larry lived at the Knickerbocker Hotel in Hollywood and I think the evening before we started shooting we all got together at Larry's and read the script and went over it. It was a very casual 'get to meet you' kind of thing with some of the cast.

"He was my favorite of the guys," she says, "because he was always there first thing in the morning, waiting with a joke. He was so real and warm and funny. I adored him and thought the world of him. He was so easy to talk with and he always had a silly little joke just waiting for me, every single morning. I looked forward to seeing him. He was, without question, more personable than the other two."

Vicki Trickett, who costarred with the team in *The Three Stooges Meet Hercules,* went away from the experience with the same impression during

The tank-helicopter-submarine, a $15,000 monstrosity custom-built for *The Three Stooges in Orbit,* was the most expensive prop the Stooges employed.

The Stooges consciously toned down the violence in their films. Moe was adamant because "Kids do emulate," he told a reporter in 1960, "and you've got to take that into consideration . . . a poke for the sake of a poke isn't funny anymore."

The Stooges film in front of a process screen in *The Three Stooges in Orbit.* In the finished footage, it would appear they are soaring through the air.

The Professor (Emil Sitka) prepares the boys for his new invention, something to revolutionize television production. According to a studio press book for the film, the Stooges are actually shown in a brief animated sequence produced from a new film technique called "Artiscope," invented and patented by Moe's son-in-law (as well as the film's producer), Norman Maurer.

A few scenes from *The Three Stooges Go Around the World in a Daze* (1963), a favorite of both Curly-Joe and Moe. Critiquing the team's later feature films, Moe stated his favorites in 1973: "I lean toward *Around the World in a Daze.* That was a real smart film. Of course *Hercules* I liked very much. Especially when we were in the slave slave ship. We had a great special effects team on that. I can find no fault with *The Three Stooges in Orbit.* I didn't like too much the last feature we made with Columbia, *The Outlaws IS Coming!* by comparison. Didn't care much for *Have Rocket, Will Travel.* It was contrived a lot. The pies were dragged in at the tail end and not only that, the unicorn business and all that . . . ugh."

her short weeks alongside the guys: "I liked Larry the best because he was more social, he'd come over and tell stories and talk for a while with you or the crew or any visitors to the set. Moe was businesslike; he was off on his own making calls, doing business deals and real estate. Moe was very serious most of the time. I don't remember what Curly-Joe was doing, but he didn't socialize much.

"Years later, I'd run into Larry shopping at Hughes Market in Hollywood and he'd recognize me and we'd stop from our shopping to talk for a while. He was a genuine guy with a terrific sweet sense of humor."

Larry was an abstemious eater and did most of the shopping. Not because he was Jewish, because Larry did not keep a kosher house. In fact, he had to be careful about what foods he ate following his doctor's orders. While undergoing a routine checkup, Larry's physician ran some tests that indicated that he had diabetes and required a structured diet to combat the disease. Fortunately, it had not progressed to the point where Larry would have to inject himself with insulin. Larry loved driving to a bakery on Fairfax Boulevard, not too far away, which offered goodies and candies for the diabetic. Not long after, Larry underwent prostate surgery with great success, and his recovery was a quick one. He didn't like hospitals, although the pretty nurses kept him occupied—or diverted his attention enough that his anxiety for hospitals didn't matter as much.

There were other habits and quirks Larry had that often amused his partners. It was that "flakiness" thing again. Larry, ever the theater performer, was also superstitious: absolutely no whistling in the dressing room or backstage. No hats ever rested on a bed. Even nights when they worked early the next morning, Larry stayed up until 1:00 or 2:00 a.m., either reading or watching television. When he did hit the sack, he was most comfortable in a long nightshirt. Rather than sleeping in his underwear, nude, or in pajamas, Larry preferred those "sleeping coats," a fashion that had gone *out* of fashion long before. He wore the same style nightshirts, in fact, that the Stooges wore in their bedroom scenes.

The next few years were mega-productive for the team, with prime-time television appearances, licensing agreements, recording for children's record albums, weekend appearance tours, and more feature films: *The Three Stooges Go Around the World in a Daze,* released in 1963, and appearances in Stanley Kramer's *It's a Mad, Mad, Mad, Mad World* (1963) and *4 for Texas* with Dean Martin and Frank Sinatra (1963). In October 1963, the Stooges made their third appearance on *The Ed Sullivan Show* on CBS, performing the old standby "Niagara Falls" routine, earning the team a whopping $10,000 for that appearance alone. By the end of May 1964, the team had wrapped what ended up being their last feature film: *The Outlaws IS Coming!* (The original full title of the film was *The Three Stooges Meet the Gunslingers; Or How the Stooges Won the Wild, Wild, Wild West.*) In the film, the Stooges tangle with the Wild West's most notorious outlaws and reform them into gentlemen—and one lady, Belle Starr. The film's final scene has the Stooges riding into the proverbial sunset with costars Adam West and Nancy Kovack, an eerie and prophetic parallel to their actual movie career.

In the summer of 1964, Larry and Mabel carefully planned out a long-needed vacation together; in August of that year the couple boarded the S.S. *Lurline* and set sail on the luxury liner for an extended ten-day cruise to the Hawaiian Islands in their first-class stateroom. Christy and the grandkids drove down to Long Beach to see them off at the port and wish them well on their getaway.

Southern California's hot August made for perfect weather for their cruise. While Mabel wasn't much for sunning on the deck, she was happier than Larry had seen her in a long time. She had gone shopping in preparation for the cruise, picking out new muu-muus for the days and glamorous evening dresses for their nighttime activities. The couple were invited to dine at the Captain's table more than once and loved the evening entertainment, which blended an orchestra and dancing. Larry could be found most days laid out in the sun and working on his golden tan, enjoying the extravagant buffets between swims in the pool and the bridge games in the lounge. Naturally, word got around quickly that he was aboard and fans interrupted the couple around every corner for autographs or snapshots. Mabel was used to sharing Larry with the public, but at least Larry and his "Angel" were afforded some time together at last.

WAIKIKI VACATION—Larry Fine, one of the Three Stooges, and his wife arrived on Matson's flagship, the Lurline for a vacation in the Islands. They will return to Los Angeles by ship.   —Matson Photo

Mabel and Larry vacationed on a Hawaiian cruise in August 1964.

• • •

The Hollywood Reporter announced in May 1965 that the Three Stooges would begin recording the voice tracks for their new animated cartoon series for Cambria Studios the next month. The series of 156 five-minute animated cartoons would be produced by Heritage Productions in a co-production deal with Norman Maurer and the Stooges' company, Normandy Productions. In July, the live-action full-color introductions and closings starring the Stooges would be shot in Southern California. Moe, Larry, and Curly-Joe recorded their voice tracks at an old Technicolor stage/studio on North Cole Street in Hollywood, while the live-action segments were filmed in several different scenic locations.

Right, In this rare photo from a sequence mostly cut from *The Outlaws IS Coming!,* the comedians land in a horse trough one by one, nearly drowning when Curly-Joe hits. According to screenwriter Elwood Ullman, the timing these guys once had was gone. Consequently, many gags in this feature were scrapped. "It looked pathetic at times," Ullman admitted. *Below,* Larry and Curly-Joe wind up in a hotel room filled with women and must quickly disguise themselves to escape.

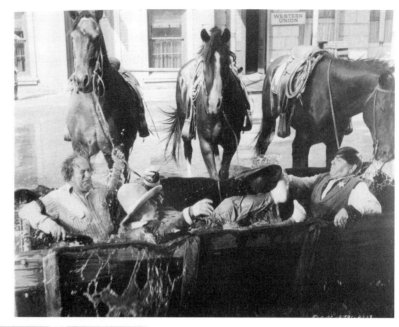

The New 3 Stooges cartoon series was as close as the team got to actually starring in a color television series. Norman Maurer, Moe's son-in-law, brought in director Edward Bernds to handle the live on-camera action. The end result was a bundle of cute cartoons for kids, but hardly the comedy that hardcore Three Stooges fans preferred. If you were to introduce a viewer to the team's slapstick style, the cartoons could be considered a good Stooge "primer," you might say, but generally for the wee ones.

"A man named Ritchard Brown, with a 'tch' in the middle, financed this thing, in a deal with Norman Maurer," Bernds explained. "He owned an animation company named Cambria and he was going to partner with Norman in making these cartoons."

Outside of recording the vocal tracks, read into the microphone in a studio, the Stooges had no hands-on or creative control regarding the actual animation process for the cartoons. The animation was limited at best, with some bright, colorful styles handled by several different animators and layout artists employed by Cambria. The live-action sequences, such as scenes that took place in a barbershop, a living room set, a haunted mansion, etc., were another matter. When the Stooges went on location for "safari" scenes and beach scenes, an entirely new set of problems arose.

By mid-1964, *The New 3 Stooges* color cartoon series, with live-action wraparound segments, were well into production and being sold in syndication to markets around the country.

ONE FINE STOOGE

Emil Sitka, Stooges, mini-bikes . . . it all spells disaster.

You know where this is leading.

While filming at the Balboa Bay Club in Newport Beach one day, Curly-Joe wasn't too happy with Emil Sitka and decided to really let him have it with a cake once the cameras rolled.

Director Ed Bernds goes over the scene with Moe and Larry, filming a cartoon wraparound in Newport Beach, California.

"Filming the live action could be a problem," admitted Ed Bernds, who also wrote much of the boys' material for these segments. "The production values all around were cheap. We shot a lot of the indoor scenes in what had been an abandoned supermarket that was converted into a small studio. It was not equipped as a studio, not up to the measure of studio standards.

"Ritchard had an animation cameraman under contract and used him for the live action. Well, those styles are so different. It was like putting an absolute novice out doing live action. He proved to be very slow, very unsure of himself and the quality was not good. He was probably a very skilled animation cameraman, but a poor live-action cameraman. He didn't know how to start. Outdoors he was not bad. With days you just read the light and set your exposure. But when we moved inside and he had to light the set, oh boy, he was all at sea."

Larry's grandson, Eric Lamond, a teenager at the time, worked on the crew as a grip; Moe's grandson, Jeffrey Maurer, appeared in a handful of episodes. Some of the outdoor episode wraparounds were shot at the Rancho

ONE FINE STOOGE

ANIMATED IMBECILES

This rare gem, an original complete storyboard for one of the *New 3 Stooges Cartoons* produced in 1965, illustrates how the animated segments were first mapped out by storyboard artists. The storyboard then was checked, altered, and approved by associate producer Dave Detiege, and off it went to the layout artists and animators who would further flesh it out.

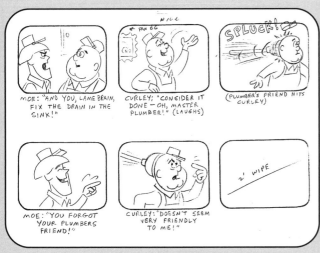

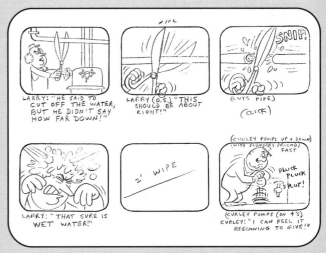

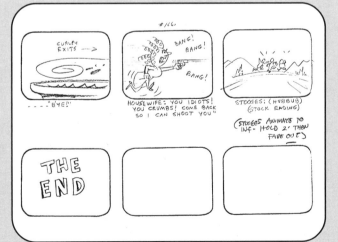

147

—the San Juan Star

A SUBSIDIARY OF COWLES MAGAZINES AND BROADCASTING, INC.
Member of the Audit Bureau of Circulations   AFME Citation, 1950

Pulitzer Prize 1961   San Juan, Puerto Rico, Wednesday, December 23, 1964.   10¢

Vol. VI No. 1652   Entered As Second Class Matter Post Office, San Juan, P. R.

Today's Thought

No pleasure is comparable to the standing upon the vantage-ground of truth.

—Francis Bacon

U.S. Warns S. Vietnam On Political Stability

★ Khanh Supports Army Move ★

Right Claimed To Participate In Govt. Affairs

By MALCOLM W. BROWNE

SAIGON, Vietnam (AP) — Lt. Gen. Nguyen Khanh put the United States on the spot last night. The ex-premier who commands South Vietnam's armed forces threw his prestige behind the young generals who ousted the High National Council on Sunday.

Khanh declared the military retains a right to take a hand in civilian governmental affairs if disputes and differences create a climate favorable to communism and colonialism. He pointedly warned against foreign intervention.

A beneficiary of U.S. support through the nine months that he was the nation's military ruler, Khanh made clear in a radio address he would not accede to American demands for restoration of the High Council or quick creation of a suitable equivalent.

Shock and dismay were evident among American officials.

The High Council was formed three months ago as a 17-man agency to steer South Vietnam from military to civilian rule and to serve as an interim legislature. American authorities approved. They hoped it would help stabilize governmental affairs for the war against the Vietcong, in which

(See KHANH, Page 30)

STAR Photo By Gunter Hett

CURLY, LARRY, AND MOE IN CHARACTER AT AIRPORT
...better known as the Three Stooges

Wild Day At Airport —3 Stooges Arrive

By JIM DOUGLAS

The Three Stooges arrived in San Juan yesterday to the waiting arms of more than 100 kids and grownups. A few giddy newspaper people, airport personnel and tourists also viewed the performance as the big jet sat down at 4:23 p.m. at Isla Verde International Airport. "Hiya, Moe," waved one tourist-class passenger aa he disembarked from the rear of the plane and noticed the Three Stooges (known locally as Los Tres Chiflados), sans costumes, posing for the photographers on the ramp outside the first-class cabin.

They stood in a row: Moe, Larry and Curly—but in neat suits, ties rnd hats. The smaller children had a difficult time telling which was which and kept checking blue and white handbills to make sure.

"Grab his hair, Moe," one of the older children yelled, and Moe obliged and bent Larry's head to one side with a twist of a handful of Larry's curly locks. Ah, the same grimaces and laughs some of us have been

(See STOOGES, Page 30)

Military Heads Cautioned Not To Interfere

By SPENCER DAVIS

WASHINGTON (AP) — The United States warned South Vietnam's restive military leaders last night that continued U.S. support is based on existence of a Saigon government "free of improper interference."

The terse U.S. statement, was issued with President Johnson's knowledge and approval, after South Vietnam's armed forces commander, Gen. Nguyen Khanh, criticized U.S. opposition to military domination of the civilian government.

State Department press officer Robert J. McCloskey, in making the statement public, declined to say whether the tough wording amounted to a U.S. ultimatum that there would be a cutoff in U.S. aid if the South Vietnamese military do not leave the civilian government alone.

However, the statement seemed to come closest yet to hinting such a possibility.

It also fully endorsed efforts of U.S. Ambassador Maxwell D. Taylor to restore civilian authority over the South Vietnam military.

The statement, read at a news conference, said:

"I and others in the department have had inquiries growing out of allegations critical of our ambas-

(See VIETNAM, Page 30)

Sharp Earthquake Hits S. California

SAN DIEGO, Calif. (AP) — A stong earthquake rumpled through Southern California and its neighbor, the Mexican state of Baja California, at 12:55 p.m. (7:55 Puerto Rico time) yesterday. There was widespread minor damage.

This coastal city of 670,000 appeared hardest hit. Walls were cracked, Christmas tree ornaments and pictures shaken down, and a chimney toppled.

In the Mexican resort town of Ensenada, 60 miles south, two plate glass store windows were shattered.

The rolling temblor was felt, barely, in Los Angeles 120 miles north. More than a score of Southern

(See QUAKE, Page 30)

Benitez Bemoans U.P.R. Budget Cut

By JULIO ROSADO

University of Puerto Rico Chancellor Jaime Benitez —angered by drastic slashing of his construction budget— yesterday accused the Planning Board of working against the interests of education in Puerto Rico, terming the board's action "senseless."

Benitez, whose $3 million budget request for construction of additional facilities at five U.P.R. campuses around the island, declared in an interview yesterday:

"It is unfortunate indeed that while professing to work in the interest of higher education in Puerto Rico, the Planning Board has disapproved funds which would

(See BENITEZ, Page 30)

Golf Course in Century City and at the Balboa Bay Club and Resort in Newport Beach.

The cartoons feature a noticeably slower-paced pack of Stooges. Moe, who was sixty-five at the time, talked with a reporter from the *San Francisco Chronicle* about the cartoon series and the Stooges' style of comedy. Suddenly, the elder Stooge was doing an about-face regarding their traditional style and how it had come to be perceived. Long known as the archetype for slapstick comedy, the Three Stooges have even been listed in encyclopedias under the very heading. Now, after years of becoming the most famous practitioner of slapstick, Moe was twisting the nostrils of semantics: "Get one thing straight," he told the reporter. "We don't do *slapstick*. That's a circus word to describe two barrel staves with an exploding torpedo between them. What we do is pure farce—the kind that's been popular since Grecian and Roman days, since the kings had jesters.

Headin' out to the beach for some fun in the sun during production of the cartoon live action segments.

"Our formula," he continued, "is a simple one: the upsetting of dignity. You can't throw a pie at a poor man and get away with it. But throw it at a millionaire, get his spats and vest gooey, and the people love to laugh. They love to see the dignified man brought down to size. And our Stooge-like behavior is excusable because we usually pose as common working men who don't know any better, who unintentionally cause all the trouble. And the

PHOTO BY TERRY BORIS

Camping in the great outdoors in a live-action segment of the *New 3 Stooges Cartoons*.

Larry joins comedienne Ruth Buzzi and announcer Johnny Grant at a celebrity baseball night with the L.A. Dodgers (1967).

trouble, as you now, always leads to total chaos—without which we Stooges could not survive."

The scenes filmed on the golf course were among Larry's favorites, as he was the only one of the trio who actually hit the links for pleasure. Granted, Larry was, by his own admission, a lousy golfer. "He never got good," says his son-in-law, Don Lamond. "I think he enjoyed being out with the guys and playing. I don't think he cared that much about the competitive part of it.

"I got Larry started playing golf. He played with the Hollywood Hackers for several years and loved it because he was playing with other actors and performers. They'd play tournaments for charity benefits in Hollywood and they traveled.

"On a good day, Larry would do 110 or 115 and he was happy with that," says Lamond. "Most of the time, he never bothered to keep score. He loved playing the celebrity golf tournaments with the Hackers because there would be dinners afterwards and the Hackers would do a show. Different guys would perform, singers, a band, I played in a group with a band. Larry would do things in the show. He and one of the other guys, Jack Albertson I think it was, would do the Abbott and Costello routine 'Who's on First?' together."

Lamond, who divorced Larry's daughter Phyllis in 1968, remarried but retained a very close relationship with his former father-in-law in the later

Producer Lee Orgel poses with the Stooges at the golf course during production of a wrap-around scene for the cartoon series.

PHOTO BY TERRY BORIS

ONE FINE STOOGE

'60s. "My wife Susie lent him her clubs to play in one of the tournaments," remembers Lamond with a laugh. Back then golfers covered their club heads with simple snug fabric or knit covers that fit over the club heads. This was long before Tiger Woods sported little "tiger" heads over his clubs. But in the late 1960s, any type of cutesy animals covering the clubs was strictly for women and would have gotten most guys laughed out of the clubhouse.

"He didn't have any clubs so Susie lent him hers. All of her head-covers were little animals. Larry looked at these and said, 'I can't do this!' He was embarrassed, but he did it anyway and it was marvelous. He could get away with it. And the women's clubs were good for him because he had small hands."

Lamond also recalled one tournament with Larry in San Diego. "Larry was riding in a cart with one of our writer-friends, Sid Morse, who's got a great sense of humor. It was a long par four, and everybody's down on the green and two are routed in two or three. And Larry lays seven. And he's not to the green yet. So he gets out of the cart and he takes out a nine iron and looks at the shot and he shakes his head; he takes out a wedge and says, 'I think I'll gamble.' He was serious. Sid fell out of the cart. Here he is, already three over par, not there yet, but he's gonna *gamble*!"

● ● ●

Truth be told, Larry loved to gamble; like golfing, he didn't take it too seriously. It was purely a hobby. He'd play the horses from time to time, but probably not as much as has been rumored over the years. There are conflicting stories about the extent of Larry's losses to bookies. Some is true, and some has become Hollywood myth. Stories of Larry gambling away every cent he ever earned are greatly exaggerated, say his relatives. Granted, he was not a wealthy man, because he and Mabel simply did not save their earnings. Larry put money into a few dead investments, like a restaurant in Hollywood called Mi Patio, which got swept away two years after its opening.

"Larry told me in 1970 that he squandered maybe ten million dollars in his life," says his friend Jim Malinda. "That's how much he made over his career and here he was late in life without very much to show for it."

A Hole in None Larry knew he wasn't a great golfer, but as a member of the Hollywood Hackers, he competed in charity tournaments for fun and exercise and eventually learned to love the sport.

Squandered and gambled are two separate things, of course. There was a time, near the end of his life, when Larry probably wished he'd socked away much of his fortune; instead he and Mabel lived life to the fullest with very few regrets. Larry and Mabel loved socializing with Hollywood types and spent much of their life living in hotels and enjoying the comforts they offered. For many years, they maintained an apartment on both coasts: The President Hotel in Atlantic City and the Knickerbocker Hotel in Hollywood. Larry was a well-dressed, manicured man most of the time. On nights out with Mabel, he looked immaculate. He wore custom-made shoes, monogrammed shirts and jackets, silk socks always. Mabel had a closet full of fine furs and an elegant collection of diamond rings; Larry was excessively generous with his money when it came to family.

There are rumors that he sank—and "sank" is the operative word here—several thousand dollars into someone's crazy investment scheme to manufacture an unsinkable bathing suit. And in addition to lovingly helping relatives who needed assistance over the years, Larry was overly generous to down-and-out show business friends who needed cash.

"My pet extravagance is good cars and buying presents for my wife," said Larry in a 1959 interview. "My wife has every kind of mink and she loves fur. My greatest pleasure is to buy things for my wife and children and grandchildren. I spoil them.

"I collect lighters and watches, and I love gadgets. Any kind of gadget on the market, I'm the first to buy it. I have a drawer in my kitchen full of gadgets. Some of them don't work too well, but I buy them to help me cook in the kitchen. I do all the driving because my wife doesn't drive and I shop, squeeze the tomatoes, smell the cantaloupes, the whole works."

Said Larry's brother, Moe Feinberg: "Larry was a gambler at heart. He loved to gamble . . . cards, dice, horses. He loved the horses. He loved boxing and the fights because we had a history of boxing in our family. My dad was a fights man and we went to the fights from way, way back when we were five, six years old. I don't think Larry did too well with his gambling, that was the problem."

The sight of Larry and his pal Phil Silvers, and sometimes Lou Costello, out at Santa Anita was a familiar one to regulars at the track. Larry's gambling would not have been considered chronic, and certainly he never bet as recklessly or even ventured in the same league as

As the only surviving vintage comedy team working in the 1960s, the Stooges made a brief silent appearance in Stanley Kramer's star-studded comedy classic, *It's a Mad, Mad, Mad, Mad World*. No dialogue. Just the sight of these guys as firemen spelled trouble.

ONE FINE STOOGE

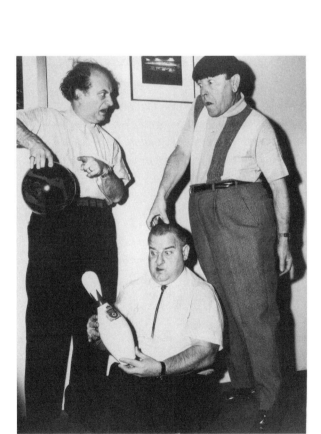

Idiots Deluxe The Stooges were experts at huddling and posing—in a moment's notice—and whipping up overall wackiness for any camera, at any time, in any surroundings. With lightning speed, they could clown or create chaos for the lens, whether at a theater, a bowling alley, or simply as guests in someone's den.

Phyllis Diller looked at this photo years later and recalled, "I think this was taken in Las Vegas," and then cackled about her hair being wilder than his for once.

Silvers or Costello. And to his credit, Larry made sure everything was always in check with the I.R.S., unlike his friends Bud Abbott and Lou Costello, who were found to owe millions in back taxes when fully investigated.

So with his well-known affinity for gambling, Larry and Las Vegas was a match made in heaven. He loved the lights and the glitter and seeing the Rat Pack perform at the Sands. When Shecky Green, George Burns, or Buddy Hackett were headlining, Larry and Mabel drove out to Vegas to catch their show, stay the weekend, and take in the Vegas nightlife. Mabel, who played cards but didn't gamble as much as Larry, kept herself occupied in other ways. The craps tables called out to Larry. He said in his book *Stroke of Luck:* "We did play the Flamingo and subsequently, at the Stage Line in Lake Tahoe. Frankly I would not care to play at either hotel again, because I lost more money at their gambling tables than I made in salary. I figure that no matter how much they pay you to appear there, it's a good thing they feed you!"

Moe's daughter, Joan Howard Maurer, told *Nit & Wit* magazine in 1983: "My father was a very serious man; he was the manager of the act, off-screen as well as on, and he'd worry for all three of them. Larry was a real will-o'-the-wisp. He enjoyed his life. He went to the track and spent money like a crazy man. The minute he got his check, it was gone. My dad invested in property. He was trying to leave an estate for his children, which he did. He was cautious and more practical. And Larry, if it wasn't for my husband Norman who incorporated them in the Sixties when they had one of their

Larry waves from the deck of his ship in Hawaii, August 1964.

ONE FINE STOOGE

Boppin' and a-bashin' in Larry's home state in 1968.

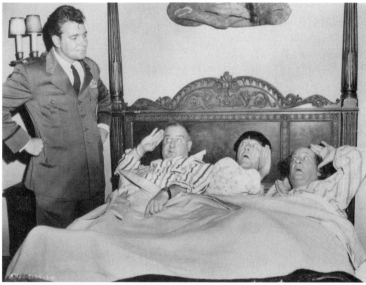

Above, Larry's son-in-law, Don Lamond, interrupts the boys' slumber in this posed publicity photo on the set of *The Three Stooges in Orbit. Left,* Larry, a partner of famed hosiery designer to the stars Willys of Hollywood, presents Willys' annual "Golden Calf" award trophy to voluptuous B-movie actress Edy Williams in 1968.

THE REVIVAL

Ship-a-Who? In one of their last prime-time network television appearances, the Stooges play the hapless Three Men in a Tub, who harmonize a novelty song called "The S.S. *Nowhere.*" This half-hour episode, titled "Who's Afraid of Mother Goose?" on the ABC-TV prime-time series *Off to See the Wizard,* took viewers on a musical visit to the colorful land of children's stories (October 13, 1967).

resurgences, Larry wouldn't have had a dime."

With the exception of gambling, "Larry did what Moe told him to do," said director Ed Bernds. "Moe was the boss in every way. When the series was finally terminated by Columbia, Moe and Larry had had the same salary for many, many years. Larry was nearly broke and Moe was a rich man. So that when their new career started, Moe took care of Larry's money and made sure he didn't blow it the way he did in the two-reeler years. Money just slipped through Larry's fingers. Lots of times, when we were shooting, we'd have to go find Larry because he'd be behind the set, listening to the radio, a ballgame or something, because he'd bet on it."

Don Lamond heartily disagreed: "Larry liked to go to the track, but he did not gamble away his fortune," he says. "He did not do that. He bet and played within his means at all times. He was never one of those guys to go out and throw caution to the wind. He enjoyed it. He'd go to the fights and bet on the fights, but not as much as people think he did."

● ● ●

One thing Larry hadn't gambled on was losing his wife so soon after losing Johnny. On Memorial Day in 1967, Larry got the call that shattered his life.

While on the road, Larry routinely called his wife at home at least once a day. He worried about her endlessly. Once, while Larry was gone, Mabel fell down the stairs in their home; the family doctor gave her a stern warning: "If you don't stop drinking, you're going to kill yourself." So when he was out of town and Mabel was alone in their apartment at the Knickerbocker, he phoned constantly to check up on her. Larry remembered one particular day:

> We were appearing as the star attraction at a large community picnic in Providence Rhode Island. It was four o'clock Eastern time and one o'clock California time. I was in my dressing room and decided to call my wife Mabel who was in Hollywood. Mabel answered the phone and I said, "Hi Honey . . ." She answered back and said, "Larry, will you please call me back in fifteen or twenty minutes? I'm washing my

hair." I said, "Okay, honey, I'll call you back in a few minutes." I hung up the phone and fifteen minutes later I get a call from my daughter, Phyllis. Her first words were, "Mother just died!" I thought, it can't be. I just spoke to her. I was stunned. I just couldn't believe it. She had suffered a sudden heart attack minutes after I spoke to her and passed away. I told my daughter: "I'm coming home immediately on the first plane I can get on."

Lyla Budnick recalled the day as well. "Mabel was bleaching her hair in her apartment and she collapsed in the bathroom and died immediately. They had maid service and the maid came in and found her and she called Phyllis. Then Phyllis called Nate and told him that her mother died and Nate didn't want to be the one to tell Larry. So, roundabout, things went back and forth and Phyllis finally told her father. First, she was going to tell him she was just sick, but she did tell him she had died.

In *Star Spangled Salesman*, the Stooges join an all-star cast in pitching the payroll savings plan in a special color short made for the U.S. Treasury Department (1968). Larry would've been wise to enroll.

"We didn't want him to go home alone," explained Lyla, "so we made arrangements and I flew to New York and he flew to New York, we met and I went back to California with him and stayed with him all during the arrangements, the burial, and I stayed with him for three weeks after that. It was a rough, rough time. They were married forty-one years. These sad things come up in life. People think you're a comedian and everything is funny and wonderful and don't realize sad things happen in private life."

Nate and Lyla's daughter, Phyllis Budnick, saw the side of Mabel that all of the family prefers to keep in their heart. "Mabel was my favorite aunt and when she died, I was devastated. She was outrageous. She'd buy us outrageous gifts. Not the normal aunt. She had such tiny feet and as kids we'd go and get in her shoes, she'd put makeup on us and do our hair. She enjoyed that. She knew we didn't have a lot then and she wanted us to have things. That was important to her. She was outgoing, beautiful, blonde hair, glamorous. A magnificent lady. I adored her, as much as I adored Larry, if not more. There was nothing she would not do for us."

• • •

The Stooges deliver an expensive, risqué painting to Dean Martin in the 1963 Warner Bros. film *4 for Texas*. After some nonsense, Martin delivers a vintage Stooge triple slap to the boys.

ONE FINE STOOGE

Above, The boys perform the old "point to the right" bit. *Left*, Catastrophe, Stooges-style.

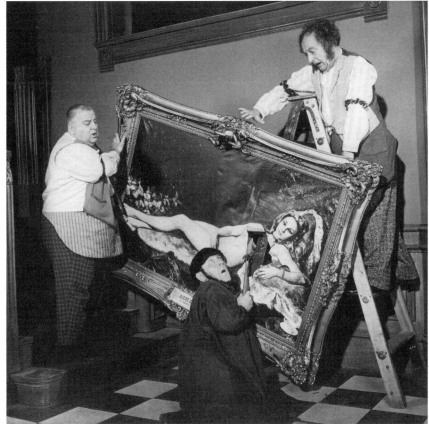

It wasn't long before Larry made the decision to leave the memories of Mabel at the Knickerbocker and attempt to continue his life with a bit of a fresh start. He moved to a smaller apartment at 7135 Hollywood Boulevard, # 401, a Hollywood high-rise located less than a mile west of his former residence at the Knickerbocker. He wanted to stay in the Hollywood area. Most people

found his new apartment to be a comfortable living space, with a small bar area set up against one wall and a kitchenette; Larry had it furnished sparsely the way he liked. He preferred very little clutter. On the coffee table in his living room were displayed several small ceramic figures he had made. There were photo collages of the Stooges framed on the wall, as well as a huge portrait painting that a very talented artist had sent to him as a gift.

To get his hands into something new, Larry directed a small production at a Hollywood playhouse. "It was a play that was just on Broadway," Larry said at the time. "It was written by George Kaufman called *If Men Played Cards As Women Do*. They never got to play cards, it was just a gossip thing."

In August 1968, the Stooges headed to Hawaii for an extended personal appearance tour and Larry couldn't wait to hit the beaches and lay out in the sun. The team was booked to be the star attraction at the International 3-Ring Circus taking place at the Honolulu International Center

Coffee, Tea or Moe?
This is *not* what United Airlines had in mind when they said, "Fly the Friendly Skies."

Larry visited with some fans at The Memory Shop while in New York City and posed for a snapshot (1968).

ONE FINE STOOGE

arena (HIC), August 8 through 18. This was the same arena from which Elvis broadcast his famous live by satellite *Elvis, Aloha from Hawaii* concert in 1973.

The Stooges did their stuff, center ring, with a single spotlight on them each night at 8:00 and matinees on the weekends. The kids went wild. Also appearing at the circus was Polynesia the Parrot and Chee Chee the chimp, who both appeared in the film *Dr. Doolittle,* plus a lineup of jugglers, high wire acts, a mini rodeo act, a French sway-pole breakaway act, and trampoline artists. During their days on the Big Island, the Stooges—as they did in most cities they visited for an extended stay—took time to

You can tell which Stooge was the sun worshipper in this rare photo, taken outside their hotel near Waikiki Beach, during their stay in Hawaii in August 1968.

meet some children at the Shriners' Hospital for Crippled Children to cheer up some tots. The team toured the islands as well and took in some of the local traditions, a luau and the like. And of course, who doesn't want to see Don Ho perform when they're in Hawaii? Well, the Stooges, that's who.

"Don Ho sent his kids back to meet the Stooges at the circus," remembers Nate Budnick, who had brought along his wife, Lyla, for the trip. "Don Ho called later and invited the Stooges to his show, but they had never heard of him. Had no idea who he was and they really didn't care."

Nate and Lyla urged Larry to go with them to an evening show and he agreed, but hesitatingly. The three of them took a cab to the hotel where Ho was performing and saw his nightclub act; afterward, Larry admitted that he loved the show and was glad he went.

"I remember there were a lot of soldiers lined

COMICS--Famous comedy team The Three Stooges arrived via Pan Am to be special stars for the International Three-Ring Circus now featured at Hono'ulu International Center Arena with wild animals, clowns and circus acts from all over the world. Left to right, Moe Howard; Joe Derita and Larry Fine.
                                                                --Pan Am Photo

Going Coconuts The Stooges performed in Hawaii (actually Honolulu, on the island of Oahu) in August 1968.

THE REVIVAL   161

up to see the show. They were on the island for R and R.," said Nate Budnick. "Don Ho knew we were coming so he had us in front, right in front of the stage. He came out and introduced Larry and brought him up on the stage and sang to Larry. We had to push Larry out of his chair to get him to go up on stage with Don Ho. He was so embarrassed, he froze. Once he was up there, he smiled and relaxed."

• • •

A twenty-four-year-old New Yorker named Walter Mitchell met with Moe and Larry for an interview on August 23, 1969, at Larry's high-rise apartment on Hollywood Boulevard. While visiting Southern California, Moe, in his usual punctilious way, left word for Mitchell to meet him at a precise time at his partner's apartment and the young Stooges fan would have the duo all to himself. Mitchell had been corresponding with Moe since 1962 and hoped to finally have the opportunity to meet his film idols. The result can only be described as a testament to how much the Stooges appreciated their loyal fans.

The boys appeared at a Los Angeles charity event co-organized by Larry's friends, Edna Earle and "Eddie" Crispell in 1968.

"When I started writing to Moe, I found that instead of getting a letter typed by a secretary, I was getting letters handwritten by Moe," says Mitchell. "He conscientiously answered his own fan mail and all the fan mail addressed to the Three Stooges. By 1969, I think he knew who I was."

Moe and Mitchell actually met face to face in the lobby of Larry's apartment and the elder Stooge graciously offered to help carry the young fan's reel-to-reel recording equipment up the stairs. "Moe only knew me from correspondence and Larry didn't know me at all, but both treated me like a friend they'd known for decades," Mitchell says. "We visited for an hour. It was heaven. Nobody else was there. Most of the questions on my tape were asked of Moe, but I wanted to be polite and remember that I was a guest in Larry's home and I did not want Larry to sit by and listen to Moe and I talking. Larry was naturally quieter than Moe, so I made a point of asking him questions. I loved that nasal tone in Larry's voice, it was like Arthur Godfrey."

It truly was soup to nuts, as Mitchell sat with Moe and Larry and asked the pair a wide variety of questions touching on all periods of their professional and personal life, from their first film to their current project. Moe and Larry, having been interviewed hundreds of times over the decades, courteously responded with standard replies they had given many times before. One question, however, seemed so appropriate at this time in their lives and in their association together. As a team, how did they manage to stick together all those years? What was the secret to their longevity? Moe answered:

It's a combination of things. A happy home life has something to do with it. Not to mingle too much socially. We see each other enough at our work without watching our footsteps every way along the sidewalk to see if somebody's around to talk to, any of us of the group. We meet fairly often to talk business. We go out socially on many things, public relations wise, publicity wise. Temperaments of the people are such: I'm a nervous excitable type of guy under certain occasions. There's whooping and hollering, but never any divisiveness.

Larry chimed in:

I believe it all stems back to our youth. We were both happily married men. And you know, when teams get together, they're single, they fight about girls, jealous of each other, and that tends to break 'em up mostly. But Moe and I were married young, and we respected each other as married men and so that's why I think we got along.

Seventy-two-year-old Larry hugs Higgy the chimp during a trip through California's Lion Country Safari park in August 1974.

THE STROKE

"My advice to anyone: Don't get sick in America . . . you simply can't afford it. Another thing: Don't get sick on Wednesday. All the doctors are out on the golf course."
—LARRY FINE, 1973

By the late 1960s, Larry really began showing his age and the years of taking a beating were becoming evident. His apartment was on the corner of LaBrea and Hollywood Boulevard, and it had similar amenities to those at the Knickerbocker, but it was a smaller dwelling since he was now living alone.

Seeking some companionship, Larry began dating a young woman he was introduced to at one of the studios in town. She was thirty years younger than him, which caused some raised eyebrows among his friends and family. Far from heading to the altar, the relationship nonetheless put some spirit in the old Stooge's step.

Larry confided in his lady friend and barber, Eddie Crispell, assuring her everything was in check: "We were having lunch one day and talked about this," says Crispell. "I didn't want to see him hurt. I said, 'Larry, I have to talk to you. I don't want you hurt by this relationship.' He smiled and patted me on the hand and said 'Sweetheart, I know, I know. I'm spending a lot of money on her and that's what she wants, but I'm having such a good time.' I said, 'Okay . . . okay.' And those were the kinds of moments we had."

"Larry was a little bitty guy," says Jim Malinda, one of his closest pals at the time. Malinda, then in his early thirties, was an actor, constantly testing and auditioning for television and film roles and trying to get ahead in the business. "Larry was a nicely dressed, simple man. He didn't have much in his apartment. I spent a lot of time with him before and after the stroke. We were friends. I think some of his grandkids were suspicious that I wanted something more out of him, but I didn't

The Three Stooges film their last scene in *Kook's Tour*, in 1969. It was to be their last performance together. Larry's final words on film: "I quit."

want anything from Larry. We were friends, nothing more. His daughter Phyllis and sister Lyla trusted me and that was that.

"Larry and I used to go to the movies a lot and we'd have to leave at least forty-five minutes early just to walk down Hollywood Boulevard where all the movies were at the time, even to go to the Graumann's Chinese down the street, for Chrissakes, because it took us that long. He was signing autographs along Hollywood Boulevard. People stopped him everywhere."

Malinda remembers how Larry would walk over the stars on Hollywood Boulevard and wonder if he and the Stooges would ever be honored with such a cemented landmark. "He wanted a star on the Boulevard in the worst way," says Malinda. "And he'd say, 'It's f—ing politics that we can't get the star.' He knew. That burned Larry. I think he inquired about it once and they told him something like 'We're not doing groups.' It was a shame because he lived there and saw the Boulevard every day."

Larry's exercise of choice was walking, but he was moving a little slower and also beginning to have difficulty with his speech. Some of his family even suspected he had suffered a minor stroke that went undiagnosed. In his later television appearances with the Stooges, it's easy to detect his speech beginning to slur and becoming thicker than normal, especially during their final television appearance as a team—as guests on *Truth or Consequences* with host Bob Barker in 1969. Larry spoke but a few words. During the production of their television travelogue pilot, *Kook's Tour,* which was shot on location in several different states, Larry's energy seemed zapped. Moe, assuming that his partner was also having some slight difficulties with his motor skills due to an onset of arthritis, convinced Larry to join him in some ceramics classes where he could regain some nimbleness in his hands. Larry really loved going to the ceramics classes and created some interesting pieces, which he molded and glazed himself and then presented to his friends and family as gifts.

Nate and Lyla Budnick and their youngest daughter, Joan, visited with Larry for the Christmas holidays. "Larry had a big New Year's Eve party for his friend, Jim Malinda, and his family," remembers Lyla. "Jim was taking Joan all over Hollywood, and we all had a wonderful time. We went out to dinner quite a lot. At that time, Larry had been seeing this young woman, she worked at the studios. A very lovely young woman. We went out to dinner a lot and she would have an after-dinner drink or something and she'd say, 'Come on Larry, have something to drink.' And he'd say, "No, no . . ." And then she'd say, "Oh, come on, Larry, I don't like to drink alone.' And then he'd have a drink or two. He'd have a drink here, a drink there, and he did it to please her. You know, a little wine or something. Well, he shouldn't have because he was a diabetic and he was on medication.

"Our entire family, Larry, my father, Phyllis, myself and a few other members of the family, we all suffered from diabetes," admitted Lyla. "My father didn't take care of himself, that's why he died when I was five. Larry didn't take care of himself that well, and that's what he died of, and Phyllis had a stroke from that as well."

• • •

In the early evening of January 9, 1970, while Larry waited for his daughter to arrive at his apartment for dinner, a massive stroke took hold of him. That evening would devastatingly alter Larry's existence for the rest of his days; he recalled it three years later:

Center Stooge Larry appears onstage in a one-man show to benefit Southern California's Loara High School on March 2, 1974. Students Jeff and Greg Lenburg organized and hosted the event; years later the brothers co-wrote the definitive biography on the Three Stooges with Moe's daughter, Joan Howard Maurer.

I was all by myself in my apartment and I had a date with my daughter. I came back from ceramic class and my daughter was going to have dinner with me and I started to get dressed for dinner and I felt nauseous. It was a terrible rainy day outside and I didn't feel too hot. I don't know what was wrong, just upset stomach, I thought. I called my daughter up to tell her, "Let's make it some other night," and my granddaughter told me she had already left for the restaurant. So I called the restaurant and I told them to tell my daughter that I wouldn't be there, to have dinner and I'd pay the check. I knew the man that owned the restaurant. But when she got there and he told her that, she said, "My father must be pretty sick if he won't come out and meet me." So she came right to my apartment.

In the meantime, I laid down thinking I'll feel better and I had a creeping feeling up my leg and up

my arm and my face. No pain, but a numbness. I said to myself, am I getting a stroke? My daughter came and rang the bell and I was laying on the bed and I got up. It was a struggle to go answer the door. The minute I put my leg down, I collapsed. I broke my arm. I just laid there. I really couldn't get up. When I didn't answer the door, she got panicked. She had no key so she went to the manager and said, 'Go open my father's door. There's something wrong.' When they opened it, I was on the floor. I wasn't unconscious, but I was helpless. She sent for the ambulance and my doctor met me at the hospital. You know, I'm a diabetic, eleven years now. My blood count then was about 140 and 120 is normal. When I got to the hospital, it was 548 and my blood pressure was over 300 and something. The doctor thought I was a dead man.

Homemade get well cards sent to Larry by young fans Mike Dimoff (above) and Mike Waiken (right) in 1971.

The doctors in the emergency room were positive in their diagnosis, and the news was given to Phyllis and the rest of the family: Larry had suffered a massive stroke, and the prognosis was not good. The next few days would be delicate ones as his condition was grave. The effects of the stroke went beyond just paralysis on his left side. His vital signs were off the wall, he nearly lost sight in one eye, and his voice was gone. Larry's vocal chords were temporarily stricken and he could not move his tongue. His ability to swallow was severely limited and for three weeks he was fed baby food to help regain the ability to use his pallet normally. Larry's left side was 95 percent paralyzed. His arm and leg was not totally dead as he detected some feeling and blood was circulating, and that was encouraging to the doctors and to family. Larry wasn't sure what had taken hold of his body.

"The spasm in my face is

ONE FINE STOOGE

gone, my tongue was paralyzed, my mouth was paralyzed. My eye was near my ear and that took a long time to come back," Larry recalled to Mike Mikicel three years later. "They had to tape up one eye, because I couldn't focus and had no sight in the left eye . . . I went through it all."

It took weeks, but Larry seemed to improve and the outlook finally brightened; all didn't appear as grim as first thought. Directly following the stroke, Larry kept reflecting on the sad ending suffered by his old partner, Curly, and how a series of strokes slowly and painfully dimmed the comedian's life. He wondered if this was to be his fate, too. Moe was dreading the worst for his partner, having visited Larry in the hospital almost immediately after hearing the news of the stroke. Larry remembered:

When Moe saw me the first time, he was surprised. You know, after my stroke, then about a few months later, he said "Larry, you're living . . . you're gonna live. You're coming to." Because he was going by Curly. He saw Curly go down and down and finally, Curly was so paralyzed, only his eyes moved.

Curly suffered seven years. He got well enough to work, but he didn't talk any better than I do now. You can tell the years he was sick. The voice changed. I hate to see a person suffer and suffer then die.

As for the future of the Three Stooges, that story looked like it was at the end. Granted, the noose had hung over the team's head before. It seemed these three guys were at the end of their rope several times in their lengthy career, but this time, without Larry, the end was in sight. Since their color television pilot, *Kook's Tour,* had not yet wrapped, some scenes had to be scrapped altogether and one scene was salvaged by using a double for Larry. Actually just his hands. In a cutaway with his face not shown, Larry is fingering a bowl of corn flakes at breakfast; director/producer Norman Maurer put on Larry's wardrobe and doubled for his hands. *Kook's Tour* was basically completed, but it was never sold for television broadcast. There was a reason for that: It was unfunny and, at times, pathetic. It was a sad swan song for this legendary team.

Jim Malinda remembers Larry's surprising outlook directly following the stroke. Laying in bed, tubes stemming his nose and arms, Larry was attempting to talk, but no one could understand his garbled speech. "He was at the Bratman Center in Culver City, and I lived in Hollywood," Malinda says. "I went over there every day. Larry had really slow speech. I couldn't understand him at all, his speech was so thick. He asked me to get him a pad. He was right handed. I get him a pad and what do you think this crazy son-of-a-bitch writes on the pad? The latest joke! He's writing jokes on a pad to me. I told him, 'Larry, you're insane.' It was a funny joke. He never told the same joke twice and he told jokes twenty-four hours a day."

Eventually Larry was moved to the home of his daughter Phyllis and her boyfriend, a lawyer, a two-story house they owned on Commonwealth Avenue in the Los Feliz area. "She had a garage at her house, and they remodeled the garage into an apartment, and that's where he was living," says Malinda. "I helped put the phones in and did some work on it for him to make things comfortable."

Malinda helped move Larry into the small converted apartment, a separate building from the main house, and a visiting nurse administered therapy to help rehabilitate Larry in weekly sessions. His speech was stymied, and for a man who loved to tell jokes, it meant infinite frustration. The body would not do what it was told. Malinda constantly encouraged Larry to walk again. "I really had to browbeat him," he says. "I had to nag him. I told him 'Walk! Damn it, walk!' And he got off his ass and he walked. He was so excited. He walked across the room with me and I got him to actually take steps. The most he walked was across the room, but he was so proud of himself he couldn't see straight. He was a proud guy."

In June 1970, Phyllis Fine Lamond, who already had power of attorney regarding her father's interests, also petitioned the Los Angeles County courts to become conservator for her father and take responsibility for his finances and health care. He didn't wish to be completely reliant on others, but he was aware of his dependency and begrudgingly accepted this fact. With the full consent of her father and the recommendation of Larry's doctors, Phylllis was granted the conservatorship. At the time, documents showed that his total concrete assets totaled about $10,000, and just under $1,000 was in cash. He owned some shares in the Arden Mayfair Company and City National Corp., some jewelry, and a small interest in a local real estate firm, but he owned no property and his automobile was valued at just $1,200. In addition, Larry owned 24 percent interest (book value) in the Stooges' own company, Comedy III. This was valued at $13,555, but those were just intangible figures on paper, hardly anything to cash in or borrow on. The Stooges, as a team and as an entity, had nearly ceased earning money in the early 1970s.

After a lifetime of work in motion pictures, that's all Larry had to show for it. Altruistic to the end, Larry "spent his money the way he wanted," says his daughter-in-law, Christy Fine Kraus. "He supported many people in his family and his wife's family. That's where a lot of his money went."

After about eight months, Larry and his family realized he would require more care and a more concentrated level of therapy than they could provide at home. Larry suffered another stroke, a minor one, but it affected his right arm much more so than the first stroke. Confined now to a wheelchair, but gaining some confidence and movement, Larry applied for admittance into the Motion Picture Country Home and Hospital in Woodland Hills, California. The process was difficult as there was a waiting list and Larry's financial situation was grim. Although Larry was not broke, he was far from flush, and the thought of being a "burden," as he called it, was something he hated. A nursing home was something he wanted to avoid. The home therapy had nearly drained his bank account and he wasn't receiving much money from the Stooges' residuals—profits from the 1960s forward. The old Columbia shorts provided no remuneration at all. Larry recalled:

I had difficulty getting in here. They didn't have this area, the Lodge area, built, and they didn't have room. I was under the impression when they took one and a half percent of my salary, that that was entitling me to come here when I got sick, but that's not true. That's a donation. Now if you're sick and broke, they will keep you here. But you gotta be broke. If you can pay, you pay like every other hospital, but the price is about one third as [much as] other places. But you have to be a member of show business a certain amount of years and earn a certain amount of money to be entitled to come here.

I'm almost glad I got sick. . . . It made me realize how well off I was. You go through life where you're well, you don't stop to think what a great gift health is. People ruin their health, trying to get wealth, which is number two as far as I'm concerned. Your first consideration is your body and your health. Without that, you've got nothing.

PHOTO BY ED MCCOLLOUGH

Fine Friends Some of Larry's pals also residing at the Motion Picture Country Home were Allyn Joslyn and Bess Flowers—the latter a recognizable character actress who costarred in several early Stooges shorts, usually playing society matrons.

Larry was finally accepted into a newly constructed wing at the Motion Picture Country Home and Hospital. It was called the "Lodge" area, and the residents lived in nicely furnished private rooms with constant care and regular activities, and, best of all, they were surrounded by others in the entertainment industry. One of Larry's pals there was Oscar-winning actor Donald Crisp, who was in his early nineties. Crisp, one of the founders in 1921 of the

During a poignant moment in the January 1972 "Ding-a-Lings" show at the Motion Picture Country Home, Moe was reunited with his old pal Larry onstage, but the audience didn't quite recognized him until he pulled out the comb and flashed those famous bangs.

Motion Picture Relief Fund, was now a recipient of its aid. The forty-one-acre facility in Southern California's San Fernando Valley featured a fully equipped hospital with nearly two hundred beds, a country house, and sixty cottage apartments for private living, plus "the Lodge" with some sixty rooms accommodating patients/residents who required some degree of care. The complex also featured a barbershop, beauty salon, theater, chapel, and beautifully manicured grounds. (Today, the facility is still in operation, including a wing dedicated to Jules White—a result of the generous contribution left to the Country Home in his will. Prominent in the lobby is a large wall-sized display of benefactors' names engraved in plates, including the names of Ernie and Joe Besser, who also left a sizeable portion of their estate to the Motion Picture Relief Fund.)

Larry was content once he got settled into the Lodge. He knew his golfing days were behind him and it was time to retire and attempt to just enjoy life as it came and make his health a priority. It was a great relief for him to be in an atmosphere with constant care, but any earnings that came his way went directly to the Relief Fund.

"Larry . . . you got spunk!" Ed Asner helps Larry with his game of shuffleboard. Asner recalled, "Larry was such a sweetheart of a man, and what an honor it was to meet him, that's what I remember."

Most people became accustomed to calling it the "old actors home," which was fine by Larry. He loved it there, surrounded by other actors, some of whom he'd known for years: Blossom Rock, Babe London, Emory Parnell, and Carter DeHaven among them. The facility didn't just accept actors. There were members of all aspects of film and television work, from grips to lighting technicians, from directors to producers. Bud Abbott was a resident for a while, as was cinematographer Benjamin "Bennie" Kline, who captured the Stooges on film in some of their best performances—including *Men in Black* (1934), their Academy Award–nominated short.

Maybe what Larry enjoyed most about living at the Country Home was the activities. He was never bored. In addition to a constant flow of fans who found out Larry was open to hosting visitors and took advantage of meeting him, the more challenging activities included art classes, bingo tournaments, trips out to local plays and movies, and shuffleboard tournaments (of course), and there was the annual Wheelchair Parade, which Larry really looked forward to. This was an annual tradition at the home, an activity anticipated not only by the residents who took part, but also the spectators who lined the parking lot and nearby street where the parade traveled a short route. To Larry, it was theatre; the more ridiculous the costume, the better.

Most entries in the parade were veterans of the film industry who decorated their wheelchairs in outlandish manner—with the aid of volunteers and friends, of course. Some of the wheelchair entries were highly creative and elaborately constructed little "floats" in and of themselves. One memorable motif was from Julius Cindrich who had a mini house cleverly built around his wheelchair with himself poking out of the shingled rooftop. Cindrich wore a floppy cap atop his head, sported a long dark beard, and played the violin as he scooted along. He named his entry "Fiddler on the Roof."

It was common to have maybe thirty or forty entries in each parade, with a theme assigned each year. For the May 22, 1974, Sixth Annual Wheelchair Parade, Larry dressed in garish pale-faced drag and held a giant vodka bottle, calling his float "Whatever Happened to Baby Jane?" (an homage to Bette Davis). He ended up grabbing the top prize for Most Original entry that year from the judges.

In the early 1970s, Larry's picture appeared in the Los Angeles area newspapers many times, usually hamming it up at functions sponsored by the Motion Picture Home. It was an event getting together with Milton Berle and a group of comedians and actors at the Friar's Club annual Thanksgiving dinner in Beverly Hills, where photographers were always present. Treated to a bountiful feast of turkey, sweet potatoes, and pumpkin pie, the residents from the Country Home felt at home at the Friars Club—a famous summit for

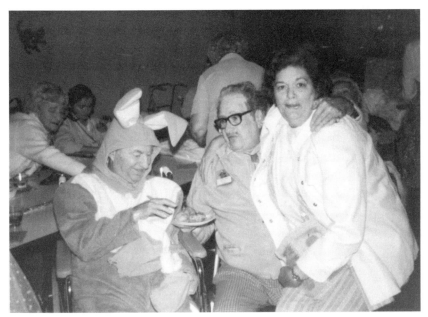

Frizzy Hare Larry has some fun at a Halloween party on October 22, 1974, with fellow friends Ted Waldman and actress Jean Hagen at the Motion Picture Country Home.

showbiz folk. There was always a lineup of top entertainers to perform for the retired veterans and hand out gifts—folks who had known Larry for years like Frankie Avalon, Ken Murray, Jack Carter, Red Buttons, and midget actor Billy Curtis.

And then there was the annual Ding-A-Lings Show, which was a night of skits and acts put on by residents as well as top name performers onstage at the Country Home's theater. For the January 1974 Ding-A-Lings Show, stars Jack Lemmon, Gavin MacLeod, Ed Asner, Jackie Joseph, and Pat Morrow joined more than thirty residents performing in sketches, telling jokes, and singing songs. At the January 1972 Ding-A-Lings Show, Moe Howard joined Cesar Romero, Lee Meriwether, Gene Raymond, and two of the Wiere Brothers for the fun onstage; Moe took the mike, only his hair was combed back and the audience didn't quite recognize him at first. With his flair for timing, Moe introduced himself, then pulled out the comb and let the hair down to thunderous applause before doing a brief routine with Larry who remained in his wheelchair.

Moe drove himself to Woodland Hills to visit Larry at the Country Home—as much as he could, anyway, which ended up being at least every month, with regular phone conversations in between. Interestingly, neither Joe DeRita, Joe Besser, nor Emil Sitka ever took the time to visit Larry in his last few years there at the Country Home. Fans who met with the former Stooges offered to take them to see Larry, but the offers were always declined. It was something that Emil Sitka later said he regretted.

"When I visited Joe Besser, I asked him if he'd like to go up to see Larry," says Mike Mikicel, "but he didn't want to. He said he felt strange doing that since he really didn't keep in touch. I would have loved to have been there and get the two guys together again."

Scott Reboul, who visited Larry in April 1974, remembers him openly commenting about Moe. "I got a sense that Larry was light-heartedly irritated by Moe," says Reboul. "He made a few comments when I was there. He'd say, 'How do you like this picture?' And he pointed to a picture, a composite of each group of the Stooges. 'Well, Moe Howard just had two hundred of them made, so big-hearted Moe gives me one. Seventy-six years old and still working. That guy doesn't know when to quit. I knew when to quit. Moe, that guy would take a job in a phone booth.'

"I think he was hurt by the brevity of Moe's visits, when Moe would only come by and see him for ten minutes," says Reboul. "I remember he made the comment, 'Moe was over here last week. He stopped by for ten whole minutes.' On one hand, he was irritated with him, on the other hand, he wanted him to stay. I think it illustrated the dynamics between the two men. He said Moe stopped by regularly, but I remember he said, '. . . but he never stays very long.'"

It had to have been hard on Moe, physically and emotionally, to get to the retirement home and see his partner deteriorating in a wheelchair. Moe also knew that Larry was

> Dear Ed,
>
> I'm sorry, I thought when you wrote me you knew I had a stroke, which has left me partially paralyzed and in a wheelchair, but I am happy to say I am getting along pretty good, and am feeling pretty good. I just got word on the book. It will not be sold in bookstores but by mail order. It will be published around Aug. 15th. If you are interested in buying the book here. how you can buy it. Send $7.95 to Larry in check or money order ℅ P.O. Box 313 Hollywood Calif. 90028. This is the commercial I had referred to in my letter. It will be about the book. I can tell you a little more. It will contain over 100 rare and collector item still photos from many of our movies, a lot with the original Curly and Shemp, I think you'll like the stories of the early beginnings of the Stooges. Cordially,
>
> Larry Fine

> Dear Ed,
>
> I am writing you to straighten out a few facts. In the first place Moe gave out that interview, and while trying to lie about our ages, did it stop to think. I was born On October 5th 1902 and I will be 71 years old. Unfortunately Mabel Haney (my wife) for almost 41 yrs passed away in 1967, I am at the Motion Picture Country Hospital. I had a stroke, which left me partially paralyzed. I see Moe very often. you can write him to Moe Howard P.O. Box 69785. Los Angeles Calif. 90069. Now please do me a favor. I'd like to have the address of the Nostalgia Book Club, as I have written a Book, about myself and the 3 Stooges called "A Stroke of Luck." and I'd like to write them about it. Thank you
>
> Sincerly,
> Larry Fine

COURTESY OF ED MCCOL-

THE STROKE   175

JIM MALINDA REMEMBERS HIS PAL LARRY

I met Larry when I was in my early thirties, he was in his sixties. I met him through his girlfriend. I'd actually dated her first and later she was dating Larry. Larry had no problem with that. One day she simply asked me if I'd like to meet Larry of the Three Stooges. I said, "Are you serious? I'd love to!" I had idolized the Stooges since I was a little boy.

The first night I met him, she had invited me over to her house to watch the landing on the moon. That's where I was in 1969 when I met Larry. We all sat around her TV and watched Neil Armstrong land on the moon with the rest of the world. Larry and I were just looking at each other and saying, "Can you believe this?" We were all in awe and I think our heads were messed up from that. We couldn't believe our ears and our eyes, in our lifetime, for this to happen. Here I am watching this with one of the Three Stooges.

So Larry and I immediately hit it off. I never drank or did drugs, and that was something Larry liked about me. In a way, I think I became a surrogate son to him because he told me that I was the same age as Johnny. He was devastated by Johnny's death. I think it hurt that man big time, but he didn't show it much.

I loved his timing, his endless jokes. He always had a good joke to tell, no matter where you were or what mood he was in, he'd have a story or a joke. His voice and his mannerisms were so great. He wasn't the most graceful of guys, he kind of walked funny, come to think of it.

We spent a lot of time together and I did get to meet the other Stooges. When they were making the TV pilot *Kook's Tour*, Larry had gotten me a little part of a man laying down sleeping or dead in the forest. I can't remember completely. I think they cut the scene, but I did work with them once. Being around Larry and Moe, you could tell they loved one another. They were very close. I went with Larry to Moe's house for dinner once. Man, he made the best lasagna I've ever tasted. I'll always remember that.

Larry and I talked about everything, especially women. And occasionally he'd tell me weird stories about the early days and Curly and show business. I remember he told me they were in the Midwest, touring in Vaudeville. It was Thanksgiving and they gave Curly a live turkey. The Stooges had a kitchenette in the apartment they were living in and Moe told Curly to take the turkey up to the room and put the turkey in the refrigerator. Curly pulled the feathers off the thing and stuck him in the refrigerator. Later on, they came back and there it was, sitting in the refrigerator shivering, still alive.

We used to go to the Dodgers games, but we'd sit in the dugout with the players and Larry used to go when they had celebrity night. We went three or four times and he loved being in the dugout, talking with the players. He loved sports. He used to play golf with the Hollywood Hackers. He'd play with people like Alan Hale, Max Baer, Don Porter, Clint Eastwood. In fact, Larry also helped me get a part in a Clint Eastwood film, *The Beguiled,* which was filming down in Baton Rouge where I'm from. I mentioned to Larry that Clint was filming down there and Larry said, 'You want me to call Clint and see if we can get you on the film?' I told Larry, "Oh man, would you really do that?" Larry had known Clint from playing celebrity golf tournaments with him and the celebrity Dodgers games. He called him and I went in and read for a part. Clint put me in the film as a one-armed vigilante and we shot it in Louisiana. That was great because I got to go see family and some friends at the same time.

Larry was such a good friend. I remember I went on the TV show *The Dating Game* as a contestant, and Larry and I had it all planned out. Larry went with me to the show and he sat in the audience in the front row. We had a signal worked out between us. I could see him in the audience and when the girl comes out, if she's really beautiful, whistle three times. If she's not, just whistle once. I listened for his whistles . . . and he

Larry and his friend Jim Malinda in December 1969, just weeks before Larry's stroke.

The guys get a little playful with Larry's girl-friend in December 1969.

did it. When she came out, I heard the signal. He was right, too, she was beautiful. I lost the show . . . I didn't win. But when I went around the corner to meet the girl, I went crazy. I waited for her backstage and we ended up making a date after the show.

This story will show you how caring Larry was. Not long after I had gone on *The Dating Game* I had some nose surgery, in my sinuses. Now, you have to understand, Larry was the worst driver ever. He'd scare the hell out of you and frustrate you in a car. When I had my nose worked on, I was in the hospital for a few days. The doctor told me not to do anything strenuous. Nothing. I wasn't supposed to lean over, pick up heavy objects, nothing. Well, to make a long story short, that girl from *The Dating Game* came over that night and we started to fool around. We went crazy and it was a few hours of some real fun. She no sooner left my place that I started bleeding out of my nose. My nose was hemorrhaging and I didn't know what to do, so I called the doctor, and then I called Larry.

I had a bath towel, holding it up to my nose. I said, "Larry, I'm in trouble. I'm bleeding and I called the doctor and he said to go to his office, not to the hospital because he had the equipment at his office." Larry just said, "I'm on my way." Larry picks me up. I swear to god, you would have thought he was Paul Newman in a race car driving through Hollywood at sixty-five miles an hour on Wilshire Boulevard. And this time, he was driving good. I remember I was trying to talk and he said, "Shut up, you're gonna bleed some more!" The towel I had was soaked. They fixed me up and Larry stayed

with me the whole time. He wouldn't leave me until all hours of the night because the doctor had actually put me back into the hospital. That's what kind of friend he was. And come to think of it, that was the only time I saw him drive really well.

After Larry had his first stroke at his apartment on Hollywood Boulevard, I took him to Palm Springs and we stayed for a couple of months at The Spa. I didn't know what a stroke was. . . . I had to read up on it in order to try to help him. Larry loved Palm Springs and it was down there I tried to get him back to walking, and I did. He could walk across the room with his walker. He was slow, but he could do it. He had to be encouraged and I had to keep on him, but when he finally did it, he was so proud of himself. Larry laid out at the pool in Palm Springs . . . man, he had a great tan. We would use the Jacuzzi and the steam-room to relax. I remember we saw Truman Capote in the same steam room one day, all of us sitting there in towels. Larry looked at him, then looked at me with a crooked face. It was hilarious. For the most part, Larry was in a wheelchair, but he was getting stronger. We also went out to dinner a few times with Colonel Parker, Elvis's manager. He really liked Larry and he'd invite us out for dinner.

I have to say, I cherish those memories of Larry. He was such a neat guy to know. I think about him all the time. One thing I regret is being out of town when the Stooges finally received a star on the Walk of Fame. Larry wanted a Star in the worst way and I remember him saying so. He loved Hollywood and being right there in the heart of it.

Larry and Jim compare schnozzes.

being well cared for and he was not the only visitor to stop by and chat with Larry.

"Jimmy Cagney used to visit Larry at the home," said Nate Budnick. "One of his best friends was Jimmy Cagney. Larry and he would correspond on the road. He saved all his letters from Cagney, piles of them. When Larry was in the home, his granddaughter, Crissy, would visit him. One time, the nurse told her 'No, you can't go in there now, you'll have to sit outside and wait.' About a half hour later, the nurse comes in and says 'Okay, you can go in.' She went into the room and asked him 'Pop-pop, what were they doing?' He said, 'Jimmy Cagney was just here.'"

Cagney wanted to keep a low profile while visiting his pal, Larry, so he entered the back way and would knock on the sliding glass door Larry had in his room which opened up into a terrace area outside. When he left, he preferred to exit through the same way rather than going through the lobby and causing a stir.

VISITING WITH LARRY

Academy Award–winning actor Kevin Spacey remembers quite well the day his high school choir took a field trip to the Motion Picture Country Home and sang for the residents. It was the day he met Larry Fine, among other old-timers there at the home, but he mostly remembered the Stooge. And that visit and his experience that day is one of the reasons he has such fondness for the retirement home and still visits with some frequency. In the late 1990s, just weeks before he took home his Oscar, Spacey accepted the Screen Actors Guild award for his performance in the film *American Beauty*. In his speech, he dedicated the trophy to the residents at the retirement home where Larry lived out his life, a trophy for all the talents in their twilight years who'd contributed so much to the profession in which he was now being honored. "Tonight," he said, "they are not forgotten." Spacey is not the only A-list actor to selflessly wander the grounds of the home on any given afternoon and spend time with the retirees. Tom Hanks, Robin Williams, Catherine Zeta-Jones, Tony Danza, Clint Eastwood, Kirk Douglas, and countless others in the entertainment industry have all spent time visiting the grateful residents.

It's easy to see why Larry felt completely at home around other show-biz folks. Prior to his own residency, Larry had been to the Motion Picture Home as a visitor and knew what it meant to those who lived in the retirement community. He told Mike Mikicel: "I visited once in a while to see people. The fellow who used to double me and was my stand-in was out here. And Curly

THE STROKE

was here, you know. But not in this place. This section wasn't here. He was in the hospital. This is the lodge. There is a country house, cottage, lodge, and the hospital. The country house is for retired actors who aren't sick, who have been in the business for so many years and earned a certain amount of money."

During Larry's stay as a resident at the retirement home in the early 1970s, his door was always open, and not just to celebrity friends who wished to pop in and say hello. Kids, adults, and fans of all ages found out—mostly from newspaper interviews and magazine stories—that Larry was alive and well and amenable to having company and sharing a few memories; visitors came from across the country just to meet him and get an autograph from a Stooge, and without a doubt, he received more mail and more visitors than any other resident at that time. There were some weeks when Larry received two hundred pieces of correspondence in the mail, and the chore of responding to these requests became an overwhelming pleasure for him. He became the consummate congenial host, and by all accounts it was tremendous therapy for him—not to mention the thrill of a lifetime for his visitors.

Larry also frequently checked out of the home for the day and made personal appearances at local high school and college campuses. After he'd made a few of these appearances, he had a speech prepared. He would show a few shorts from his meager 16mm collection (which included *Scrambled Brains, Men in Black, Cuckoo on a Choo Choo, Woman Haters, Micro-Phonies, The Yokes on Me,* or *Three Little Pigskins,* depending on his mood that day) and open the final portion of his presentation to questions. All in all, it was usually a loose and fun experience, which is why Larry accepted the invitations.

One of his earliest appearances was in early October 1971. Larry thought he would test out this notion of speaking to students, although he was nervous because he wasn't sure how the kids would react to seeing him in a wheelchair and adjusting to his distorted speech. This was at El Camino Real High School, right there in Woodland Hills, a close drive from the Motion Picture Home. As reported in the high school newspaper, *King's Courier,* reprinted here are a few of Larry's responses to questions posed by the school newspaper's cub reporter. Interestingly, he hedged the young reporter's question about his own education, most likely because he did not graduate from high school himself and thought it might present a negative example for the fertile minds in front of him. It's also interesting to note how Larry described sustaining painful slaps despite Moe's precision with delivery. Larry rarely put this revealing detail—as simple as it is—into perspective so succinctly.

KC: *You've told us that you started your career off early. I was just wondering how many years of schooling you have had?*

Fine: In high school, I was with the band. I really play the violin, and I played it then. I always had the tendency to play popular music, so I went up to the publishers and there I met Gus Edwards's (famous songwriter) brother who was trying to find a replacement for the "Newsboys Quartet" which included George Price, Georgie Jessel, Eddie Cantor, and Herman Timberg. He was looking for a replacement for Timberg.

KC: *What do you think of kids today?*

Fine: I have a grandson older than you. So I love the kids of today. I think they're wonderful, they have a mind of their own, not like when we were around. I was eight years old before I could say "mama."

KC: *Not only are you popular with kids, but you seem to have fans of all ages.*

Fine: I think there's a lot of kid in all of us. You know, even if you think you have grown up, you still like to see slapstick. When I went to Philadelphia my sister brought me to her bank to introduce me to the president of the bank and he said, "Oh, I know all about your brothers." I said to him, "Why do you watch the Stooges?" and he said that he gets so much grief all day long, he likes to go home, take off his shoes, relax with a drink and watch other guys get it. We did what people would like to do to their own boss. That was before everyone claimed violence was no good in movies. When you look back, however, you see nobody ever got killed in one of our pictures . . .

KC: *Did you ever get hurt because of all the nonsense that went on in your movies?*

Fine: When Moe hit me over the ear; I had to learn to take the slap without moving, because Moe had a spot previously picked out to hit me. Once in a while, I tried to duck and then I got it and it hurt . . . We did almost anything and we really got hurt, because coming from the stage like we did, we didn't understand the intricacy of a double or a stand-in.

Following this positive response to his intimate and lively campus appearance, Larry was invited to—and appeared at—many more schools over the next few years: UCLA, West Los Angeles College, Pierce College, Taft High

THE SENIOR CLASS OF 1974 AND THE
FINE ARTS BOOSTERS OF LOARA
PRESENT

The Larry Fine Benefit Show

☆ CURLY JOE ☆

☆ MOE ☆

☆ LARRY ☆

"THREE STOOGES DAY"
Saturday, March 2, 1974

Larry often made personal appearances to aid educational fundraisers in Southern California.

School, Van Nuys High School, and Gaspar De Portola Junior High among them. One of the more auspicious appearances at a southern California high school campus took place on March 2, 1974, at Anaheim's Loara High School, orchestrated by twin high school fans named Greg and Jeff Lenburg.

Publicized as "The Larry Fine Benefit Show," this appearance raised funds for needed equipment in the school's auditorium. The school went all out for Larry on what was dedicated as "Three Stooges Day" on the campus: The school band performed for the audience, and Larry presented his show with films and fielded questions from the audience. This was followed by an award presentation to honor the elder Stooge. Larry knew it would be a huge success and that he was in good hands; he was eager to participate in the charity event, mainly because of the two organizers—Stooges enthusiasts whom he'd befriended.

The Lenburg twins from Loara were old-time film fanatics and collectors who appreciated all of the old classics—Laurel and Hardy, Abbott and Costello, and the Marx Brothers—not just the Stooges. The two studied the Stooges and met with Larry many times, traveling more than an hour from Anaheim to visit the Motion Picture Home and conduct interviews. In conjunction with their high school's student activities director and speech instructor, the twins borrowed the high school's bulky videotape recorder and conducted an interview with Moe Howard, which they presented as a class project. These fans were in high school, but they were hard-core. The local *Anaheim Bulletin* newspaper reported that the twins were so preoccupied with the Stooges that they formed a Three Stooges Band with their pals Bill Parsley and Kent

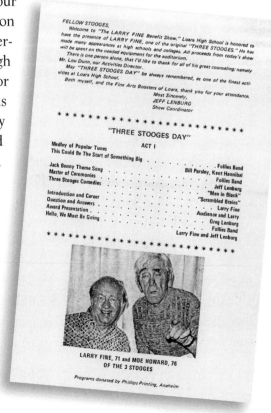

FELLOW STOOGES,

Welcome to "The LARRY FINE Benefit Show." Loara High School is honored to have the presence of LARRY FINE, one of the original "THREE STOOGES." He has made many appearances at high schools and colleges. All proceeds from today's show will be spent on the needed equipment for the auditorium.

There is one person alone, that I'd like to thank for all of his great counseling: namely Mr. Lou Dunn, our Activities Director.

May "THREE STOOGES DAY" be always remembered, as one of the finest activities at Loara High School.

Both myself, and the Fine Arts Boosters of Loara, thank you for your attendance.

Most Sincerely,
JEFF LENBURG
Show Coordinator

* *

"THREE STOOGES DAY"

ACT I

Medley of Popular Tunes	
This Could Be The Start of Something Big	. . . . Follies Band
Jack Benny Theme Song	. . . . . Follies Band
Master of Ceremonies	Bill Parsley, Kent Hannibal
Three Stooges Comedies	. . . . . Follies Band
	. . . . . Jeff Lenburg
	"Men in Black"
Introduction and Career	"Scrambled Brains"
Question and Answers	. . . Larry Fine
Award Presentation	Audience and Larry
Hello, We Must Be Going	. . . Greg Lenburg
	Follies Band
	Larry Fine and Jeff Lenburg

* *

LARRY FINE, 71 and MOE HOWARD, 76
OF THE 3 STOOGES

Programs donated by Phillips Printing, Anaheim

ONE FINE STOOGE

Hannibal, "adding their talent to a Spike Jones type of musical representation."

Eventually, the Lenburg brothers went on to careers in the field of communications and became professional writers—even representing their close friend, Joe Besser, as his agents during the last few years of his career. The Lenburgs co-wrote Besser's autobiography, *Not Just a Stooge* and collaborated with Joan Howard Maurer on the exhaustive volume *The Three Stooges Scrapbook,* which today remains one of the most comprehensive books published about the comedy team.

This was among Larry's favorite caricatures, sent to him by a fan, Tom Bertino.

Stooges fan Stephen Alpert was a graduate student in the Geology Department at UCLA in 1972 when he learned of Larry's accessibility at the Motion Picture Country Home. "I phoned the facility and asked to speak with Larry Fine, and I got through to him almost instantly! I was amazed how quick and easy it was to reach one of the Stooges in person on the phone," Alpert wrote, describing his experience in the *Three Stooges Journal.* "For fun I was conducting the 'Alpert Personality of the Year' award to honor people (mostly offbeat) who were worthy of recognition, but not receiving it elsewhere. Nominees (about twenty per year) had to have their picture appear in a newspaper. Every November, the people in the Geology Department voted for their choice . . . usually the person most likely to appear in person at the school to receive the award was selected. Thus, Larry Fine was voted the winner in 1972."

Alpert described the invitation and tongue-in-cheek award to Larry on the phone and followed up with a written invitation on UCLA stationery. Larry agreed to be picked up on November 30 and said he would bring some 16mm films to show as well. Alpert couldn't wait and drove to escort Larry himself. "The show was held in the largest available room I could get in the Geology Building, about a hundred seats, and the room was overflowing with students, professors, and staff anxious to meet one of the Three Stooges.

"After I introduced Larry and awarded him a trophy, Larry gave a ten-minute comedy monologue. He mentioned that he didn't have much money, but Moe was so rich that he kept falling off his wallet. Larry's joke about how to know when you're getting old brought down the house: 'There are three ways to tell that you're getting old. One, you forget things . . . (pause) . . . I forget the other two.' About fifteen years later, I heard President Reagan tell the same joke on TV."

Alex Jackson, from
Moorestown, New Jersey,
sent this artwork to Larry in
April 1974. Larry liked it
so much he sent this reply
complimenting the young
artist, also noting he was
planning another book.

Dear Alex

Didn't I write you thanking you for the
picture you drew of us. That was stupid of
me. I have it framed, and am very crazy
about it. About my book, I am having a
legal battle about it, and it would take too
long to write about it. However I am thinking
of writing another one, and if it all right
with you, I'd like to use your cartoon for the
cover. I would say, cover by Alex Jackson.
Enclosed find a few pictures of the 3 Stooges.
Thank you

Sincerely yours
Larry Fine

LARRY   LARRY

Alpert drove Larry home following the ninety-minute appearance and presented him with a gift for his appearance: a cribbage set. "Fortunately, Larry knew how to play," Alpert said. "Looking back now, I wish I had visited Larry more after the UCLA show. At the time, I was a busy student and didn't want to be a pest, but now I think Larry probably would have enjoyed my visits. Bringing Larry to UCLA was a truly great experience."

● ● ●

Comedian Bob Saget was in his early teens when he witnessed Larry speaking at his high school. "I have a picture of me and Larry," Saget admits. "And I got a head like a pumpkin, head full of hair, glasses. I looked like a nice fat Jew boy."

Saget outgrew the gourd-ish appearance, even forsaking his initial plans to attend medical school, and his career took a different direction. Knowing at age twelve that deep down he wanted to be a filmmaker or enter some area of show business, Saget eventually made a name and handsome bank account for himself as a successful comedian and actor, all the while keeping the Stooges close at heart. In the late 1980s he became a hip TV dad as star of the sitcom *Full House* and then in 1990 guided *America's Funniest Home Videos* (as the show's original host) to the number-one spot in prime time at ABC.

He never forgot the first time he saw a Stooge in person. Saget attended Southern California's Mulholland Junior High and later Birmingham High, and it was at the latter where Larry Fine was invited to speak at an assembly. "It might have been 1972 or '73, and he also ran some of his shorts and took pictures with people. I went nuts. So when they said he was at the Motion Picture Country Home, I called and talked to him and told him I'd like to visit. He was a lonely guy, he'd had a stroke. He talked kind of curmudgeon-like, but really nice. My mom drove me there to see him because I was about fourteen or fifteen.

"When I was a kid, like nine years old, I used to make these regular 8mm movies and then I moved up to Super 8, so I used to get Blackhawk films and get silent movies with subtitles on Super 8. I had some of the Stooges films, silent, that had been doctored by Blackhawk Films. It was fascinating. The first time I went to see Larry, I didn't bring the movies and we just talked. I called and asked Larry if he'd want to see any of his movies and he wanted to watch them.

"So the second time I went, I took an 8mm projector, without sound," Saget remembers. Larry helped young Bob set up the projector and draw the shades in his room. "It was really a wild scene, it was like one of those movies

FRANKIE AVALON REMEMBERS LARRY

I first met Larry and the Stooges when I was doing a picture called *Voyage to the Bottom of the Sea* at 20th Century Fox and they were doing *Snow White*. That's where we got together. I knew Larry was from Philadelphia, and we'd just hit it off right away because of Philly and we did nothing but discuss South Philly, cheese-steaks and Levi's hot dogs, the Mummers Parade. I felt an immediate friendship with him. Naturally, I'd watched him as a kid, and aside from that, I pushed away his celebrity status and really just enjoyed hanging out with him as a friend. I was about twenty-two, maybe. He was in his sixties, maybe. But

that didn't matter. I knew the Stooges were legends even back then. I just loved their films and loved Larry's character, so yes, I was in awe, but there was an immediate friendship with Larry.

I found him to be a pal, a hangout guy. You felt very comfortable with Larry right away. He always wore a suit with an open shirt or a sport jacket, never casual, that's what I remember about him. He liked to laugh and talk about gambling, a full of life guy. Larry and I would spend time, not only in between shooting, even after that I'd meet him for coffee and we'd just hang out. He used to live at the Knickerbocker, and we'd have lunch

Larry's pal from Philly, singer Frankie Avalon, visits his film idols on the set of *The Outlaws IS Coming!*

186

there. He was that kind of guy, just a terrific guy who loved to tell stories and reminisce and have some laughs.

I remember I told Larry at the time that the thing that made a lot of their comedic value on screen was the sound effects. In watching them there live on the soundstage, I missed that because they went through all the motions of doing the slaps and the slugs, but those effects were put in after the scene. I found that very amusing not being able to hear those wonderful sounds.

The set was not like what you might expect a Three Stooges set to be. I found it to be very low-key instead of up with a lot of laughs. But don't forget, these guys were older guys, they'd made hundreds of films and I think it was really a job. That's how they went into it. There wasn't a lot of laughter on the set or a lot of people playing and joking around.

I have a photo of the Stooges taken with my two sons, Tony and Frank. At the time I only had two boys. The Stooges did some kind of an appearance with Batman. In town here, Batman was the hottest television show, you know. Batman and Robin were appearing with, I think, a circus. Batman and Robin were to come out in the Batmobile and wave to the audience and the Three Stooges came out as well; they were on the bill. They did their little routine in front of the circus audience and then after there was a little greenroom where everybody got together and they had little sand-wiches and Coca-Colas and things like that. That was the last time I saw the three of them together and we took photographs together with my two boys at the time, who were maybe six and seven.

It was a little disheartening later on, even an emotional thing, to see Larry the way he finally wound up in a wheelchair and his speech was difficult to make out. He'd look at me and I'd just imagine what was going through his mind, but he couldn't communicate well at the time. Not a very pleasant sight.

I remember I got a call from Milton Berle. He said, "Frankie, we're doing a show for the Motion Picture Home and I want you to come along and be a part of the show." I said, fine, I'll be there. Of course, I went and I took out all of the things that the folks in the Motion Picture Home would really want to see or hear. . . . I sang, I took out impressions that I did, like Cagney, and I did the dance and everything. I'll never forget all these people that I've seen through the years on screen are sitting there. I got off the stage after the show and said to Berle, "You think it went over?" He said, "Of course it went over!" I said, "But there was no reaction." And he said, "They're not well! They're in wheelchairs!"

That was the last time I saw Larry.

I'm glad somebody is recognizing Larry because he was a hell of a guy. A great talent. He was a guy's guy.

where you see Chaplin and he would sit and look at his old movies. We just sat there and watched, like, three of them."

Saget remembers quite a lot of his visits with Larry. Maybe his favorite memory is one of the oddest: "I was there visiting one day, I remember, and he was in his wheelchair and I remember because of his stroke, he was wheeling backwards in his chair. It was comedic in a way, but not really. Depends on what you find funny. He was going to pick up his teeth at the front desk, which had just been mailed to him. With one leg he was wheeling himself backwards. He goes to the desk, opens up a parcel post envelope, rips it open in front of me and takes his teeth out of a bag and puts them in his mouth. That was cool. I liked that. Really a comedic moment. To replace them in front of you, that's just too hip for the room. The only thing cooler would have been if he'd unscrewed his leg and put another one on."

Saget says he's always felt an affinity for older people. "I had really cool grandparents and I've always seen the value of older people. These people have the gems. They've been around, and if you can sit and talk with them, you're lucky. Rodney Dangerfield was a friend of mine. And what Larry went through in show business is incredible.

"He was really nice to me, very gentle, grandfatherly like. He told me stories how Moe would get a little rough. Sometimes his real hair got ripped with the fake hair. There was always pain involved and how they didn't get the money and got screwed for the most part—except they became legends until the end of time . . . B movie shorts that turned out to be organically funny forever. I think he realized they were something special because everybody told him. I know he felt he did *something.*"

No matter how you feel about the Three Stooges, says Saget, the team was funny. Period. "Some people don't find them funny," he says flatly. "In my opinion, they are just wrong. They committed one hundred thousand percent. It was very tight what they did. Brilliance. Lightning struck for what they were doing."

Saget grew up on the comedy of the Stooges and defends them today. "The Three Stooges were a fourteen-year-old boy's dream," he explains. "You go through adolescence, and you're out of control. When you get hyper—they Ritalin everybody today—but you just bounce off the walls and you want to just poke holes in stuff and cause destruction. It's nature. That's what the Stooges did. They did everything that you shouldn't do, which is to grab a guy's nose with scissors or put pliers in his nostrils."

Inspired by Larry and the Stooges, Saget often allowed slapstick to seep into his own productions, with occasional parodies that popped up *Full House* and in his own voice-over bits during *America's Funniest Home*

Videos. When *Videos* premiered, its violence factor was debated among television critics and outspoken media watchdogs, and Saget couldn't help recall the same treatment suffered by the Stooges years prior. Did the more mature television audiences of the 1980s really want to see actual home video footage of an obese lady harnessed up in a futile attempt at parasailing—only to lose her balance running along the sand, fall flat on her face, and get dragged by the line? Sure they did! And the network's through-the-roof ratings proved Saget right.

"It was an edge that came out of real stuff and you laugh at it," Saget says. "It's human nature. The problem with that show when it started was a concern that people would stage stuff and really get hurt. The video show is like nothing compared to *Fear Factor* and shows where you have people doing things where they could literally die."

● ● ●

Adding credence to the notion that not all Three Stooges fans are knuckleheads, Scott Reboul proudly shares his memories of tracking down Moe Howard and Larry Fine in the early 1970s. Proof is found on his computer at work where his screen-saver is a bold black and white image of young Reboul and old Moe clowning around. Reboul is certainly proud of the opportunities he made and undertook to meet these comedy legends, he says.

Reboul was an amateur filmmaker and magician growing up in Philadelphia, an unabashed enthusiast for the classic comedians like many kids his age—Philly has always been known as strong Stooge territory. Today, Reboul is a husband and father and works as a nuclear environmental engineer. "Actually, I'm what's called a radiochemist," he clarifies. It didn't take a scientist, however, to find Larry Fine in 1973 when Reboul, in his teens, took to the hunt.

"I like Laurel and Hardy, the Bowery Boys, Little Rascals. . . . I watched all of these guys and I always thought, 'Are those guys still alive? Whatever happened to them?' I knew of the '60s Stooges cartoons, but in the '70s, you never heard of them anymore. I did the math and figured they might still be alive. Then I saw an article in the *Evening Bulletin* with the headline *Larry Fine's Brother Relates History of the Three Stooges* and I thought, this is what I've been looking for. I read that and immediately went to the library to find a phone book for Los Angeles to find this Motion Picture retirement home. I called information and got the number."

Reboul was one of many to write to Larry Fine and receive a personal message and autograph from the retired Stooge. But he would shake the hand of Moe Howard before meeting Larry Fine, as it turned out. "I went and saw

THE STROKE

Dear Arthur:

    Please excuse this form letter, but as you know I cannot possibly answer every letter I get personally, although I would like to.

    Thanks for wishing me well, and I am happy to be able to write you that I am getting better. However I will answer any personal questions at the bottom of this letter, and will also send an autographed picture.

    Thanks again for remembering me. Please write again, as I hope soon to be able to answer all my mail personally.

Gratefully yours,

Larry Fine

In answer to your letter, first let me inform you, I had a stroke, which left me partially paralyzed. I was born in Phila. Pa. Oct 5, 1902. I met the Howard Brothers in a shubert show in New York called "A Night in Spain" in 1927. I was a musician, and decided to go in show Business in 1920 with two girls in an act called "The Haney Sisters + Fine." I am at the Motion Picture Country Home, 23388 Mulholland Dr. Woodland Hills Calif. 91364. The Phone number here is 347-1591 and I would be glad to see you any time you can get out here.

Sincerely

Larry

LARRY

Even though he was seriously debilitated, Larry attempted to respond to all fan mail with at least a brief handwritten greeting.

Moe at the Walt Whitman Theatre in Penn-sauken, New Jersey, in April 1973," says Reboul. "I was sitting in the front row, and there were no more than fifteen people in the audience. It was an old movie theatre and he came out, introduced himself, showed one or two shorts and answered some questions. But I could not understand it. Maybe the word didn't get out, I don't know. It was only a dollar fifty to get in to this afternoon show."

The presentation was a disappointing experience for Moe, actually throwing terror into the little old guy. He wondered if all future personal appearances were going to be so ill attended. Had fans forgotten about the Stooges? To Moe this personal appearance was a bomb, but the feeling certainly was not shared by the intimate group of people who were treated to a relatively private audience with the elder Stooge. It's a scenario fans can only dream of now. Reboul was determined to meet his film idol after the show, and he managed it when he came face to face with tiny Moe Howard outside the theatre and snapped some photos with him.

"Later I went to the *Mike Douglas Show,* which taped here in Philadelphia, and I knew Moe Howard was going to be on the show," says Reboul. "It was the show in August of 1973 with Soupy Sales as a guest. I sat next to Larry Fine's brother, Moe Feinberg, in the audience and we had a chance to talk about the Stooges. Later I met Moe Howard after the show again and gave him a photograph that I'd taken of him. Years later, he ended up using that photo in his book."

By the reaction Moe Howard received from his repeated appearances on the *Mike Douglas Show* over the next few months, the old Stooge was relieved and assured that fans had not forgotten him and his partners. Moe

Howard trudged along and committed to further onstage appearances at college campuses. He simply didn't want to quit.

"Once I met Moe I really wanted to meet Larry," says Reboul. He inched closer to the opportunity, but it was actually his father who met Larry next. "My dad was making a business trip to Los Angeles and I wrote to Larry to tell him and asked if my dad could stop by to visit him and interview him for me. My dad brought Tastykakes [a staple on the east coast similar to Hostess treats] for him.

"I knew Larry loved Tastykakes, so I filled up a very large shoe box with every variety of Tastykakes—about three dollars' worth, and at that time they cost twelve cents a pack, so this was about twenty-five packs."

Scott Reboul took a bus trip from the East Coast with his father and finally met his pen pal and friend, Larry, in California at the Motion Picture Country Home on April 16, 1974.

Larry was taken by the gesture from his young friend and loved the goodies. He admitted to Reboul's father, however, that he was a diabetic and treated himself to such confections only rarely. Larry eventually thanked Scott in a letter and told him that he'd save the bakery goods for his grandkids.

Reboul kept up a correspondence with Larry and finally, in April 1974, the time to meet the Stooge arrived. Reboul eagerly handwrote a letter to Larry to tell him he'd be visiting Los Angeles with his father and ask if he could drop by the Home. Larry answered affirmatively. Reboul and his father boarded a bus, the Silver Eagle, traveling from Philadelphia to Los Angeles, a trek that took three days and three nights. The sole purpose of the excursion: to meet Larry Fine. Any other Stooges he might meet would be whipped cream on the pie. (With Stooges, you don't talk in terms of cake.)

Larry was sitting in the sun room and waved the Rebouls in when they arrived. After a little tour of the facility and grounds outside where they took photographs together, Larry asked Reboul to wheel him into his private room and there, the young fan got to privately chat and interview him in person—for a while anyway. Reboul helped Larry get comfortable in his room, all the while his eyes fixed on the odd plaque with Larry's name painted on it, dried up glue dripping from one side, kind of cockeyed and affixed to his doorway. Inside Larry's tidy standard room, like a studio apartment, was a single bed, a desk, some chairs, and a little bathroom area. Larry's desk was piled high with correspondence, pictures, and drawings that children had made him.

THE STROKE

Hold That Lion Larry gets a roaring welcome from a leonine mascot at a premiere event for the film *Frasier, the Sensuous Lion* in June 1973.

Some of those very drawings—albeit more professionally created—were those sent to him by Reboul and another pal of his from Philly named Alex Jackson. On the walls were framed photos depicting different stages of Larry's Stoogedom.

"I remember several people came in to see him," says Reboul. "It wasn't long after we'd gotten in his room, and it still sticks in my mind. The receptionist called him on his intercom and said, 'Larry, there's some men here from the gas company to see you.' And Larry said, 'You better tell them to take some Di-Gel and send them in.' He was sort of winking at me when he was saying it and laughing. These guys came in and wanted to meet him.

"I also remember this was at the time Patty Hearst was missing. One of the visitors said, 'Can I get a picture signed for my daughter?' And Larry said, 'Sure . . . what's her name?' The guy told him, 'Patty.' And Larry asked him, 'That's not Patty *Hearst,* is it?'"

About three different encroachments of company dented Reboul's precious time with Larry, but the visiting student didn't mind at all. Each intrusion brought about a new experience to remember. One visitor asked to show Larry some films on the wall with a projector, so everyone in the room was treated.

"He was very hospitable," Reboul says, trying to sum up Larry's personality. "I went in there thinking: Here's this talented guy, one of the Three Stooges, the greatest guy in the world, a guy that everybody in the world knows, and he would answer any questions I had, but he never put the attention on himself. He'd crack a few jokes and laugh, but his main interest from the time I got there until the time I left, was me. What are your favorite subjects in school? What are your hobbies? And then, everybody that came in, he'd repeat to them, 'Scott here came to see me from Philadelphia.' And at the time, my biggest hobbies were making movies and doing magic shows at kids' birthday parties. Larry would tell these people who came in, 'You know this guy does magic at birthday parties, and he makes his own movies, and he's only fifteen.' He put all the focus on me and made me feel like I was the most important person in the world. I was just enamored with this guy. He was interested in everybody who came in, but not making a big show. He had this talent for making you seem important and showed interest in you."

For Reboul, the Stooging involved in this vacation did not stop at Larry. Although Moe Howard was unavailable, he was able to meet briefly with Joe

Besser and Joe DeRita, chatting briefly with the former Stooges at their respective North Hollywood homes and taking snapshots outside in the California sunshine. Both retired Stooges were receptive to the polite young fan who'd crossed the country to meet his film idols.

"I was surprised to learn that Joe DeRita had never been to see Larry at the Home," says Reboul. "Five years Larry was there and the three couldn't reunite once? But, it was a job, so I guess Larry and Joe didn't socialize together.

"I remember Joe DeRita told me he never thought the Stooges were funny. He told me, 'I never saw what anyone thought was funny about the Stooges,' and that hit me. I guess, if he feels he's in this thing, feeling like he's a prop, not really contributing much to the act, but he's there because he looks just a little bit like Curly with the shaved head and the belly, he doesn't feel too good about it. Whenever fans came to see him, they wanted to see Moe and Larry and didn't care about him, comparing him to the others. I can't imagine him feeling good all around about the whole thing."

● ● ●

Mike Mikicel made his trek to California to meet the Stooges in 1973 and again in 1974, with luck on his side both times. Mikicel was a young college graduate of the University of Toronto, aspiring to enter the field of communication arts in some capacity, and like many guys his age he became swept up in the resurgence in popularity for the classic comedians like the Marx Brothers and the Three Stooges in the 1970s. While most visitors from Canada might do the touristy things and hit Disneyland and Universal Studios first, Mikicel's priority was to meet Moe and Larry.

"I figure Disneyland and the rest will always be there whenever I might like to experience these things," he told a local Canadian newspaper reporter who described his venture in a feature story. "I went down to meet some fascinating people in my estimate . . . while they were still living."

Mikicel met and shared meals with Larry at the Motion Picture Country Home; it was the first time he'd feasted on one of Larry's favorite entrees: an overstuffed Denver omelet, jammed

Fine Points Longtime Stooges' fan Mike Mikicel traveled from Canada in the fall of 1974 to meet his comedy idols, the Three Stooges. Here, Larry demonstrates the art of Stooging.

THE STROKE

thick with ham, green peppers, some cheese, and the rest. In his room, Larry pointed and asked, "How 'bout those pictures on the wall?" Then he pointed to a row of small trophies arranged neatly on his desk. "I'm the shuffleboard champ. I'm gonna quit now because everybody's getting jealous. Too many trophies. It's a sure way to get hated around here, you know?"

Mikicel also took time to conduct some extensive interviews, which he recorded for posterity. "I think I may be the last one to tape him," says Mikicel whose last visit with Larry was in September 1974. Larry's health was waning and his speech was more garbled than ever before. The two discussed Moe Howard's college appearances and interviews on the *Mike Douglas Show* on television. Larry totally negated any notion that he might fly back for an appearance with Mike Douglas, although an open invitation from Douglas stood. Some degree of noticeable depression was setting in, and Mikicel tried his best to help cheer up the aging comedian, but Larry's morale was sliding along with his health.

"Personally, I don't feel like I sound too good. I sound a little sickly, I think," Larry admitted candidly on tape to Mikicel. "I want to leave the people remembering me as I was, see what I mean? After you make a wonderful impression for forty years, there's no use spoiling it. I want to get my voice back, my healthy look . . . I think I've lost some self confidence. People said, 'Oh, you'll be out of here in no time.' When a year or two goes by you lose your confidence. What the hell happened? I was getting along so well and all of a sudden, you start thinking about it. Why am I down in the dumps? Why is my leg still bad? All I know, this is as far as I'm going to go. There's no guarantee. I'll be eighty years old before I drive a car again, and by then, who cares?

"I saw Groucho on the Academy Awards and thought he looked terrible," Larry said. "The minute he opened his mouth, I thought 'Oh my God . . . is that Groucho?' I feel that's what people would say about me. 'Oh my God, look at Larry!' I don't care about my arm and leg, that can't be helped, but my voice. I don't belong in show business with my voice in this condition."

Larry spent more of his time these days watching television and even caught parodies of the Stooges on the *Carol Burnett Show* and the cartoon show *Scooby-Doo.* He understood why he was not asked to voice the cartoon character, but he couldn't understand why Moe was passed by as well. He gave Mikicel an update on Moe and the other surviving Stooges. "Joe DeRita tried out a new act that called themselves the Three Stooges with two other guys last year," Larry said in an irritated tone. "They tried it in Massachusetts or Providence, Rhode Island, and they closed them out. Didn't work. People wouldn't buy it. They said, 'That's not the Three Stooges.' I don't know what Joe's doing now.

"Moe does what I do, only he gets a lot of money for it. I've made appearances at high schools and colleges. There's a frame of a letter they sent from Granada Hills. I've been to Canoga Park, Birmingham, even UCLA and Pierce. I have about four shorts and I show a couple of them and answer questions. Moe's doing it in the East along with the *Mike Douglas Show.* And he's advertised as 'The last of the remaining Stooges.' They've got me written off."

● ● ●

As the old commercial has it, "Only her hairdresser knows for sure." That timeworn line could be applied to Larry as well. Eddie Crispell was a curvaceous and lively blonde-haired barber in her late thirties when she met Larry at a B'nai Brith affair in the mid-1960s. Larry adopted her as his personal hairstylist for more than ten years, but more than that, Eddie became a friend in whom Larry put much trust. Eddie and her husband, Nick, ran a popular barbershop on La Cienega Boulevard for decades, and it became a nice haven for Larry to come in and leisurely get his hair cut and kibitz for a while. Eddie even accompanied Larry to some events after Mabel died—with her husband's consent, of course. Larry and Eddie's friendship was purely platonic; he simply enjoyed the company of females and in Eddie he found a confidante with whom he could discuss anything. Nick and Eddie Crispell ate out with Larry, attended events, and were guests of Larry's in his home during the Christmas holidays; they shared a bond that Larry valued and counted on.

Fine Tooth Comb
Larry's barber, "Eddie" Crispell, tried a new comb-over on Larry in 1968. He seemed to like it.

Both Eddie and her husband visited Larry several times in late 1974 at the Motion Picture Home and they saw his health taking a turn. As 1974 drew to a close, Larry was complaining that he felt lousy. He didn't want to alarm his family and friends, but he confided in his close friend, Nathaniel Davis, his longtime personal physician of more than forty years, that he knew his health was on the downswing and he felt helpless about it. Dr. Davis attempted to keep Larry's mood up and encouraged him to take care of himself while he consulted with the facility's physicians to make sure his blood pressure and blood sugar were in check. In late December, Larry suffered additional strokes, which laid him up completely and eventually he slipped into a coma. By this time, he had been transferred to the hospital area of the Motion Picture Country Home, and his vitals signs were not strong.

On Thursday, January 23, 1975, Eddie and Nick Crispell went to the Motion Picture Home's hospital to visit with Larry. "He'd had another stroke and he was in a coma," she remembers. "What alarmed me was that they had stopped giving him any nourishment. I'd made an inquiry about it. And when I found out they had not given him any nourishment from Wednesday on, I was furious. I wanted to see the doctor and he was out of town. I guess they knew he was dying and there wasn't anything they could do.

"Larry laid there still with his eyes closed. I washed his hair, combed his hair and bathed him and I kept talking to him. I told him, 'It's Eddie . . . I'm here and Nick is with me. . . .' I kept telling him to show me a sign, move a finger, move a toe. I really hoped that he would either come out of the coma or show me some sign that he could hear me. A tear came out of his eye and ran down his cheek and I knew that he knew I was there with him. It was really heartbreaking to us."

In the early morning hours of Friday January 24, 1975, Larry died peacefully. "We really lost a good friend when we lost Larry," says Crispell. "He was one of my truest friends. I had bought a chai for him and put it on his gold chain. When he died, Phyllis took it off of his body and gave me the chain and the chai."

Word of Larry's death traveled fast and hit newspapers around the world that very day. The network television's evening news broadcasts covered the passing as well:

Walter Cronkite on the CBS Evening News announced: "Larry Fine, the frizzy haired member of the Three Stooges comedy team, died today of a stroke in Woodland Hills, California. Fine was seventy-three."

Howard K. Smith at ABC provided a little more detail on his prime-time news broadcast, with a clip of the Stooges performing the "point to the right" bit accompanying his broadcast. Smith announced: "Larry Fine, one of the original members of the slapstick comedy team called the Three Stooges, died today in Los Angeles of a stroke. He was seventy-three. The team banded together in the 1930s and made more than two hundred short films over a twenty-four-year period, many you can still see on television. In this trademark segment of one movie, Fine is the man in the middle."

On Sunday morning in Philadelphia, a memorial service was held for Larry at the Beth Israel Temple on Roosevelt Boulevard, with his brother Moe and sister Lyla and their families in attendance, along with a great crowd of people who knew Larry and many folks who didn't but merely wanted to pay their respects; they loved him for his body of work and for all the laughs he provided. Following the service, Larry's younger brother, Moe Feinberg, hosted an open house at his home where a crowd of family and friends gathered to celebrate the life of their famous native son.

Services for Larry in Los Angeles were held the next day, on Monday, January 27, in the Church of the Recessional on the hillside grounds at Forest Lawn Memorial Park in Glendale, California. Larry and Mabel, along with their son, John, and Mabel's sister, are entombed in the marble-encased wall of the Freedom Mausoleum, in the wing known as the Sanctuary of Liberation.

Larry's afternoon services were well attended, and his casket was open for viewing. "I remember my son John crying his head off," says Larry's daughter-in-law, Christy Kraus. "John was very young, but he cried a lot. The grandkids called Larry 'Pop-Pop' and he loved his Pop-Pop."

Emil Sitka recalled Larry's funeral service in a 1979 interview: "Larry looked almost in death as he did in person. They prepared him nicely. They had his coffin open and he was propped up slightly, you know. His hair was sort of curly, but not real big, not as much as when he played a Stooge, you know.

"There was a big crowd there, it was open to the public," recalled Sitka. "That's where I had met with Christine McIntyre after all those years. She was the pretty blonde who played in a lot of comedies with the Stooges. It'd been years since we talked, and I was so glad to see her. I greeted her and we talked for a while and that was the last time I saw her. Moe, Joe DeRita was there. I didn't see Joe Besser there. An awful lot of public, but quite a few fans came around to me, believe it or not, and a lot of them wanted to know if I was still alive and all that. I'd say, 'Here I am.'"

Larry left no will. Phyllis divided his personal effects between her family and her late brother's family. His pinkie ring (which can be seen in most of his films) as well as his precious violin went to the grandchildren, who eventually sold the items in the late 1980s. His violin is currently kept safely in a case, part of a private collection in Larry's home state of Pennsylvania.

Near the close of his life, Moe Howard appeared at a few colleges and theaters to reminisce about his experiences as a Stooge. Scott Reboul artfully captured the comedy elder here at the Walt Whitman Theatre in Pennsauken, New Jersey, on April 29, 1973.

AFTERWORD

Throughout Larry's illness in the early 1970s, Moe Howard nervously strived to stay busy. It wasn't because he needed the work; he had all the money in the world from wise investments. The ham in him never disappeared. He answered as much fan mail as he possibly could handle, appeared on radio shows from coast to coast, and traveled to Philadelphia for the taping of a few appearances on the *Mike Douglas Show.* On the East Coast he also accepted and performed some college lecture dates. A fan once asked him what his last movie was. Moe responded sharply, "Never say last, say most recent." With white hair, in an un-Stooge-like role, Moe made a brief appearance in a low-budget horror film, *Doctor Death, Seeker of Souls,* in 1973. This was his last.

Moe recognized that the Stooges were on the brink of another wave of discovery, all the while he was making notes for an autobiography. An annoying aspect surrounding the whole resurgence, however, was the fact that the Hollywood Chamber of Commerce refused to honor him and his partners with a coveted star on the Hollywood Walk of Fame. Moe just couldn't figure out why producer/director Jules White had one and the Stooges didn't. Abbott and Costello had several, honoring their radio, film, and television work separately. Most of their motion picture peers had been bestowed a star.

In a moment that has been called apocryphal, Moe made his opinion clear and told one radio show host, "They can take their star and I can show them where to put it—one point at a time." True story. Tape exists.

So driven to keep the act going, and keep himself moving, Moe was even willing to form yet a fifth group of Stooges, appointing Stooges' costar Emil Sitka the role of the middle Stooge, although he would not have been called "Larry."

"Even when Larry was still at the hospital, a producer from Manila, in the Philippines, had a story for a feature film with the Stooges. Moe and Norman Maurer called me in for this and asked me, 'How would you like to become a Stooge?' I thought they were kidding," Sitka admits. "I never pictured myself as being a Stooge, but they were serious. Moe was very serious.

Old Moe, as he looked in the 1970s.

Curly-Joe in his final years.

Norman and Moe assured me that I'd have to act it in my own way. I was much taller than they are, so that was a problem.

"I was a little apprehensive about it at first," says Sitka of becoming a Stooge. "My character would not have been a duplicate of Larry. I was going to be totally smart, so smart that I was stupid. I know you can't imagine that, but I'd thought about the character and even talked with Moe about it and he liked the idea."

The new Stooges were called together twice for meetings, the second at the Sheraton Universal Hotel in North Hollywood, to discuss a film and take some fresh publicity photos. Norman Maurer came along and drove Moe to the meeting. Moe once again dyed his thin hair jet black, combed it down, but his face was gaunt and both Curly-Joe and Emil Sitka were aware that he wasn't well. Moe painted his face with a thick coat of pancake makeup in an effort to erase some age, but it really didn't help. His energy level was low and he was nervous, much more so than ever before, recalled Sitka. Wearing the Stooges' wild stage outfits, the new boys posed for a photographer who simply placed them in front of a white stucco wall at the hotel. The three tried to laugh and capture some comical spirit in the still photography, just like old times.

"After we took the pictures, Moe motioned to me to follow him into the lobby bathroom to talk about something," Sitka recalled. "I went in there with him and he was talking about the film and he wanted to get away from his son-in-law, Norman, for some reason. He had some concerns about the production—that I know. He pulled out a little pillbox from his pocket, and just as he was about to take one out, Norman stormed into the bathroom and yelled at him. The pillbox went up in the air and pills flew all over. I was on the floor helping Moe pick up the pills. I don't remember what Norman was upset about, but it really scared Moe. Ohhh, I remember that very well."

Plans were being made to film in Palm Springs with Moe, Emil, and Curly-Joe, but that "never came through," Sitka remembers. There were no more meetings, no contracts were signed. As the dates drew nearer, technical difficulties were blamed for further delays. Moe became weaker and those around him knew his health was sharply declining.

Moe's physical deterioration continued, and his little body was noticeably frail. Even in interviews where he was miked, his voice was just above a whisper; at times it was an effort for him to communicate. Meanwhile, all plans for any more filmmaking were put on hold. Moe had finally curtailed his longtime habit of cigarette smoking, but the efforts were really too little, too late; he knew he was suffering from lung cancer the last year of his life. Moe Howard died in the early evening of May 4, 1975, at the Hollywood Presbyterian Hospital, just a few weeks shy of his seventy-eighth birthday.

Emil Sitka recalled Moe's intimate funeral services. "It was at a more exclusive temple as I remember, and not nearly as many people as Larry's funeral, but the directors were there, Jules White, Ed Bernds, and the writers Elwood Ullman and some others. That's where I learned what his real name was. His name was Moses, and Horwitz was the last name. Joe DeRita was there, but he sat in his car. He didn't come out. He was close by, but I didn't see him go into the temple or where the services were held."

PHOTO BY SCOTT REBOUL

Joe Besser and Joe DeRita became the surviving Stooges, although they both admitted they'd never met. They resided just minutes from each other and there were fans who offered to introduce them, but they weren't interested. Both Joes were unwittingly carrying the torch and representing a comedy team whose popularity was on the rise in the 1980s. In fact, it became pandemic. A new generation of young fans rediscovered the Stooges yet again, and they looked to Besser and DeRita to answer their questions and comment on their association with Moe and Larry—whether they liked it or not.

By the late 1970s, Curly-Joe had gained a considerable amount of weight in his retirement, limiting his mobility. He suffered from arthritis and failing eyesight, yet for years he graciously talked with fans who hunted him down by phone, and on good days, he even met with many of them at his small North Hollywood home.

For the most part, Curly-Joe enjoyed the rediscovery in his full retirement, occasionally appearing on radio shows by telephone and welcoming visiting fans inside his quaint North Hollywood home. Joe Besser did the same, but he was, at times, agitated by his recognition as a Stooge because it seemed to him that fans had forgotten the rest of his body of work in the entertainment field. "Oh my God, I've done other things, you have to remember," Besser told one young interviewer. "I've worked with Jack Benny, Olson and Johnson, and Abbott and Costello. My two years with Moe and Larry were wonderful, but I started in vaudeville, long before I worked with those boys." Poof! A whole career went by the wayside as fans pestered him repeatedly about getting smacked in the gut in the Stooge two-reelers at Columbia. They

Star Struck The author peered just over Joe Besser's shoulder and shot these images as the former Stooge unveiled the Star on Hollywood's Walk of Fame in 1983.

PHOTOS BY STEVE COX

AFTERWORD

just wanted him to yell those signature lines one more time: "Oh ya craaaaazy you!" and "Not so louuud!"

Except for some occasional voice-over work in Hanna Barbera cartoons—a job that was physically nearby, involved no on-camera work, and paid fairly well—Besser was retired. In the last few years of his life, he successfully kept his weight down due to a diabetes scare. His wife, Ernie, actually handled most of the correspondence from his fans, handwriting his letters. Besser himself always handled the chore of autographing photographs. He relished that job and tried to accommodate the volume of requests, but it was nearly out of hand, he admitted. Although he had made very few public appearances in the early 1980s, Joe happily represented the Stooges at a film festival in Southern California in 1982 and the next year accepted the invitation to unveil the Three Stooges' star on the Hollywood Walk of Fame. The gleam in Besser's eye the day of the star ceremony could not convey the honor he felt. There was no mistaking that he was proud to be able to do this, especially for Moe and Larry.

On August 30, 1983, in front of record crowds and a celebrity dais that included Milton Berle, Gary Owens, Emil Sitka, Jamie Farr, and Adam West, the Stooges finally received their star on the legendary Walk of Fame. Due to the overwhelming number of fans—literally thousands—who came to witness the event, streets had to be blocked off to control the crowds and the press in attendance. A host of Stooges' relatives were in attendance, including members of Curly's family as well as Shemp's. There were brief speeches and then Joe Besser carefully knelt down on one knee next to the star as the crowd quieted. With Moe's daughter Joan on one side and Larry's daughter Phyllis at the other, the threesome jointly unveiled the fresh shiny monument to a cacophony of applause and a battery of paparazzi the likes of which Besser had never experienced before. Besser's benediction, as one of the Stooges, was all the fans could hope for.

Paul Howard (Moe's son), Lyla Budnick (Larry's sister), and Jane Howard Hanky (Curly's daughter) represent their respective families at a Three Stooges convention in Philadelphia, 2001.

Joe DeRita was, of course, invited to take part in the ceremony. Fans wanted him to be there as well, but he was nearly immobile and rarely ventured out of the house because of obesity and failing eyesight. Jean, his wife, accepted the honor on his behalf that day and revealed that Joe just wasn't up to it. Due to his girth and the onset of arthritis, it was an effort for him just

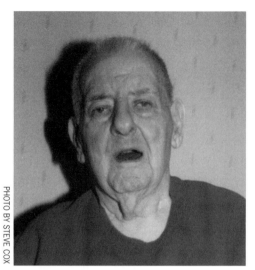

The last photo of Curly-Joe DeRita, taken at the Motion Picture Country Home, in 1993.

to get dressed, so his wife, a registered nurse, took care of Joe and helped him live out his life in the comfort of their home with their little dog by his side and a pack of cigars always at arm's reach. His humor, however, never diminished. One fan, while visiting DeRita at his home, hesitated before taking a snapshot of him while he relaxed in his giant boxer shorts and t-shirt. DeRita wasn't one to be shy, in or out of clothes. He told the fan to snap away. "What's the matter with my underwear? It's clean!"

The world held in esteem these two old Stooges, survivors of the legendary comedy team, for a few more years until the death of Joe Besser. The eighty-year-old comedian had collapsed in the hallway of his home and died on March 1, 1988, the victim of a sudden heart attack.

In the last year of Joe DeRita's life, he was cared for at the Motion Picture Country Home and Hospital, the same facility in which Larry had lived out his life. Due to a lengthy illness, DeRita had dropped an inordinate amount of weight, to the point where he was nearly unrecognizable. DeRita developed multiple health problems and also suffered from advanced dementia in his final months, so the news of his residency at the Motion Picture Country Home was kept from the press. Only family and close friends knew he was there. His devoted wife Jean visited him regularly and made sure he was comfortable. Joe DeRita died of heart failure on July 3, 1993, at the age of eighty-three. He was buried with a ten-dollar cigar tucked in his suit pocket. DeRita's passing marked the true end of the legendary comedy team. On his black granite grave marker, under his name, it reads: The Last Stooge.

APPENDIX A: STOOGES ON STAGE

Buried deep in the USC Cinema-Television Archive is the original vault copy of a twenty-two page treatment titled "Suggested Bits and Scenes by Ted Healy and Moe Howard." This typed treatment, dated April 19, 1933, was submitted to Metro-Goldwyn-Mayer Studios for possible use in the film Hollywood Revue *(later retitled* Hollywood Party*) and contains several original Healy/Stooges onstage vaudeville routines. Since only a fraction of Healy's act with the Stooges was ever filmed or recorded in any fashion, most of their live performances were unfortunately lost to the ages—comedy material never to be recreated or even recognized. These brief sketches, some published here for the first time, provide a rare glimpse into the vintage nature and flavor of their vaudeville act from the 1920s and early 1930s.*

QUEEN BIT WITH KEYS

Queen (to Healy)

You are so nice.
                (rubbing Healy's chest with each word)
So sweet, so beautiful.

Healy

Lemme do it to you now.

Queen

I like you. Here I have two keys. This one is for my room, and this one is for your room, right next to mine. Now, so I will know you, you will wear the royal purple pajamas.

Healy

What is it, a joint?

Queen

Oh, no. It's the royal palace.

Healy

Let me get this straight. This key is for your room and this key is for my room, right next to yours.

Queen

Yes. You will be there?

Healy

It won't be my brother.

Queen

Au revoir.

Healy

Skip the gutter.

(Queen exits.)

First Man

You'd better watch out. Every one of the Royal Guards is in love with her, and if they find you asleep in your room next to hers, they'll stab you.

All - in unison

Stab him!

Healy

Now don't get excited. If they find me asleep in my room next to hers, I deserve to get stabbed.

BLACK OUT

LAPSE OF TIME

Scene in one.

EXTERIOR OF QUEEN'S ROOM. Three Stooges rush on, attired in royal purple pajamas. Coming from different directions, they meet in front of door.

First Stooge

How are you? You're looking fine. Didn't expect to meet you around here.

Second Stooge

I'm feeling swell. You're getting fat.

First Stooge

Well, so long. I'll see you later.

APPENDIX A

(They turn to go, take two steps and immediately turn back and reach for doorknob. Repeat ad lib conversation.)

First Stooge
Now, I know what we're here for. Let's get it over with.
(he knocks on door)

Queen's Voice (from behind door)
Who is it?

Second Stooge
It is I, your King, in the royal pajamas. Have you nothing to say?

Healy
(opens Queen's bedroom door, hands Stooges suit of clothes)

Yes. Have this suit pressed.

BLACK OUT.

*   *   *

THE BONNIE AND MOE BIT
Bonnie and Moe interrupt Healy.

Healy
What happens here?

Moe
This is where she sings her special song.

(to Bonnie)
Go ahead. Give him an audition.

Bonnie (singing special song)
"She lives in the cottage on the edge of—"

Healy (interrupts – to Moe)
What are you out here for, son?

Moe
I'm out here for protection.

                              Healy
Oh, protection.

                               Moe
Yes, she sang a song in Buffalo last week and a fellow
cracked her right here, with a stick.

                              Healy
Oh, he hit her with a stick.

                               Moe
Yeah, and the brains and the blood—oh, it was beautiful!

                       Healy (to Bonnie)
You'd better sing.

  She starts again. "She lived in the cottage on the edge of—"

                   Healy (interrupting)
Oh, where you from, son?

                               Moe
I'm from Lake Winnepesago.

                              Healy
Lake what?

                               Moe
Lake Winnepesago.

                              Healy
I never heard of that lake. How do you spell it?

                               Moe
No, I'm from Lake Erie.

                       Healy (to Bonnie)
Sing.

                             Bonnie
"She lives in the cottage—"

                  Healy (interrupts – to Moe)
What do you do for a living . . . you're not an actor, are you?

208   APPENDIX A

                    Moe

No.

                    Healy

Well, what do you do for a living?

                    Moe

I raise rabbits.

                    Healy

How many rabbits do you raise?

                    Moe

Oh, that's up to the rabbits.

                  Healy (to Bonnie)

Please sing.

                    Bonnie

"She lives in the cottage—"

                 Healy (interrupting)

How old are you, girlie?

                    Bonnie

For goodness sake! Will you let me get out of that cottage!

                    Healy

Go ahead and sing.

(Bonnie goes through song to the finish. At finish, Healy grabs
Moe by the back of the pants.)

                 Moe (slaps his hand away)

Hey!

                    Healy

What's the matter with you?

                    Moe

What's with those hands? Ain't nothing sacred to you?

                  (after ad lib)

Moe

(raising coat sleeve, exposing three wrist-watches on one
arm)

Have we time for another song?

Healy (seeing watches)

What are you doing with three wrist-watches?

Moe

I always wear three wrist-watches.

Healy

Oh, you always wear three.

Moe

Yes, that's how I tell the time.

Healy

I see.

Moe

You see this one on the end? That runs ten minutes slow every two hours. You see the one on the other end? That runs fifteen minutes fast every four hours. The one in the middle is broken; it stopped at two o'clock.

Healy

I see. But how do you tell the time?

Moe

I was waiting for you to ask me that.

Healy

I knew you were waiting for something.

Moe

You see the ten minutes on this end? Well, you subtract that from the fifteen on this end, then you divide by the two in the middle.

Healy

Well, what time is it now?

Moe

(pulling a fourth watch from vest pocket)

It is 9:30.

Healy (after ad lib)
I think the whole mob of you are daffy.

Bonnie
That's not so.

Healy
You all belong in the insane asylum.

Moe
You're not bad either.

Healy
Well, I'm the boss.

Moe
All right, boss, can you stand a mental test?

Healy
Can I stand a mental test? Me—a guy that's worked for
Shuberts all my life! Can I stand a mental test!

Moe (insistently)
Yes, but can you stand a mental test?

Healy
Certainly I can stand a mental test.

Bonnie
All right, do what we tell you.

Moe
Put your right hand on your right ear.

(he does)

Bonnie
Put your right foot behind your left foot.

(he does)

Moe
Now put your hand on your hip.

(he does)

APPENDIX A   211

                    Bonnie
Now turn your head this way.

                    (he does)

                    Moe
Now throw your head back.

 As he completes the final picture, Bonnie and Moe, each putting hands on their own hips, say "Whoops!" and run.

                  BLACK OUT.

                    * * *

                SAND BAG BIT

While Healy is conducting his band, a singer in the band
starts broadcasting. On Healy's signal, a sand bag falls close
to the singer, in front of the mike. The singer moves the mike.
Healy repeats business, ad libs.

                    * * *

              NOEL COWARD BIT

             (For Healy and the Boys)

Three boys enter, interrupting Healy. General ad lib.

                    Moe
Right here's where we do our vaudeville act.

                    Healy
Oh, you're old troupers?

                    Moe
Yes, comedy singing, dancing, and talking.

                    Healy
You do enough, all right.

                Moe (to other two boys)
We'll give them the same routine we gave them in the other
joints.

Healy

This is no joint. This is the so-and-so Theatre, one of the finest theatres in the country.

Moe

O.K. This'll do.

Larry

It's a swell dive.

Jerry

You don't mind if we wear our tuxedos?

Healy

No. You've got on heavy underwear, haven't you?

Boys

Yes.

Healy

Well, that's all right. So long as you don't catch cold.

Moe

Spread out.

Jerry

Right here's where we go into a snappy gag. I walk down the street and I meet the straight man.

Healy

Who's that, hatchet head?

Jerry

Yes. I walk down and give him the first swift gag. Hello, Moe.

Moe

Hello, Curlie.

Healy

Wait a minute. What did you call him?

Moe

That's Curlie.

Healy

I thought you said girlie.

                          Jerry
Hello, Moe.

                          Moe
Hello Curlie.

                          Jerry
What would you do if a girl kissed you?

                          Moe
I'd kiss her back.

                          Jerry
Ah! Supposing she was a big, tall girl?

               (general ad lib and pushing around)

                          Moe
Spread out.

                     (to Healy)
Do you care for the drama?

                          Healy
You mean that high-class stuff?

                          Moe
Yeh, that Noel Coward chatter.

                          Healy
Sure, I like the drama.

                     Moe (to boys)
We'll slug him with a drama.

                     (to Healy)
Now I've got a part here for you if you'll help us out.

                          Healy
Sure, I'm an old trouper. I'll help you out.

                     Moe (handing him the part)
That's fine. Now, when the music plays, "The Gates of Hell
Are Open"—that's where you walk in.

(to Jerry)
Take this part.

Jerry

Not me.

Moe (smacks Jerry)

Oh, mutiny.

(walks to Larry)
Take this part.

Larry

I'll take it when I'm ready.

Moe

Are you ready?

Larry

Yeh, I'm ready.

(general ad lib)

Moe

Now I'll give you a resume of the next scene.

Healy

Get that guy with those high words. Putting on the dog—getting high class. How do you like that?

Larry

Is he getting high class?

Healy

Yeh.

Larry

Hey, Curlie, throw a louse on him.

(general ad lib, pushing and eye-gouging)

> **Moe**
> Now, in the next scene, I play the part of a count. I drive up to the castle on horseback. Hop into my castle, into my bedroom and there's two ladies in my bed. What do you think happens?

> **Healy**
> I don't know; what happens?

> **Moe**
> I say "One of you broads has gotta get outta here."

> (general ad lib)

> Spread out.

> Gladys! Gladys! What, not here! She has deceived me. She promised to meet me at the old bridge at ten o'clock. It is now half past eight and she's not here yet.

> **Jerry**
> I think she'll be coming round the mountain when she comes.

> **Moe (smacks Jerry)**
> How the wind blows!

> (Larry rushes up to Moe's ear, making a loud sound of wind blowing. Moe smacks him. General ad lib.)

> **Healy**
> Is this my part?

> **Moe**
> Yeh, that's where you come in.

> **Healy (to Jerry)**
> Pay me the $50,000 or I'll foreclose the mortgage. Heigh-ho! Cheerio! How are you? Smack!

> (slaps Moe)

> **Moe**
> I will not give you the money.

Healy

(showing Jerry the part in his part which calls for the slap and starting again)

Pay me the $50,000 or I'll foreclose the mortgage. Heigh-ho! Cheerio! How are you? Smack!

Moe

Verily, I repeat, I will not give you the money.

Repeat business

Healy

Pay me the $50,000 or I'll foreclose the mortgage. Heigh-ho! Cheerio! How are you? Smack!

Jerry (to Moe)

For God's sake, pay him the money.

(general ad lib)

Moe

With Gladys as my wife, and those papers in my possession, I can laugh at the world.

Jerry (gives prop laugh)

Healy

If you want to lay an egg, go over there.

Jerry

How can a big guy like me lay an egg?

Larry

There's a big basket over there.

(which is a musical cue for "Hey – Hey!")

* * *

HEY – HEY!

Music plays "Dinah" as Larry starts recitation of "I'm from the South; Welcome home your ever-loving sonny, Sam, from sunny Tennessee, etc. Hey – Hey!"

Moe and Jerry bow and punch. Larry continues. "I'm from the South; I can see my mammy and pappy waitin' at the garden gate with the ever-loving buck-wheat cakes . . . Hey Hey!"

Moe and Larry bow to each other and punch. Larry continues: "I'm from the South; I'm headin' home back to the Southland; I'm on the old train . . . Hey Hey!"

Healy smacks Larry, tears shirt in half, as Moe and Jerry dance back and forth around Healy and Larry.

> Larry
> I'm from the South; I'm from the South . . . (ad lib)

> (ending with)

Hey – Hey!

Healy smacks Larry, tears top shirt as Moe and Jerry repeat dance around Larry and Healy.

> Larry
> I'm from the South. I can feel the honey oozing down my mouth and the waffles and the corn . . . Hey – Hey!"

Healy slaps Larry, tears undershirt, as Jerry and Moe repeat dance around Larry and Healy.

> Larry
> I'm from the South—

> As he says this, his pants fall. Boys run off.

* * *

DOCTOR—PICTURE BIT

Healy walks into office which has three or four pictures on the wall of prominent men, such as Roosevelt, Washington, Lincoln, and Napoleon.

Healy picks up picture of himself, puts it on the wall and the other four pictures fall down.

* * *

APPENDIX A

MAN WITH GLASSES

Man enters wearing glasses. Healy tells him that it is silly to wear glasses; it is only his imagination, he really does not need glasses. "Don't tell me you have to wear glasses."

Healy

Take your glasses off. I'll prove to you that you don't need to have them.

(takes card out of his pocket)

Do you see this card? How many people on it?

Man (without glasses)

Two.

Healy

No. You better put on the glasses; there's ten people on here. Have you got your glasses on now? Now you see this card?

Man (looking)

What card?

APPENDIX B: FILMOGRAPHY

Compiled by Brent Seguine

THE TED HEALY YEARS

Soup to Nuts	28-Sep-30	Fox Studios
Nertsery Rhymes	6-Jul-33	MGM
Turn Back the Clock	25-Aug-33	MGM
Beer and Pretzels	26-Aug-33	MGM
Screen Snapshots Series 13 #5 Hollywood Nightclub	18-Feb-33	Columbia Pictures
Hello Pop!	16-Sep-33	MGM
Plane Nuts	14-Oct-33	MGM
Meet the Baron	20-Oct-33	MGM
Dancing Lady	24-Nov-33	MGM
Myrt and Marge	25-Nov-33	Universal Studios
Fugitive Lovers	5-Jan-34	MGM
Hollywood on Parade #B-9	30-Mar-34	Paramount Pictures
The Big Idea	12-May-34	MGM
Hollywood Party	1-Jun-34	MGM
Newsreel: Jack Dempsey Spars with Max Baer and Primo Carnera	1934	MGM

THE COLUMBIA SHORT SUBJECTS

Woman Haters	5-May-34	Columbia Pictures
Punch Drunks	13-Jul-34	Columbia Pictures
Men in Black	28-Sep-34	Columbia Pictures
Three Little Pigskins	8-Dec-34	Columbia Pictures
Horses' Collars	10-Jan-35	Columbia Pictures
Restless Knights	20-Feb-35	Columbia Pictures
Pop Goes the Easel	29-Mar-35	Columbia Pictures
Uncivil Warriors	26-Apr-35	Columbia Pictures
Pardon My Scotch	1-Aug-35	Columbia Pictures
Hoi Polloi	29-Aug-35	Columbia Pictures
Three Little Beers	28-Nov-35	Columbia Pictures
Ants in the Pantry	6-Feb-36	Columbia Pictures
Movie Maniacs	20-Feb-36	Columbia Pictures

Half Shot Shooters	30-Apr-36	Columbia Pictures
Disorder in the Court	30-May-36	Columbia Pictures
A Pain in the Pullman	27-Jun-36	Columbia Pictures
False Alarms	16-Aug-36	Columbia Pictures
Whoops, I'm an Indian!	11-Sep-36	Columbia Pictures
Slippery Silks	27-Dec-36	Columbia Pictures
Grips, Grunts and Groans	15-Jan-37	Columbia Pictures
Dizzy Doctors	19-Mar-37	Columbia Pictures
3 Dumb Clucks	17-Apr-37	Columbia Pictures
Back to the Woods	14-May-37	Columbia Pictures
Goofs and Saddles	2-Jul-37	Columbia Pictures
Cash and Carry	3-Sep-37	Columbia Pictures
Playing the Ponies	15-Oct-37	Columbia Pictures
The Sitter Downers	26-Nov-37	Columbia Pictures
Termites of 1938	7-Jan-38	Columbia Pictures
Wee Wee Monsieur	18-Feb-38	Columbia Pictures
Tassels in the Air	1-Apr-38	Columbia Pictures
Healthy, Wealthy and Dumb	20-May-38	Columbia Pictures
Violent Is the Word for Curly	2-Jul-38	Columbia Pictures
Three Missing Links	2-Sep-38	Columbia Pictures
Mutts to You	14-Oct-38	Columbia Pictures
Flat Foot Stooges	25-Nov-38	Columbia Pictures
Three Little Sew and Sews	6-Jan-39	Columbia Pictures
We Want Our Mummy	24-Feb-39	Columbia Pictures
A Ducking They Did Go	7-Apr-39	Columbia Pictures
Yes, We Have No Bonanza	19-May-39	Columbia Pictures
Saved by the Belle	30-Jun-39	Columbia Pictures
Calling All Curs	25-Aug-39	Columbia Pictures
Oily to Bed, Oily to Rise	6-Oct-39	Columbia Pictures
Three Sappy People	1-Dec-39	Columbia Pictures
You Nazty Spy!	19-Jan-40	Columbia Pictures
Rockin' Thru the Rockies	8-Mar-40	Columbia Pictures
A Plumbing We Will Go	19-Apr-40	Columbia Pictures
Nutty But Nice	14-Jun-40	Columbia Pictures
How High Is Up?	26-Jul-40	Columbia Pictures
From Nurse to Worse	23-Aug-40	Columbia Pictures
No Census, No Feeling	4-Oct-40	Columbia Pictures
Cookoo Cavaliers	15-Nov-40	Columbia Pictures
Boobs in Arms	27-Dec-40	Columbia Pictures
So Long, Mr. Chumps	7-Feb-41	Columbia Pictures
Dutiful but Dumb	21-Mar-41	Columbia Pictures
All the World's a Stooge	16-May-41	Columbia Pictures
I'll Never Heil Again	11-Jul-41	Columbia Pictures
An Ache in Every Stake	22-Aug-41	Columbia Pictures
In the Sweet Pie and Pie	16-Oct-41	Columbia Pictures
Some More of Samoa	4-Dec-41	Columbia Pictures

Loco Boy Makes Good	8-Jan-42	Columbia Pictures
Cactus Makes Perfect	26-Feb-42	Columbia Pictures
What's the Matador?	23-Apr-42	Columbia Pictures
Matri-Phony	2-Jul-42	Columbia Pictures
Three Smart Saps	30-Jul-42	Columbia Pictures
Even as IOU	18-Sep-42	Columbia Pictures
Sock-a-Bye Baby	13-Nov-42	Columbia Pictures
They Stooge to Conga	1-Jan-43	Columbia Pictures
Dizzy Detectives	5-Feb-43	Columbia Pictures
Spook Louder	2-Apr-43	Columbia Pictures
Back From the Front	28-May-43	Columbia Pictures
Three Little Twirps	9-Jul-43	Columbia Pictures
Higher Than a Kite	30-Jul-43	Columbia Pictures
I Can Hardly Wait	13-Aug-43	Columbia Pictures
Dizzy Pilots	24-Sep-43	Columbia Pictures
Phony Express	18-Nov-43	Columbia Pictures
A Gem of a Jam	30-Dec-43	Columbia Pictures
Crash Goes the Hash	5-Feb-44	Columbia Pictures
Busy Buddies	18-Mar-44	Columbia Pictures
The Yoke's on Me	26-May-44	Columbia Pictures
Idle Roomers	16-Jul-44	Columbia Pictures
Gents Without Cents	22-Sep-44	Columbia Pictures
No Dough Boys	24-Nov-44	Columbia Pictures
Three Pests in a Mess	19-Jan-45	Columbia Pictures
Booby Dupes	17-Mar-45	Columbia Pictures
Idiots Deluxe	29-Jul-45	Columbia Pictures
If a Body Meets a Body	30-Aug-45	Columbia Pictures
Micro-Phonies	15-Nov-45	Columbia Pictures
Beer Barrel Polecats	10-Jan-46	Columbia Pictures
A Bird in the Head	28-Feb-46	Columbia Pictures
Uncivil War Birds	29-Mar-46	Columbia Pictures
The Three Troubledoers	25-Apr-46	Columbia Pictures
Monkey Businessmen	20-Jun-46	Columbia Pictures
Three Loan Wolves	4-Jul-46	Columbia Pictures
G. I. Wanna Home	5-Sep-46	Columbia Pictures
Rhythm and Weep	3-Oct-46	Columbia Pictures
Three Little Pirates	5-Dec-46	Columbia Pictures
Half-Wits Holiday	9-Jan-47	Columbia Pictures
Fright Night	6-Mar-47	Columbia Pictures
Out West	24-Apr-47	Columbia Pictures
Hold That Lion!	17-Jul-47	Columbia Pictures
Brideless Groom	11-Sep-47	Columbia Pictures
Sing a Song of Six Pants	30-Oct-47	Columbia Pictures
All Gummed Up	18-Dec-47	Columbia Pictures
Shivering Sherlocks	8-Jan-48	Columbia Pictures
Pardon My Clutch	26-Feb-48	Columbia Pictures

Squareheads of the Round Table	4-Mar-48	Columbia Pictures
Fiddlers Three	6-May-48	Columbia Pictures
The Hot Scots	8-Jul-48	Columbia Pictures
Heavenly Daze	2-Sep-48	Columbia Pictures
I'm a Monkey's Uncle	7-Oct-48	Columbia Pictures
Mummy's Dummies	4-Nov-48	Columbia Pictures
Crime on Their Hands	9-Dec-48	Columbia Pictures
The Ghost Talks	3-Feb-49	Columbia Pictures
Who Done It?	3-Mar-49	Columbia Pictures
Hokus Pokus	5-May-49	Columbia Pictures
Fuelin' Around	7-Jul-49	Columbia Pictures
Malice in the Palace	1-Sep-49	Columbia Pictures
Vagabond Loafers	6-Oct-49	Columbia Pictures
Dunked in the Deep	3-Nov-49	Columbia Pictures
Punchy Cowpunchers	5-Jan-50	Columbia Pictures
Hugs and Mugs	2-Feb-50	Columbia Pictures
Dopey Dicks	2-Mar-50	Columbia Pictures
Love at First Bite	4-May-50	Columbia Pictures
Self-Made Maids	6-Jul-50	Columbia Pictures
Three Hams on Rye	7-Sep-50	Columbia Pictures
Studio Stoops	5-Oct-50	Columbia Pictures
Slaphappy Sleuths	9-Nov-50	Columbia Pictures
A Snitch in Time	7-Dec-50	Columbia Pictures
Three Arabian Nuts	4-Jan-51	Columbia Pictures
Baby Sitters Jitters	1-Feb-51	Columbia Pictures
Don't Throw That Knife	3-May-51	Columbia Pictures
Scrambled Brains	7-Jul-51	Columbia Pictures
Merry Mavericks	6-Sep-51	Columbia Pictures
The Tooth Will Out	4-Oct-51	Columbia Pictures
Hula-La-La	1-Nov-51	Columbia Pictures
Pest Man Wins	6-Dec-51	Columbia Pictures
A Missed Fortune	3-Jan-52	Columbia Pictures
Listen, Judge	6-Mar-52	Columbia Pictures
Corny Casanovas	1-May-52	Columbia Pictures
He Cooked His Goose	3-Jun-52	Columbia Pictures
Gents in a Jam	4-Jul-52	Columbia Pictures
Three Dark Horses	16-Oct-52	Columbia Pictures
Cuckoo on a Choo Choo	4-Dec-52	Columbia Pictures
Up in Daisy's Penthouse	5-Feb-53	Columbia Pictures
Booty and the Beast	5-Mar-53	Columbia Pictures
Loose Loot	2-Apr-53	Columbia Pictures
Tricky Dicks	7-May-53	Columbia Pictures
Spooks!	15-Jun-53	Columbia Pictures
Pardon My Backfire	15-Aug-53	Columbia Pictures
Rip, Sew and Stitch	3-Sep-53	Columbia Pictures
Bubble Trouble	8-Oct-53	Columbia Pictures

Goof on the Roof	3-Dec-53	Columbia Pictures
Income Tax Sappy	4-Feb-54	Columbia Pictures
Musty Musketeers	13-May-54	Columbia Pictures
Pals and Gals	3-Jun-54	Columbia Pictures
Knutzy Knights	2-Sep-54	Columbia Pictures
Shot in the Frontier	7-Oct-54	Columbia Pictures
Scotched in Scotland	4-Nov-54	Columbia Pictures
Fling in the Ring	6-Jan-55	Columbia Pictures
Of Cash and Hash	3-Feb-55	Columbia Pictures
Gypped in the Penthouse	10-Mar-55	Columbia Pictures
Bedlam in Paradise	14-Apr-55	Columbia Pictures
Stone Age Romeos	2-Jun-55	Columbia Pictures
Wham-Bam-Slam!	1-Sep-55	Columbia Pictures
Hot Ice	6-Oct-55	Columbia Pictures
Blunder Boys	3-Nov-55	Columbia Pictures
Husbands Beware	5-Jan-56	Columbia Pictures
Creeps	2-Feb-56	Columbia Pictures
Flagpole Jitters	5-Apr-56	Columbia Pictures
For Crimin' Out Loud	3-May-56	Columbia Pictures
Rumpus in the Harem	21-Jun-56	Columbia Pictures
Hot Stuff	6-Sep-56	Columbia Pictures
Scheming Schemers	4-Oct-56	Columbia Pictures
Commotion on the Ocean	8-Nov-56	Columbia Pictures
Hoofs and Goofs	31-Jan-57	Columbia Pictures
Muscle Up a Little Closer	28-Feb-57	Columbia Pictures
A Merry Mix-Up	28-Mar-57	Columbia Pictures
Space Ship Sappy	18-Apr-57	Columbia Pictures
Guns a Poppin!	13-Jun-57	Columbia Pictures
Horsing Around	12-Sep-57	Columbia Pictures
Rusty Romeos	17-Oct-57	Columbia Pictures
Outer Space Jitters	5-Dec-57	Columbia Pictures
Quiz Whizz	13-Feb-58	Columbia Pictures
Fifi Blows Her Top	10-Apr-58	Columbia Pictures
Pies and Guys	12-Jun-58	Columbia Pictures
Sweet and Hot	4-Sep-58	Columbia Pictures
Flying Saucer Daffy	9-Oct-58	Columbia Pictures
Oil's Well That Ends Well	4-Dec-58	Columbia Pictures
Triple Crossed	2-Feb-59	Columbia Pictures
Sappy Bull Fighters	4-Jun-59	Columbia Pictures

FEATURE FILMS & OTHER THEATRICALS

The Captain Hates the Sea	22-Oct-34	Columbia Pictures
Screen Snapshots Series 14 #6: Graumann's Chinese Theater	22-Feb-35	Columbia Pictures
Screen Snapshots Series 15 #7: The Captain Hates the Sea	28-Feb-36	Columbia Pictures

Start Cheering	3-Mar-38	Columbia Pictures
Screen Snapshots Series 18 #9: San Fernando Valley Horse Show	12-May-39	Columbia Pictures
Screen Snapshots Series 19 #5: Art in Hollywood	28-Feb-40	Columbia Pictures
Screen Snapshots Series 19 #6: Hollywood Recreations	29-Mar-40	Columbia Pictures
Screen Snapshots Series 20 #3	22-Nov-40	Columbia Pictures
Time Out for Rhythm	5-Jun-41	Columbia Pictures
Screen Snapshots Series 21 #3: Flying Cadets Graduation	7-Nov-41	Columbia Pictures
My Sister Eileen	24-Sep-42	Columbia Pictures
Screen Snapshots Series 22 #8: Hollywood's War Effort	31-Mar-43	Columbia Pictures
Rockin' in the Rockies	17-Apr-45	Columbia Pictures
Screen Snapshots: Celebrity Baseball Game	1945	Columbia Pictures
Swing Parade of 1946	16-Mar-46	Monogram Pictures
Three Stooges Festival of Fun Compilation	1949	Columbia Pictures
Gold Raiders	14-Sep-51	United Artists
Three Stooges 3-D Fun Feature Compilation	1953	Columbia Pictures
Laff Hour Compilation	1956	Columbia Pictures
Three Stooges Fun Festival Compilation	1957	Columbia Pictures
Three Stooges Fun-O-Rama Compilation	1959	Columbia Pictures
Have Rocket, Will Travel	1-Aug-59	Columbia Pictures
Stop! Look! and Laugh! Compilation	1-Jul-60	Columbia Pictures
Fox Movietone News: Return to Peyton Place premiere	2-May-61	20th Century-Fox
Snow White and the Three Stooges	26-May-61	20th Century-Fox
The Three Stooges Meet Hercules	26-Jan-62	Columbia Pictures
The Three Stooges in Orbit	4-Jul-62	Columbia Pictures
The Three Stooges Go Around the World in a Daze	21-Aug-63	Columbia Pictures
It's a Mad, Mad, Mad, Mad World	7-Nov-63	United Artists
4 for Texas	18-Dec-63	Warner Brothers
MGM's The Big Parade of Comedy, Compilation	23-Sep-64	MGM
The Outlaws IS Coming!	1-Jan-65	Columbia Pictures
Star Spangled Salesman (short subject)	9-Feb-68	U.S. Treasury Dept.
The Horror Hit Triple Threat, Compilation	1972	Columbia Pictures
The Three Stooges Follies, Compilation	Nov-74	Columbia Pictures
Curly's Movie Mayhem, Compilation	1982	Columbia Pictures
The MGM Three Stooges Festival, Compilation	1982	MGM

NETWORK & NATIONALLY SYNDICATED TELEVISION

Texaco Star Theater	19-Oct-48	NBC
The Morey Amsterdam Show	31-Dec-48	CBS
Jerks of All Trades (Unaired Pilot; Phil Berle Productions)	Oct-49	ABC
Camel Comedy Caravan (The Ed Wynn Show)	11-Mar-50	CBS
Damon Runyon Memorial Fund	29-Apr-50	NBC
Texaco Star Theater	2-May-50	NBC
Texaco Star Theater	10-Oct-50	NBC
The Kate Smith Hour	13-Oct-50	NBC
The Kate Smith Hour	18-May-51	NBC
The Colgate Comedy Hour	16-Dec-51	NBC
The Frank Sinatra Show	1-Jan-52	CBS
The Eddie Cantor Comedy Theatre	29-Apr-55	Syndicated
The Steve Allen Show	11-Jan-59	NBC
Masquerade Party	19-Jan-59	NBC
The Steve Allen Show	22-Feb-59	NBC
The Steve Allen Show	5-Apr-59	NBC
Simoniz	15-Mar-60	Commercial
On the Go	5-Apr-60	CBS
The Frances Langford Show	1-May-60	NBC
The Three Stooges Scrapbook (Unaired pilot)	Dec-60	Normandy Productions
The Arthritis Foundation	1960	Commercial PSA
Chunky Chocolates	1960	Commercial
Hot Shot Insecticide	1960	Commercial
The Ed Sullivan Show	14-May-61	CBS
Here's Hollywood	27-Jul-61	NBC
Play Your Hunch	24-Jan-62	NBC
The Tonight Show Starring Johnny Carson	10-Jul-62	NBC
The Ed Sullivan Show	10-Feb-63	CBS
The Ed Sullivan Show	6-Oct-63	CBS
Aqua-Net Hair Spray (3 spots)	1963	Commercial
The Ed Sullivan Show	9-May-65	CBS
Danny Thomas Presents The Comics	8-Nov-65	NBC
Astro Snacks	1-Apr-67	Commercial
Off to See the Wizard	13-Oct-67	ABC
Metropolitan Life	1967	Commercial
Dickie Work Pants	31-Mar-69	Commercial
The Joey Bishop Show (talk show; three appearances)	1967–1969	ABC
Truth or Consequences	27-Oct-69	Syndicated
Kook's Tour (Unaired Pilot)	5-Feb-70	Normandy Productions
Stooge Snapshots, Documentary	1984	Syndicated

The Curly Shuffle	1984		Music Video
The Lost Stooges, Compilation	1990		TNT
Disorder in the Court: 60th Anniversary Tribute to the Stooges, Retrospective	1990		Fox
Biography—The Three Stooges: The Men Behind the Mayhem	1994		A&E
The Three Stooges' Greatest Hits! Retrospective	1997		ABC
The Three Stooges 75th Anniversary Special, Retrospective	2003		NBC

THE NEW 3 STOOGES CARTOONS (television)

Live Action (wraparound) Segments:

1	Soldiers	Oct-65	Cambria Prods./Normandy Prods.
2	Lost	Oct-65	Cambria Prods./Normandy Prods.
3	Campers	Oct-65	Cambria Prods./Normandy Prods.
4	Bakers	Oct-65	Cambria Prods./Normandy Prods.
5	Orangutan	Oct-65	Cambria Prods./Normandy Prods.
6	Flat Tire	Oct-65	Cambria Prods./Normandy Prods.
7	Fan Belt	Oct-65	Cambria Prods./Normandy Prods.
8	Fishermen	Oct-65	Cambria Prods./Normandy Prods.
9	Dentists	Oct-65	Cambria Prods./Normandy Prods.
10	Janitors	Oct-65	Cambria Prods./Normandy Prods.
11	Artists	Oct-65	Cambria Prods./Normandy Prods.
12	Decorators	Oct-65	Cambria Prods./Normandy Prods.
13	Golfers	Oct-65	Cambria Prods./Normandy Prods.
14	Hunters	Oct-65	Cambria Prods./Normandy Prods.
15	Weighing In	Oct-65	Cambria Prods./Normandy Prods.
16	Telegram	Oct-65	Cambria Prods./Normandy Prods.
17	Buried Treasure	Oct-65	Cambria Prods./Normandy Prods.
18	Outdoor Breakfast	Oct-65	Cambria Prods./Normandy Prods.
19	Setting Up Camp	Oct-65	Cambria Prods./Normandy Prods.
20	Rare Bird	Oct-65	Cambria Prods./Normandy Prods.
21	Caretakers	Oct-65	Cambria Prods./Normandy Prods.
22	Seasick Joe	Oct-65	Cambria Prods./Normandy Prods.
23	Electricians	Oct-65	Cambria Prods./Normandy Prods.
24	Salesmen	Oct-65	Cambria Prods./Normandy Prods.
25	Barbers	Oct-65	Cambria Prods./Normandy Prods.
26	Prospectors	Oct-65	Cambria Prods./Normandy Prods.
27	Sweepstakes Ticket	Oct-65	Cambria Prods./Normandy Prods.
28	Sunbathers	Oct-65	Cambria Prods./Normandy Prods.
29	Inheritance	Oct-65	Cambria Prods./Normandy Prods.
30	Melodrama	Oct-65	Cambria Prods./Normandy Prods.
31	Waiters	Oct-65	Cambria Prods./Normandy Prods.
32	Athletes	Oct-65	Cambria Prods./Normandy Prods.
33	Doctors	Oct-65	Cambria Prods./Normandy Prods.

34	Shipmates	Oct-65	Cambria Prods./Normandy Prods.
35	High Voltage	Oct-65	Cambria Prods./Normandy Prods.
36	Pilots	Oct-65	Cambria Prods./Normandy Prods.
37	Turkey Stuffers	Oct-65	Cambria Prods./Normandy Prods.
38	Piemakers	Oct-65	Cambria Prods./Normandy Prods.
39	Sharpshooters	Oct-65	Cambria Prods./Normandy Prods.
40	Magicians	Oct-65	Cambria Prods./Normandy Prods.
41	Sunken Treasure	Oct-65	Cambria Prods./Normandy Prods.

Animated Segments:

1	That Little Old Bomb Maker	Oct-65	Cambria Prods./Normandy Prods.
2	Woodsman Bear That Tree	Oct-65	Cambria Prods./Normandy Prods.
3	Let's Shoot the Player Piano Player	Oct-65	Cambria Prods./Normandy Prods.
4	Dentist the Menace	Oct-65	Cambria Prods./Normandy Prods.
5	Safari So Good	Oct-65	Cambria Prods./Normandy Prods.
6	Think or Thwim	Oct-65	Cambria Prods./Normandy Prods.
7	There Auto Be a Law	Oct-65	Cambria Prods./Normandy Prods.
8	That Old Shell Game	Oct-65	Cambria Prods./Normandy Prods.
9	Hold That Line	Oct-65	Cambria Prods./Normandy Prods.
10	Flycycle Built for Two	Oct-65	Cambria Prods./Normandy Prods.
11	Dizzy Doodlers	Oct-65	Cambria Prods./Normandy Prods.
12	The Classical Clinker	Oct-65	Cambria Prods./Normandy Prods.
13	Movie Scars	Oct-65	Cambria Prods./Normandy Prods.
14	A Bull for Adamo	Oct-65	Cambria Prods./Normandy Prods.
15	The Tree Nuts	Oct-65	Cambria Prods./Normandy Prods.
16	Tin Horn Dude	Oct-65	Cambria Prods./Normandy Prods.
17	Thru Rain, Sleet and Snow	Oct-65	Cambria Prods./Normandy Prods.
18	Goldriggers of '49	Oct-65	Cambria Prods./Normandy Prods.
19	Ready, Jet Set, Go	Oct-65	Cambria Prods./Normandy Prods.
20	Behind the 8 Ball Express	Oct-65	Cambria Prods./Normandy Prods.
21	Stop Dragon Around	Oct-65	Cambria Prods./Normandy Prods.
22	To Kill a Clockingbird	Oct-65	Cambria Prods./Normandy Prods.
23	Who's Lion	Oct-65	Cambria Prods./Normandy Prods.
24	Fowl Weather Friend	Oct-65	Cambria Prods./Normandy Prods.
25	Wash My Line	Oct-65	Cambria Prods./Normandy Prods.
26	Little Cheese Chaser	Oct-65	Cambria Prods./Normandy Prods.
27	Big Wind Bag	Oct-65	Cambria Prods./Normandy Prods.
28	Baby Sitters	Oct-65	Cambria Prods./Normandy Prods.
29	Clarence of Arabia	Oct-65	Cambria Prods./Normandy Prods.
30	Three Jacks and a Beanstalk	Oct-65	Cambria Prods./Normandy Prods.
31	That Was the Wreck That Was	Oct-65	Cambria Prods./Normandy Prods.
32	The Three Astronutz	Oct-65	Cambria Prods./Normandy Prods.

33	Peter Panic	Oct-65	Cambria Prods./Normandy Prods.
34	When You Wish Upon a Fish	Oct-65	Cambria Prods./Normandy Prods.
35	A Little Past Noon	Oct-65	Cambria Prods./Normandy Prods.
36	Hair of the Bear	Oct-65	Cambria Prods./Normandy Prods.
37	3 Lumps and a Lamp	Oct-65	Cambria Prods./Normandy Prods.
38	Who's for Dessert?	Oct-65	Cambria Prods./Normandy Prods.
39	Watt's My Lion	Oct-65	Cambria Prods./Normandy Prods.
40	Which Is Witch?	Oct-65	Cambria Prods./Normandy Prods.
41	Suture Self	Oct-65	Cambria Prods./Normandy Prods.
42	The Yolks on You	Oct-65	Cambria Prods./Normandy Prods.
43	Tally Moe with Larry and Joe	Oct-65	Cambria Prods./Normandy Prods.
44	The 1st in Lion	Oct-65	Cambria Prods./Normandy Prods.
45	The Transylvania Railroad	Oct-65	Cambria Prods./Normandy Prods.
46	What's Mew Pussycat?	Oct-65	Cambria Prods./Normandy Prods.
47	It's a Bad, Bad, Bad, Bad Word	Oct-65	Cambria Prods./Normandy Prods.
48	Bridge on the River Cry	Oct-65	Cambria Prods./Normandy Prods.
49	Hot Shots	Oct-65	Cambria Prods./Normandy Prods.
50	Mel's Angels	Oct-65	Cambria Prods./Normandy Prods.
51	Bee My Honey	Oct-65	Cambria Prods./Normandy Prods.
52	That Dirty Bird	Oct-65	Cambria Prods./Normandy Prods.
53	Stone Age Stooges	Oct-65	Cambria Prods./Normandy Prods.
54	Smoke Gets in Your Skies	Oct-65	Cambria Prods./Normandy Prods.
55	Queen Quong	Oct-65	Cambria Prods./Normandy Prods.
56	Campsite Fright	Oct-65	Cambria Prods./Normandy Prods.
57	Goldibear and the 3 Stooges	Oct-65	Cambria Prods./Normandy Prods.
58	The Lyin' Tamer	Oct-65	Cambria Prods./Normandy Prods.
59	The Pen Game	Oct-65	Cambria Prods./Normandy Prods.
60	It's a Small World	Oct-65	Cambria Prods./Normandy Prods.
61	Late for Launch	Oct-65	Cambria Prods./Normandy Prods.
62	Focus in Space	Oct-65	Cambria Prods./Normandy Prods.
63	The Noisy Silent Movie	Oct-65	Cambria Prods./Normandy Prods.
64	Get Out of Town by Sundown Brown	Oct-65	Cambria Prods./Normandy Prods.
65	Table Tennis Tussle	Oct-65	Cambria Prods./Normandy Prods.
66	Phony Express	Oct-65	Cambria Prods./Normandy Prods.
67	Best Test Pilots	Oct-65	Cambria Prods./Normandy Prods.
68	Litter Bear	Oct-65	Cambria Prods./Normandy Prods.
69	A Fishy Tale	Oct-65	Cambria Prods./Normandy Prods.
70	The Unhaunted House	Oct-65	Cambria Prods./Normandy Prods.
71	Aloha Ha Ha	Oct-65	Cambria Prods./Normandy Prods.
72	Rise and Fall of the Roman Umpire	Oct-65	Cambria Prods./Normandy Prods.
73	Deadbeat Street	Oct-65	Cambria Prods./Normandy Prods.

74	Cotton Pickin' Chicken	Oct-65	Cambria Prods./Normandy Prods.
75	Larry and the Pirates	Oct-65	Cambria Prods./Normandy Prods.
76	Tree Is a Crowd	Oct-65	Cambria Prods./Normandy Prods.
77	Feud for Thought	Oct-65	Cambria Prods./Normandy Prods.
78	Bat and Brawl	Oct-65	Cambria Prods./Normandy Prods.
79	Knight Without End	Oct-65	Cambria Prods./Normandy Prods.
80	Up a Tree	Oct-65	Cambria Prods./Normandy Prods.
81	Turnabout Is Bearplay	Oct-65	Cambria Prods./Normandy Prods.
82	Pow Wow Row	Oct-65	Cambria Prods./Normandy Prods.
83	Flat Heads	Oct-65	Cambria Prods./Normandy Prods.
84	No News Is Good News	Oct-65	Cambria Prods./Normandy Prods.
85	Bully for You, Curly	Oct-65	Cambria Prods./Normandy Prods.
86	Tee for Three	Oct-65	Cambria Prods./Normandy Prods.
87	Goofy Gondoliers	Oct-65	Cambria Prods./Normandy Prods.
88	Bearfoot Fishermen	Oct-65	Cambria Prods./Normandy Prods.
89	Washout Below	Oct-65	Cambria Prods./Normandy Prods.
90	The 3 Marketeers	Oct-65	Cambria Prods./Normandy Prods.
91	Follo the White Lion	Oct-65	Cambria Prods./Normandy Prods.
92	One Good Burn Deserves Another	Oct-65	Cambria Prods./Normandy Prods.
93	Curly's Bear	Oct-65	Cambria Prods./Normandy Prods.
94	Land Ho, Ho, Ho	Oct-65	Cambria Prods./Normandy Prods.
95	Surfs You Right	Oct-65	Cambria Prods./Normandy Prods.
96	7 Faces of Timbear	Oct-65	Cambria Prods./Normandy Prods.
97	Bearfoot Bandit	Oct-65	Cambria Prods./Normandy Prods.
98	None Butt the Brave	Oct-65	Cambria Prods./Normandy Prods.
99	Three Good Knights	Oct-65	Cambria Prods./Normandy Prods.
100	Call of the Wile	Oct-65	Cambria Prods./Normandy Prods.
101	Snowbrawl	Oct-65	Cambria Prods./Normandy Prods.
102	Rob N. Good	Oct-65	Cambria Prods./Normandy Prods.
103	There's No Mule Like an Old Mule	Oct-65	Cambria Prods./Normandy Prods.
104	Squawk Valley	Oct-65	Cambria Prods./Normandy Prods.
105	Mummies Boys	Oct-65	Cambria Prods./Normandy Prods.
106	The Plumber's Friend	Oct-65	Cambria Prods./Normandy Prods.
107	Rub-a-Dub-Tub	Oct-65	Cambria Prods./Normandy Prods.
108	Under the Bad Bad Tree	Oct-65	Cambria Prods./Normandy Prods.
109	Hairbrained Barbers	Oct-65	Cambria Prods./Normandy Prods.
110	Waiter Minute	Oct-65	Cambria Prods./Normandy Prods.
111	Souperman	Oct-65	Cambria Prods./Normandy Prods.
112	Abominable Snowman	Oct-65	Cambria Prods./Normandy Prods.
113	Curly in Wonderland	Oct-65	Cambria Prods./Normandy Prods.
114	Boobs in the Woods	Oct-65	Cambria Prods./Normandy Prods.
115	The Chimney Sweeps	Oct-65	Cambria Prods./Normandy Prods.
116	The Mad Mail Mission	Oct-65	Cambria Prods./Normandy Prods.
117	Out of Space	Oct-65	Cambria Prods./Normandy Prods.

118	3 Wizards of Odds	Oct-65	Cambria Prods./Normandy Prods.
119	Three for the Road	Oct-65	Cambria Prods./Normandy Prods.
120	Feudin', Fuss'n Hillbully	Oct-65	Cambria Prods./Normandy Prods.
121	Don't Misbehave Indian Brave	Oct-65	Cambria Prods./Normandy Prods.
122	You Ain't Lion	Oct-65	Cambria Prods./Normandy Prods.
123	Muscle on the Mind	Oct-65	Cambria Prods./Normandy Prods.
124	Badmen of the Briny	Oct-65	Cambria Prods./Normandy Prods.
125	Furry Fugitive	Oct-65	Cambria Prods./Normandy Prods.
126	How the West Was Once	Oct-65	Cambria Prods./Normandy Prods.
127	Bowling Pinheads	Oct-65	Cambria Prods./Normandy Prods.
128	The Mountain Ear	Oct-65	Cambria Prods./Normandy Prods.
129	Norse West Passage	Oct-65	Cambria Prods./Normandy Prods.
130	Lastest Gun in the West	Oct-65	Cambria Prods./Normandy Prods.
131	Toys Will Be Toys	Oct-65	Cambria Prods./Normandy Prods.
132	First Glass Service	Oct-65	Cambria Prods./Normandy Prods.
133	Strictly for the Birds	Oct-65	Cambria Prods./Normandy Prods.
134	Le Stoogenaires	Oct-65	Cambria Prods./Normandy Prods.
135	The Bear Who Came in Out of the Cold	Oct-65	Cambria Prods./Normandy Prods.
136	The Bigger They Are, the Harder They Hit	Oct-65	Cambria Prods./Normandy Prods.
137	Little Red Riding Wolf	Oct-65	Cambria Prods./Normandy Prods.
138	Bell Hop Flops	Oct-65	Cambria Prods./Normandy Prods.
139	Dig That Gopher	Oct-65	Cambria Prods./Normandy Prods.
140	Gagster Dragster	Oct-65	Cambria Prods./Normandy Prods.
141	Just Plane Crazy	Oct-65	Cambria Prods./Normandy Prods.
142	From Bad to Verse	Oct-65	Cambria Prods./Normandy Prods.
143	Droll Weevil	Oct-65	Cambria Prods./Normandy Prods.
144	The Littlest Martian	Oct-65	Cambria Prods./Normandy Prods.
145	The Bear Showoff	Oct-65	Cambria Prods./Normandy Prods.
146	No Money, No Honey	Oct-65	Cambria Prods./Normandy Prods.
147	Get That Snack Shack Off the Track	Oct-65	Cambria Prods./Normandy Prods.
148	Curly's Birthday-a-Go-Go	Oct-65	Cambria Prods./Normandy Prods.
149	The Men from UCLA	Oct-65	Cambria Prods./Normandy Prods.
150	Super Everybody	Oct-65	Cambria Prods./Normandy Prods.
151	Kangaroo Catchers	Oct-65	Cambria Prods./Normandy Prods.
152	No Smoking Aloud	Oct-65	Cambria Prods./Normandy Prods.
153	The Chicken Delivery Boys	Oct-65	Cambria Prods./Normandy Prods.
154	'Sno Ball	Oct-65	Cambria Prods./Normandy Prods.
155	Rug-a-Bye, Baby	Oct-65	Cambria Prods./Normandy Prods.
156	Dinopoodi	Oct-65	Cambria Prods./Normandy Prods.

LARRY FINE SOLO APPEARANCES

Stage Mother (bit role)	20-Sept-33	MGM
Stroke of Luck (book promotion)	1973	Commercial
Three Stooges T-Shirt Commercial	1973	Commercial

INDEX

ABOUT THE AUTHORS

STEVE COX grew up in loyal Stooge territory: St. Louis, Missouri. Too young to have seen the trio live in the '60s, he nonetheless became an avid and unabashed fan of the comedy team watching their films after school in the 1970s and continued for years to research the comedians as a hobby. In his teens, he assisted Larry Fine's brother, Morris "Moe" Feinberg, in relaunching the International Three Stooges Fan Club, Inc. (a nonprofit organization that still boasts an active, healthy, worldwide membership today). In 1983, Cox represented the Fan Club and spoke on the dais alongside Milton Berle and Joe Besser, among others, when the Three Stooges received their long overdue star on the Hollywood Walk of Fame. In 1988, he graduated from Park University in Kansas City, Missouri, with a B.A. in journalism and communication arts, and later spent much of the 90s trying to get accustomed to life in la-la land (a.k.a. Los Angeles). His articles about vintage television have appeared in *TV Guide,* the *Los Angeles Times,* and the *Hollywood Reporter,* and he has written more than a dozen books on film and television (including *It's a Wonderful Life: A Memory Book; The Beverly Hillbillies; The Munchkins of Oz; The Addams Chronicles;* and *Here's Johnny!*). Cox, 40, is a member of The Authors Guild and currently resides in Southern California.

JIM TERRY. a native Californian, is a man who has worn many hats in his day and successfully dabbled in the arts. He has worked as an actor, stage and film producer, and packager at Paramount Pictures and Allied Artists. In 1956, Terry co-produced Paramount's first television pilot, a marionette presentation from Sid & Marty Krofft titled *Little Irving.* For more than thirty years Terry has been sweetly involved as an entrepreneur—he was the Hollywood Chocolatier, owner and operator of Jim Terry's Gourmet Fudge, sold nationally in fine department stores. Terry struck up a friendship with Larry Fine in the early 1970s, when the actor was living at the Motion Picture Country Home. So impressed with the illustrated book Terry had co-authored (*The Busby Berkeley Book* with Tony Thomas, 1973), Larry began working with Terry on an autobiographical work—the blueprints for this book. "I'm so glad we could finally do this for Larry" Terry says. Terry resides today with his lovely wife, Doris, in West Hollywood, and is working toward a stage production and adaptation of the life of Busby Berkeley.